DATE DUE FOR RETURN

THE FRENCH EXCEPTION

THE FRENCH EXCEPTION

Edited by
Emmanuel Godin and Tony Chafer

Berghahn Books
New York • Oxford

1004 234804 T

First published in 2005 by

Berghahn Books

www.berghahnbooks.com

©2005 Emmanuel Godin and Tony Chafer

Library of Congress Cataloging-in-Publication Data

The French exception / edited by Emmanuel Godin and Tony Chafer.
   p. cm.
ISBN 1-57181-684-4
1. France--Civilization. 2. National characteristics, French. 3. France--
Social life and customs. 4. France--Politics and government. I. Godin,
Emmanuel. II. Chafer, Tony.

DC33.7.F728 2004
944--dc22

2004049097

British Library Cataloguing in Publication Data

A catalogue record for this book is available from
the British Library.

Printed in Canada on acid-free paper
ISBN 1-57181-684-4 (hardback)

In memory of Eric Cahm

'Des institutions singulières, une cohabitation qui étonne nos voisins, un Etat-providence encore très présent dans le jeu économique et social, un sens aigü du service public, une défense farouche de la culture, films, chansons et livres: tout cela ne fait pas de la France un pays exceptionnel, mais une société où l'exception est une manière d'identité. Le "modèle français" est source de fierté ou de nostalgie. "Une certaine idée de la France", disait le général de Gaulle. Une certaine idée d'un pays devenu puissance poids moyen.

Tantôt pour préserver des archaïsmes risibles ou fâcheux, tantôt pour refuser les forces dominantes du tout-libéral, l'exception est une façon de vivre, de se vivre comme une nation affichant ses différences jusqu'à l'excès parfois. En témoignent les tristes records en matière d'alcoolisme, de consommation de médicaments – singulièrement d'antidépresseurs – ou d'accidents de la route. Ainsi que le souligne l'historien Theodore Zeldin, les Français ne sont pas si différents des autres, mais ils se distinguent par leur retard, ou leur avance.

'La France est-elle un pays d'exception?', *Le Monde*, 15 April 2002

CONTENTS

FOREWORD

This book emerges from the Annual Conference of the Association for the Study of Modern and Contemporary France (ASMCF) on the theme 'La France Exceptionnelle? Comparisons and Intercultural Perspectives', held at the University of Portsmouth in September 2001. Some of the chapters of the present book emerge from papers given at the conference, others have been specially written for it.

One of the founders of the Association for the Study of Modern and Contemporary France, Eric Cahm, served as executive editor of its journal *Modern and Contemporary France* for a number of years. Eric was an enthusiastic francophile and a fervent advocate of an interdisciplinary approach to the study of France. He played a major role in promoting French Studies in U.K. higher education. It is therefore especially fitting that this book, an interdisciplinary study of what is 'different' and special about France, should be dedicated to his memory.

LIST OF ABBREVIATIONS

ACCT	Agence de la Coopération Culturelle et Technique
AFSOUTH	Allied Forces Southern Europe
AN	Alleanza Nazionale
APS	Activités Physiques et Sportives
BNP	British National Party
CFDT	Confédération Française Démocratique du Travail
CFE-CGC	Confédération Française de l'Encadrement-Confédération Générale des Cadres
CFSP	Common Foreign and Security Policy
CFTC	Confédération Française des Travailleurs Chrétiens
CGT	Confédération Générale du Travail
CNC	Centre National de la Cinématographie
CNCL	Commission Nationale de la Communication et des Libertés
CNE	Comité National des Ecrivains
CPSU	Communist Party of the Soviet Union
CSA	Conseil Supérieur de l'Audiovisuel
CSNEP	Common Strategy for National Employment Policies
DNCG	Direction Nationale de Contrôle et de Gestion
DV	Digital Video
DVU	Deutsche Volksunion
ECB	European Central Bank
EEC	European Economic Commuity
EHESS	Ecole des Hautes Etudes en Sciences Sociales
EMS	European Monetary System
EMU	Economic and Monetary Union
ENA	Ecole Nationale d'Administration
ESDI	European Security and Defence Identity
FAR	Force d'Action Rapide
FEMIS	Ecole Nationale Supérieure des Métiers de l'Image et du Son
FEN	Fédération de l'Education Nationale
FIFA	International Federation of Football Associations
FN	Front National
FNDS	Fond National pour le Développement du Sport
FO	Force Ouvrière

FPÖ	Freiheitliche Partei Österreichs
FGSPF	Fédération Gymnastique et Sportive des Patronages de France
FSS	Fondation Saint-Simon
FSU	Fédération Syndicale Unitaire
GATT	General Agreement on Tariffs and Trade
GDP	Gross Domestic Product
IDHEC	Institut des Hautes Etudes Cinématographiques
IEP	Institut d'Etudes Politiques
IFIC	Institut pour le Financement du Cinéma et des Industries Culturelles
INED	Institut National d'Etudes Démographiques
INSEE	Institut National de la Statistique et des Etudes Economiques
MEDEF	Mouvement des Entreprises de France
MES	Ministère de l'Emploi et de la Solidarité
MSI	Movimento Sociale Italiano
NATO	North Atlantic Treaty Organisation
OECD	Organisation for Economic Cooperation and Development
OFCE	Observatoire Français des Conjonctures Economiques
ORTF	Office de la Radiodiffusion-Télévision Française
PACS	Pacte Civil de Solidarité
PCF	Parti Communiste Français
PS	Parti Socialiste
SEATO	South East Asia Treaty Organisation
SFIO	Section Française de l'Internationale Ouvrière
SOFICA	Sociétés de Financement des Industries Cinématographiques et Audiovisuelles
SUD	Solidaires Unitaires Démocratiques
UN	United Nations
UNEDIC	Union pour l'Emploi dans l'Industrie et le Commerce
UNSA	Union Nationale des Syndicats Autonomes
USFSA	Union des Sociétés Françaises des Sports Athlétiques
USSR	United Soviet Socialist Republics
VB	Vlaams Blok
WEU	Western European Union
WMD	Weapons of Mass Destruction

INTRODUCTION

During the summer of 2003, a medical doctor in the Grenoble region pinned on the door of his surgery waiting room a large and colourful poster that warned his patients of a great danger: statistics clearly showed that young French children were becoming as obese as their American counterparts. Various unappealing photos of hamburgers, chocolate bars and fizzy drinks showed that the excessive consumption of junk food was primarily responsible for this worrying trend. Of course, similar concerns are regularly expressed in the British and American press, usually with an exhortation to review the menus that schools serve to children. But in this French surgery, the argument was taken further and developed in peculiar, but not unsurprising terms. The doctor had highlighted with a fluorescent red pen the conclusion of his home-made poster: parents who had forgotten the nutritive qualities of the perfectly balanced French diet were feeding their offspring a variety of unhealthy and culturally alien products: 'The Anglo-Saxon diet is undermining the health of your children'. The doctor pressed his patients to show enough civic virtue (*responsabilité citoyenne*) to revert to a more balanced regime and to defend '*l'exception diététique française*'. It is unlikely that a British or American journalist writing on the subject of obesity among young children would make the link between dietary principles and citizenry. Although it is not entirely clear what *l'exception diététique française* and *la responsabilité citoyenne* actually mean, as an incantation it works fairly well; it conjures up the idea that something quite fundamentally French is under siege and that fraternal courage and permanent mobilisation of citizens are needed to save it from evil. Moreover, it implicitly suggests that the French have the best diet in the world and that other peoples would be better off adopting it.

This book is *not* a collection of such stories. As Sue Collard points out in her contribution to this volume, the expression 'the French exception' is now routinely 'used as a way of pointing to areas in which France is perceived as being different from other countries, [from …] road safety [to] gynaecology, [… from] the constitution [… to] the shooting of migrating birds'. As such, an *ad infinitum* review of such occurrences would be no more than a mildly entertaining exercise, whose sole value would be to state the obvious: each country has its own particularities. This book seeks to explore and evaluate how two different, but related discourses have constructed the notion of the French exception in specific ways, have ascribed certain value(s) to it and have mobilised it for specific reasons.

In this volume, the chapters are organised in three sections. In the first section, the contributions by Hewlett, Majumdar and Collard aim at problematising the French exception. This first part therefore provides the reader with the context necessary to understand how the notion of exceptionalism has been framed and defined and the reasons why it has acquired such a visibility. It also charts the limits of its heuristic value as an analytical tool. The second part looks at the exceptionalism in the field of politics, whereas the third one focuses on culture, media, and sport. The aim of this introduction is to highlight the recurrent themes that cut across the contributions gathered here.

The French exception as an analytical framework

As Nick Hewlett points out (chapter 1), whether we think that the notion of the French exception as an analytical framework is 'inaccurate or even trivial', we have to admit that it has permeated an enormous number of academic works. If the notion of French exception is not explored as such, it often looms in the background or provides a backdrop to various arguments. For instance, David Howarth and Georgios Varouxakis use the notion of French exception in their introduction with great care, to explain that France 'is, or rather [...] sees itself as being, permanently in crisis' and to discuss whether this exceptional lack of consensus has not reached the end of its tether today (2003: x). In their conclusion, they emphasise France's claim to universalism and point out that what makes it different is that it is only country that 'offers its "sister-republic", America, a mirror image through which to see itself better, and the rest of the world an alternative way of living and thinking than that of the *hyperpuissance*'. (Howarth and Varouxakis 2003: 211). Likewise, David Bell in *French Politics Today* (2002) makes the point that it could be useful to look at French political culture as 'exceptional' and introduces his argument by stating that '... the history of French politics will help explain why France is different' (Bell 2002: 3). This is done with much nuance as he also points out that France shares many common traits with other Western liberal democracies. Nevertheless, the questions that Bell puts forwards in the course of this book suggest that the notion of 'the French exception' is a useful starting point to ask interesting questions: 'What is distinctive about the French economy?' (39); 'In what ways is the French Left distinctive?' (78); 'In what ways is French foreign policy distinctive?' (240).

To be sure, saying that France is 'different' or 'distinctive' or 'exemplary' does not necessarily mean that it is 'exceptional'. The majority of the contributors to this volume are, as we shall see, sceptical if not critical of the 'French exception' as a heuristic device. Moreover, an exception only exists in opposition to a general rule or a norm and it is difficult to determine what this norm is or could be (or even if it exists at all). Indeed, how are we to decide whether any departure from the norm constitutes a variance, a deviation or an exception? Yet most academics also recognise that the notion has often been used in their field, that it has helped to generate some relevant research questions (notably about the permanence of its 'exceptional status' in a more globalised or Europeanised environment) and that it has encouraged the development of further comparative studies.

As an analytical tool, the notion of French exception is usually constructed along two different but closely related axes. The first axis maps the origins and contours of the French exception. It has its roots in a distinctive republican model, attaching central importance to the prestige of the state, the primacy of politics and the active propagation, at home and worldwide, of certain values, perceived, rightly or wrongly, to be enlightened and progressive. Thus, the 'French exception' could be defined by four core elements:

(1) The French State, in its *Jacobin, dirigiste,* republican or protectionist guise, is supposed to dominate civil society and to play a more powerful role than in any other Western democracy.
(2) France is a country divided against itself, where domestic conflicts are more polarised than in other Western countries. It displays a degree of political radicalism which ensures that debates are highly politicised and issues are solved, if at all, through confrontation, not negotiation.
(3) France has long seen itself as the depository of values inherited from the Enlightenment and the French Revolution. Its mission is to diffuse them universally. From the Napoleonic conquests to colonial expansion, from the Gaullist refusal of the cold war divide to the development of *Francophonie*, France has presented itself as a model to follow for the rest of the world. In this respect, it shares the same ambition as the U.S. and this might help to explain the periodic outbursts of anti-Americanism in France.
(4) The French republican model only recognises individuals and not communities within the nation-state. Thus, the existence of minority groups, from regional minorities such as Bretons to religious minorities such as Muslims, are not acknowledged (Rosanvallon 2004). The reluctance of President Chirac to sign the European Charter for Regional or Minority Languages and the new legislation to ban the wearing of the veil in schools by Muslim girls testify to the continuing durability of this model.

Two important points need to be made. Firstly, within academic discourse, such characteristics are obviously treated as hypotheses rather than empirical truths. Indeed, academics – and this is the second axis of the debate – have long tried to evaluate critically whether and to what extent such hypotheses make sense at all. After all, this is what their job is about. For instance, the Jacobin tendencies of the French State, its propensity to denigrate regional particularisms and to promote a homogenised national culture have often been critically re-examined by social scientists. The historian Jean-François Chanet (1996), for example, clearly shows that our traditional views of republican centralisation, both as a concept and a practice, should be empirically reassessed. Education policy under the Third Republic did not always seek to eradicate positive attachments to a regional culture. Instead, it mobilised existing regional identities to promote the development of French national consciousness. The discourse developed by the central administration was not monolithic and was characterised by constant hesitations and adjustments between Jacobin and Girondin traditions. As a result, the formulation and implementation of education policy did not display the homogenising tendencies that are usually associated with *les hussards noirs de la république*. Likewise, Pierre Grémion's seminal work on the French prefects (1976) highlighted the relations of complicity, rather than of domination, between local elites and the representatives of the central state, leading to a more subtle reassessment of the idea and practice of centralisation. Finally, Dupuy and Thoenig (1985) have described the French State apparatus as being rather fragmented, marred both by inertia and internal conflicts, a description far removed from the image of an all powerful and effective bureaucracy. In this volume, Anne Stevens (chapter 6) and Ben Clift (chapter 8) show that the traditional image of a powerful *and* efficient state, either in its Jacobin or *dirigiste* guise, has not always been supported by empirical evidence.

Secondly, until the mid-1980s, the assessment and evaluation of such hypotheses did not make, or indeed require, any explicit reference to the notion of 'French exceptionalism'. Indeed, the role played by the state, the polarised and radical nature of French society as well as the willingness to promote French *rayonnement* on the international stage, were used to described France's attempt to overcome the humiliation of her fall in 1940 and to embark, *coûte que coûte*, on a largely state-led programme of modernisation from 1945 onwards. As Sue Collard (chapter 3) shows in this volume, it is difficult to know exactly when the expression 'French exceptionalism' first appeared. What is certain, however, is that it became common currency after the publication, in 1988, of an influential book by François Furet, Jacques Julliard and Pierre Rosanvallon: *La République du centre. La fin de l'exception française*. The book argued that France's road to modernisation had run out of steam, that state intervention had become counter-productive, that the existence and radical expression of political conflicts were now irrelevant, archaic or even morally dangerous, and that France's destiny was to become a 'normal' country, with ambitions limited to her medium-sized status. It was time to bring to a close a political culture and a republican model inherited from the Revolution. France had taken a long time to complete its modernisation and had chosen a tumultuous path to do so. Now the time had come to join the European club of liberal democracies (Gauchet 2002). The argument opened a space for a heated political debate between those who called for such normalisation and those who defended a more traditional French model. Or to put it another way, the notion of the French exception started to be a popular one when it became charged with political values and an object of political ambitions.

The French exception as a political and polarised discourse

The notion of 'French exceptionalism' can be conceived not only as a framework of analysis, with hypotheses to be tested, but also as a political discourse with a specific agenda. From the late 1980s this discourse fell on fertile ground. The celebrations of the bicentenary of the French Revolution led some historians, notably around François Furet, to reassess critically the inheritance of the French republican model, particularly the dangers associated with unlimited popular sovereignty. After the fall of the Berlin Wall and the collapse of Communism, there seemed to be no alternative to neoliberal values and the rule of the market. The consensual method adopted by the Socialist prime minister Michel Rocard (1988–1991) made a sharp contrast with the voluntarist and often rhetorically *marxisant* policies pursued by the Socialists only six years before (1981–1983). The pragmatism of the left in government, the transformation of Gaullism into a 'normal' conservative party, the consensual cohabitation between Prime Minister Balladur and President Mitterrand in 1993–1995, all seemed to indicate that France was moving towards a more consensual political culture. The evolution of the EU towards an ever closer union, the further transfers of sovereignty organised by the Maastricht (1992) and Amsterdam (1995) treaties and the introduction of the euro (1999) put further constraints on the state's room for manoeuvre. New technologies accelerated the globalisation of culture, often perceived and understood as a process of Americanisation of the French life styles. Some applauded the 'end of the French exception' as the surest sign of France's ability to 'modernise' itself. Others deplored it and sought to underline both the merits of the French traditional model and the dangers of liberalisation *à l'anglo-saxonne*. In this volume, the nature and the intensity of this debate is charted by Sue Collard in chapter 3.

The distinction that has been made so far between the French exception as an analytical framework and as a political discourse is in fact an extremely porous one. Academics do not simply and dispassionately test hypotheses, they also take sides. This is still blatantly the case in France: the role of the Fondation Saint-Simon, analysed by Collard, demonstrates the interconnection between academics, politicians, civil servants and business leaders. Indeed, it can be seen as perpetuating in a lacklustre and less prestigious guise (see Kelly, chapter 14), the traditional role played by 'intellectuals' in French (political) culture. In this volume too, academics may take sides. Nick Hewlett (chapter 1), for instance, who explores the centrality of radicalism in French political culture, appears sympathetic to this tradition. He demonstrates how the primacy given to politics is related to a healthy conception of democracy and active citizenry. He explicitly challenges those 'liberals' who advocate 'the end of the French exception' in order to depoliticise the *polis*, which is a necessary prerequisite for the development of unchecked capitalism. He is also optimistic that the new radical movements that are emerging on the left of the political spectrum will perpetuate the French radical tradition. Interestingly, he also stresses that this radicalism seems to be particularly exceptional when seen from an 'Anglo-Saxon' vantage point and wonders whether an observer from Southern Europe would view French radicalism in the same way. Brigitte Rollet in chapter 12 takes sides too. She may be quite sympathetic to the intervention of the state to support French cinema against the homogenisation (Americanisation) of culture, although the effectiveness of such intervention, as she points out, remains to be demonstrated. Furthermore, Rollet questions the content of this cinema, which is sometimes defined as '*citoyen*', and develops an argument against the traditional republican universalist discourse that still refuses to grant minorities the visibility they deserve. This leads, sometimes, to the production of rather bland films, which is a pity, she argues, given the opportunities to promote cinematic originality, to celebrate overtly cultural, sexual and gender differences and to explore subjects directly related to the development of a multicultural society.

The French exception and the weight of external constraints

The political debate about the 'end of the French exception' has compelled academics to formulate new hypotheses, to revisit well-established ideas or to decipher recent shifts in traditional discourses. In particular, the increasing weight of external pressures (globalisation, European construction, and generally the central role played by the market place) have opened new opportunities for comparative analysis. In a more global context, the comparative method is still very useful (Hague and Harrop 2001). It does not presuppose that convergence is the necessary or likely outcome of the forces of globalisation or Europeanisation: the resilience of national cultures and strength and flexibility of specific institutional arrangements should be taken into account in order to understand how each nation mediates such general trends. This is a point clearly made by Parsons in chapter 7 when analysing the evolution of French industrial relations: 'Although changes in the world economy may pose common problems, [...] this does not mean that different countries will react in the same way. [...] This should not surprise us as current responses will depend, to some extent at least, on pre-existing institutional structures and the former compromises they embody, as well as upon pre-existing actors, all with their own attitudes and values that inform their past, present and future choices and strategies'. Thus in the case of industrial relations, and using a comparative framework, Parsons is able to demonstrate that, although it is possible to identify a degree of convergence towards a 'European model' with more decentralised forms of collective bargaining, France remains characterised by 'a chronically weak and divided trade union movement and the consequent need for state intervention in the area of industrial relations'.

Globalisation and Europeanisation also help to generate new questions: to what extent, for instance, has ' French *politics* acquired a European character, since much of French *policy* [...] is made within the EU (Guyomarch et al. 2001: 2)? Conversely, to what extent has France been able to influence European developments and to shape the EU to its own liking (Guyomarch et al. 1998)? Is there still some room today for the development of a voluntarist – but plausible and successful – economic policy at national or European level? These questions, of course, preoccupy most left-wing parties today (Lardech 2000, Glyn 2001). Faced with similar dilemmas, however, these parties do not necessarily produce the same answers. A comparative analysis is again useful. For instance, Clift (chapter 8) contrasts the arguments and strategies developed by the French Socialists under Jospin to 'Europeanise' employment policy with those of the British New Labour administration and the German Government led by Gerhard Schröder. The French attempt to reproduce a *dirigiste* strategy at the European level, Clift argues, received lukewarm support, to say the least, from British and German Social-Democrats and finally failed, partly because Jospin's *dirigisme* remained far too anchored in the French tradition, far too 'exceptional'.

The political visibility of external constraints today and the realisation that the EU is unlikely to become '*la France en plus grand*' fuel a variety of euro-sceptic discourses on both the right and the left of the political spectrum. The claim that French exceptionalism has now reached its end has also prompted academics to revisit the past and to question whether the notion of French exceptionalism had not been exaggerated in the first place. In some cases it has, in others it has not. For Raymond Kuhn it is difficult to argue that French television has ever had any 'exceptional status' and therefore it does not make sense today to talk about its 'normalisation'. Replacing the object of his analysis in its temporal and spatial context, Kuhn builds up a comparative study of French television in Western Europe over the long term 'since the advent of television as a mass medium after the end of the Second World War' (chapter 11). Using five different variables over the period (scale and centralisation, degree of politicisation, diversity profile, sources of finance and degree of public regulation and control), he concludes that French television 'from its origins to the present day can be satisfactorily regarded as a national variant of wider European trends, rather than a special case apart'. Yet, as Kuhn notes, this has not prevented the development of political and cultural discourses that have attempted, for specific reasons, to portray French television as remarkably different and therefore exceptional.

Universalism, anti-Americanism and the French cultural exception

The notion of a French cultural exception acquired some salience during the 1993 'Urugay Round of GATT negotiations[…] where France led European opposition to U.S. proposals for deregulating the audiovisual industries. Subsequently, the notion of the exception was extended to cover the entire political domain' (see Kelly chapter 14). The argument that French culture was under siege and threatened by progressive Americanisation generated much nostalgia about France's past cultural *rayonnement*. In particular much was written about the death of the French intellectual (Hazareesingh 1991; Ross 1991; Jennings 1993). In this volume, Kelly demonstrates that the exceptional status enjoyed by French intellectuals from the end of the Second World War to the 1970s has not been exaggerated. Equally, the progressive disappearance of this specific group from the 1980s onwards is beyond doubt. Yet Kelly shows how, with the passing years, the postwar intellectual has acquired a near-mythical status. In his contribution, he tries to 'clarify the basis on which the legend has arisen [… how] its "halo effects" have surrounded intellectual activities in France up to the present day and have also inflected the way earlier periods have been understood'. Today, 'nostalgia for the Golden Age easily leads to optimistic denials that it has come to an end and both contribute to the legend of the French intellectual as a permanent feature of the French exception'. Nostalgia might indeed be a key to understanding the vitality of the 'French exception' as a discourse. For *Le Monde* (2002), it is the discourse of a middle-range country that still thinks of itself as a major power.

Nostalgia for French cultural *rayonnement* and fears of Americanisation have their roots in France's claim to universalism. In the specific context of Francophonie, Margaret Majumdar (chapter 2) analyses the progressive discursive shifts that have affected French universalism and how such shifts have led *la Francophonie* to move from a concern with cultural and linguistic issues to a more politically-oriented organisation. France now seems to have redefined its universal project as it presents itself as the standard bearer of pluralism and cultural diversity in a world threatened by the homogenising forces of globalisation. Thus, 'Francophonie [is] increasingly seen as a vehicle for the defence of French exceptionalism in the face of "Anglo-Saxon" cultural hegemony'. Similar arguments, as Janet Bryant shows in chapter 9, have been put forward to justify French opposition to American intervention in Iraq, with France presenting itself as the champion of multilateralism. In both cases, as Majumdar argues, 'there is a perceptible gap between the idealism of the present discourse and the political and economic realities that have now come to the fore'.

The same point is made by Janet Bryant in chapter 9. She explains that the notion of French exception in the field of defence policy is more a question of rhetoric than substance. This rhetoric still serves specific political and professional interests. In particular, it can be mobilised to cajole French public opinion at a time when such opinion is likely to become too critical about the government's handling of specific domestic issues. Anti-Americanism remains a winning card in French domestic politics. The reality is rather different, as Bryant shows in her an analysis of the progressive but still partial normalisation of French defence policy, notably through a *rapprochement* with NATO.

Sheila Perry (chapter 10) is sceptical about the supposedly all-powerful influence of American models and ideas on French political culture. Through her analysis of presidential debates in France, she shows that, in this particular field at least, the Americanisation of French politics is more a myth than a reality. The overall organisation of presidential debates still mirrors the most salient features of French political culture: the 'institutionalisation of the bipolarisation process', and 'the dramatic embodiment of political conflicts' and the primacy granted to presidential elections over all others. Perry also notes the more deferential tone adopted by French journalists toward political leaders than is customarily the case in the U.K. and the U.S. Whether or not this is detrimental to the quality of the debate remains an open question. For the Communist leader Robert Hue, presidential debates in France are even vital for the preservation of democracy and for the healthy politicisation of issues. Without such debates, he argued, there is a real risk that French democracy will Americanise itself. Such debates generate further electoral mobilisation and are the right antidote to abstention rates *à l'américaine* (*L'Humanité*, 26 March 2002). The argument here is similar to that developed by Hewlett and calls for a repoliticisation of democracy in order to avoid the anaesthetic effects of *la pensée unique*. But it also shows how much the Communist discourse has changed and how far it has gone in its acceptance of the presidential nature of the regime.

Consensus and polarisation

The development of *une pensée unique* among the main parties of government and the marginalisation of other voices with a more radical agenda are of course at the heart of the debate about the French exception. The fact that the Parti Communiste Français (PCF) today is a spent electoral force (it only gained 3.24 percent of the votes in the 2002 legislative elections) is often taken as evidence that France is on the road of normalisation. Indeed, the electoral collapse of the PCF today constitutes a dramatic change in the French political landscape. Bell (chapter 4) reveals that what distinguished the PCF from other Communist Parties in Western Europe was not so much its subservience to Moscow, but its sheer electoral success, which monopolised most of the space to the left of the political spectrum and left very little room for the development of a reformist social-democratic party. This success can be explained by its ability to rework into its discourse radical and nationalist republican themes inherited from the Revolution or even the Enlightenment: 'It is the Revolution which is the key to "exceptionalism" on the French left'. If Communism is ideologically discredited today, the same may not necessarily be said of radical republicanism and new parties or movements might carry on the polarising role that the PCF once played. The relative electoral success of the French extreme left or the popularity enjoyed by the *altermondialistes* around José Bové might just be evidence of this.

The durability and the strength of the Front National (FN) also ensure continuing polarisation. Yet in this respect France is far from being exceptional. For instance, Emmanuel Godin (chapter 5) places the electoral strength and the political discourse of the French extreme right in its European context and shows that it is difficult to describe the FN as an exceptional party in Western Europe today: its electoral dynamics, the profile of its voters and the discourse it develops are similar to many other European extreme-right parties. Both Bell and Godin show the resilience of a radical tradition in France and the continuing role played by protest parties at a time when some commentators were heralding the demise of political ideologies. However, as Godin notes, other Western countries are also becoming politically more polarised, not only because the 'postmaterialist' extreme right is now a pan-European phenomenon, but also because the values it defends have permeated the agenda of other parties, notably, but not only, traditional right-wing parties. In such respects, France might well be the norm rather than the exception.

The role of the state

France, it appears, also conforms to the norm in the field of sport policy. In chapter 13, Patrick Mignon notes that countries such as Britain or Australia seem to have abandoned their traditional *laissez-faire* approach to sport and have come to endorse a more interventionist model, with the state taking more responsibility for the organisation and financing of competition level sport. Paradoxically, this is happening precisely at a time when, in France, such intervention is coming up against the limits of its effectiveness. Indeed, Mignon argues that such intervention will not be sustainable in the long term and that it has its own limits, in terms of both sporting success and the regulation of sporting activities. Nevertheless, his contribution helps us to understand both the roots and the resilience of state intervention in this sector and reminds the reader that general hypotheses about the decline of state intervention must be tested empirically rather than taken for granted. The continuing presence of state intervention is of course not limited to sport. Brigitte Rollet (chapter 12) stresses the 'almost incestuous relationship between state and culture in France' and the state's determination to defend the 'French cultural exception', but also the limited success of this strategy. The willingness to defend cultural diversity in a globalised and Europeanised context justifies and renews the legitimacy of state intervention, as Rollet shows in the case of cinema. In the end, Clift, Parsons, Kuhn, Rollet and Mignon's contributions taken together, offer a complex and varied image of state intervention and of its changing nature and intensity over time and across different sectors.

Voluntarism is one thing but to achieve the desired results is quite another. To do so in a more liberal, open and flexible context, the French State needs to reform itself, its procedures, its organisation and its culture. So far, it seems, this has been a rather difficult task. Anne Stevens (chapter 6) demonstrates this when she makes the point that 'unlike its counterpart in Whitehall or (to a lesser extent) the Netherlands, the French civil service has experienced no more than mild and incremental change'. Although the reform of the civil service has been high on the agenda of successive governments since Michel Rocard's *renouveau*, its overall characteristics have not changed dramatically since the description that Grémion and Suleiman gave of it in the 1970s. One of the main reasons put forward by Stevens to explain this limited change is the fact that France has been unable to develop 'a new, alternative or competing set of ideas to which the politico-administrative elite could appeal. Even under governments of the right, there is no presumption that the private sector is more efficient or competent that the state sector'. The weakness of a liberal political and cultural tradition in France, which the Fondation Saint-Simon both deplored and tried to remedy, made it difficult to build powerful neoliberal arguments, legitimising changes with the strength of a moral argument, in the way that Thatcherism did (Jobert 1994; Godin 1996).

This volume shows that the notion of the French exception is in a number of ways problematic. It is nevertheless a useful starting point as it obliges us to address interesting questions about contemporary developments in French society, politics and culture. In the field of French studies, it also encourages us to enrich our approach with comparative research. It compels us to examine issues related to the processes of globalisation and the Europeanisation of French society, politics and culture, and to assess how France both contributes to, and undergoes, this process. Further analyses of the discursive shifts that affect the debate on French exceptionalism must also be attempted. In this respect a historical perspective that examines the various discourses that have periodically heralded French decline would also be of interest (Baverez 2003).

Emmanuel Godin and Tony Chafer
Southsea, November 2003

PART I

Problematising Exceptionalism

Chapter 1

FRANCE AND EXCEPTIONALISM

Nick Hewlett

Anyone with more than a passing scholarly interest in things French will have encountered the notion that France is different from other countries.[1] We might disagree about the usefulness of this idea, we might think it is inaccurate or even trivial, but we have all been exposed to the view that important aspects of French society, French politics, French thought, French language and French culture are strikingly unique. From newspaper articles to the most serious historiography of the French Revolution, via an almost endless array of journal articles, textbooks, journalistic potboilers, and now websites, we find arguments and approaches whose organising principles depend on the idea that France is special (see for example Rémond 1985; Finkielkraut 1991; Halimi 1996; Lovecy 1999; Collard 2000).

It is worth saying immediately that France is not alone in being characterised in this way. One school of historians of Germany uses the term *Sonderweg*, or special path, arguing that from well before the Nazi era Germany was different from the common model to which France and Britain conform (Wehler 1973; for a critique see Blackbourn and Eley 1984). In Linda Colley's *Britons: Forging the Nation* (1992 and 1999), there is a strong sense that it is Britain that is distinct from European countries in the eighteenth and nineteenth centuries, a view expressed strongly by Perry Anderson and Tom Nairn in the 1960s (Anderson 1964) and critiqued by E.P. Thompson (1965; see Elliott 1998: 13–39). The political scientist Seymour Martin Lipset, on the other hand, argues that we must think in terms of *American* exceptionalism (Lipset 1996; 2000; also Adams and van Minnen 1994); and in Barrington Moore's influential *Origins of Dictatorship and Democracy* (1966), French history is used as an example of the 'conformist', parliamentary democratic road to political modernity and Moore contrasts it with the more exceptional histories of Germany, Japan, Russia and China.

Ultimately, of course, it is a truism to say that any particular country is unique. But although the application of the notion of exceptionalism is indeed not peculiar to France, it is far more widespread than the notion as applied to other countries. Moreover, there is nothing like the alleged end of something to provoke debate on the nature of the phenomenon itself. Thus when scholars and journalists began to talk of the 'end of exceptionalism' in the 1980s (especially Furet, Julliard and Rosanvallon 1988; Mendras 1988; July 1986), these perhaps rather premature obituaries engendered further debate on what was different in the first place, and of course about whether the alleged demise of difference was exaggerated.

In this chapter I begin by looking at what is meant by the notion of exceptionalism, discussion of which has now become almost indissociable from the supposed 'normalisation' of the 1980s and beyond. I then concentrate on the history of French politics and society, and especially the argument that France is particularly conflictual as a result of intense popular participation in politics, broadly defined. By way of illustrating this point further, I then examine the way in which the decline of exceptionalism has been associated with a decline of popular participation in politics, and just as importantly a conscious attempt on the part of intellectuals to depoliticise what was previously so political and participative. Finally, I argue that globalisation – or what I prefer to call the increased global power of capital – which is part of the decline of the individual nature of all countries, including France, has in fact provoked opposition to this process and breathed a certain amount of new life into the tradition of popular participation.

Defining exceptionalism

The claim for French exceptionalism is found in relation to many domains, from cooking to industrial relations, from language to the economy, from cinema to foreign relations. Most accounts, however, and certainly the most convincing, point to France's particularly revolutionary and conflictual tradition when attempting to explain why – as the argument goes – France is different. Predilection for conflict, revolt and revolution is often seen as informing other domains. This view of France as particularly conflictual and revolutionary, sometimes described as the *la guerre franco-française* (see for example Azéma et al. 1985) is indeed a view that has long been prevalent among writers and public figures of various different complexions. Karl Marx wrote enthusiastically in 1843 that France was 'the nerve-centre of European history, sending out electric shocks at intervals which galvanised the whole world' (Marx 1968: 6–7) and Friedrich Engels (1968: 94) commented that 'France is the land where, more than anywhere else, the historical class struggles are each time fought out to a decision, and where, consequently, the changing political forms in which they move are stamped in the sharpest outlines'. More importantly, countless rank and file activists from the early 1800s to May 1968 regarded France as having a special place in the struggles that were to point the way for humanity as a whole.

On the patriotic right, meanwhile, there is Charles de Gaulle's famous *'certaine idée de la France'*, where France 'is only really herself when she is at the forefront of nations (*n'est réellement elle-même que quand elle est au premier rang)'* (de Gaulle 1954: 1), a sentiment that underpinned much of the ideological, hegemonic power of the de Gaulle phenomenon, both in his first political heyday in the 1940s and in his second, at the beginning of the Fifth Republic. De Gaulle twinned this idea of the need for French glory with a view of France as being constantly in danger of descending into civil war and popular revolt. In his Bayeux speech in 1946, in which he famously expressed the ideas that later influenced the design of the Constitution of the Fifth Republic, de Gaulle talked of 'our long-standing Gallic propensity to divisions and quarrels (*notre vieille propension gauloise aux divisions et aux quérelles'*) and declared 'we need new democratic institutions that compensate for our constant political ferment (*il est nécessaire que nos institutions démocratiques nouvelles compensent, par elle-mêmes, les effets de notre perpétuelle effervescence politique)'* (de Gaulle 1970: 649–50).

Thus, both revolutionaries and people of the right have identified the conflictual and revolutionary nature of France as being at the root of its exceptionalism, a crucial difference being that for the left this characteristic was a source of hope, of the potential for universal emancipation, while for the right and centre it was something that needed to be combatted and corrected, and certain more conservative aspects of France consolidated. Further to the right, of course, the extreme right has drawn inspiration from the counter-revolution that often followed revolution or revolt, an extreme right that includes the Front National in contemporary France, but stretches back to Poujadism, to Pétainism, to Maurras and the Ligues of the 1930s, and to the anti-Drefusards roughly a hundred years ago (Winock 1994). All this has become part of France's polarised character, part of *la guerre franco-française* as ideologues and political leaders have stressed these conflictual aspects and acted upon them.

There is no doubt a strong element of pure patriotism, sometimes of arrogance, in many accounts that claim France is exceptional, including among historians. Jules Michelet argued that '[o]ur history alone is complete. Take the history of France; with it you know the world ... This is the tradition that, from Caesar to Charlemagne and Saint Louis, from Louis XIV to Napoleon, makes the history of France that of humanity as a whole. Through it, in various forms, the whole moral history of humanity is perpetuated. The saint of France is the saint of all nations' (Michelet 1961: 35). This intense patriotism is indeed prevalent both among some French historians and men (usually men) of letters, and of course among countless political leaders on the left, right and centre. All scholars of aspects of France are also in danger of believing in rather parental fashion that their particular object of interest is not only unique but 'especially unique', and it is necessary to distinguish between a passion for the subject and the necessary detachment that allows one to be analytical.

However, there is in my view a substantial kernel of truth in the exceptionalism argument, which I shall begin to illustrate by simply mentioning some characteristics of the post-1945 period. In November 1946, 28 percent of the voting electorate, or 6 million people, opted for the strongly pro-Moscow French Communist Party (PCF), and ten years later these figures were still 25 percent and 5.5 million respectively. The Confédération générale du travail (CGT) trade union confederation, which was very close to the PCF, was by far the strongest and the most intransigent of the confederations. Another significant point is that after France came within a hair's breadth of a coup d'état, in May 1958, de Gaulle returned to power and ruled with an authoritarian populism that seemed so out of sync with the time. It was effectively brought to an end by the events of May 1968, which most importantly included a general strike of almost three weeks. There were other well-known phenomena and events which tend also to suggest exceptional predilection for conflict and absence of consensus, such as Poujadism, the intransigence of the *patronat*, and of course the behaviour of France towards Algeria, which led to strong condemnation from other liberal democracies, and which is crucial to an understanding of the period as a whole.

But if we wish to argue that France is exceptional, instead of just radical, we need to suggest how France deviated from a rule or rules followed by other countries. For the notion of exceptionalism is necessarily comparative and suggests a norm to which other countries adhere and to which France does not. Certainly, if we compare the postwar period in France with the same period in other countries, we can conclude that there is in France a marked absence of Fordist compromise, or consensus. As I have argued elsewhere, in France there were none of the formal or informal arrangements between government, trade unions and employers, which were often the key to more consensual politics elsewhere but impossible in France because of its inherent conflictuality and polarity (Hewlett 1998: 36–59). France contrasted markedly with Britain, Germany and most of the Nordic countries in this respect, and the contrast with the U.S. is also clear.

But how about countries of southern Europe, where consensual liberal democracy was far from being the enduring norm? In Spain there was one-party dictatorship from 1939 to 1975; in Portugal the long-established dictatorship was followed by a coup d'état in 1974 and popular uprising in 1975; in Greece the colonels ruled from 1967 to 1974; and in Italy there was chronic governmental instability with a very large Communist Party, albeit more Eurocommunist as the years went by.

Could it be that France deviates from the more consensual, North European norm but conforms broadly to Southern European characteristics? Certainly, as far as social and political conflict, revolt and authoritarian rule are concerned, France seems far less exceptional when compared with Southern Europe than when compared with Northern Europe and the U.S. But what has perhaps been more broadly exceptional about France is the way in which there are many conflictual, divided characteristics combined with a truly international – arguably 'universal' – orientation, which sets France up as an international model in various ways. This is a combination that is found to a far lesser extent in most other countries: France combines some of the revolutionary characteristics of less developed countries with advanced capitalist 'sophistication' in a most unusual way, which I would venture to say is perhaps unique. This is so in many domains, from the universalist ideals of the 1789 Revolution and the Enlightenment, to the imperial designs of the two Napoleons, from the internationalist perspective of the Communist Party to the importance of France as a key player on the international stage of industrialised economies and international diplomacy in particular, not to mention the international, paradigmatic reputation in the arts, intellectual life and culture generally. Other countries also play important parts on these various international stages, including Britain, the U.S. and Germany, but they certainly tend not to be countries that also have a profound and enduring revolutionary history.

French history, revolt and popular participation

There are many reasons for France's conflictual and revolutionary history and historians such as George Rudé (1959), Eugen Weber (1977), Charles Tilly et al. (1975), Georges Lefebvre (1954) and Michel Winock (especially 1986) have each made important contributions to understanding these reasons. However, it should be noted that the political and social history of almost all countries is one of conflict and violence, including advanced capitalist societies with such mild-mannered reputations as Britain and the U.S.

However, France is a particularly interesting case. Although it has long been associated with the democratic ideals of the 1789 Revolution, ranked among the world's leading political democracies, and has been pioneering in modern cultural and intellectual spheres, its conflict-ridden and often violent modern history is evidence of a quite different political development from that of the liberal democratic models. The point about France is that although many aspects of every day life were probably no more and no less violent or conflictual than in many other countries, profound conflict became an essential element in national politics, an element that many political actors and ideologues over the years took for granted and whose history they re-enacted. This is not the place to enter into the details of this history, and I will simply mention the oft-cited fact that between the 1789 Revolution and today, every political regime has ended in coup d'état, revolution or war and that there have been fifteen different constitutions.

To explain this conflictual and violent history, we need to bear in mind the importance of: very uneven social and economic modernisation; a state that was reluctant to alienate the rural population and put substantial resources into the growing cities; an intransigent *patronat*; an often equally intransigent labour movement whose attitude was partly informed by and partly compounded by state repression; a geographical position and international relations that made for profound internal divisions; an intellectual life influenced in particular by the universal ideals of the French Enlightenment and the 1789 Revolution; and finally the tradition of revolution itself, which came to have a dynamic of its own.

In order to begin to suggest an understanding of the changes at the end of the twentieth century (what we might call at the very least the 'weakening of exceptionalism'), it is important to stress the crucial role played by ordinary people, the *demos*.

My contention is that for capitalism to flourish in the long term, there needs to be relatively little direct political involvement on the part of people, or at least only a very mild form (such as is found in most liberal democracies today), a certain 'depoliticisation' that is, incidentally, the virtual antithesis of ancient Athenian democracy. Capitalism is dependent on material inequality for its existence and success. Deeper democracy on the other hand tends to lead to many ordinary people challenging the material inequalities on which capitalism is based, leading ultimately to a challenge to the very building blocks of capitalism, just as liberal democracy challenges formal political privilege attached to birth, for example. Although France became in 1789 the land of one of the clearest modern revolutions, which in many ways laid solid foundations for capitalist enterprise, depoliticisation (or relative depoliticisation) did not take place for a long time, and the constant assertion of the will of the people was to inform the nature of political evolution for many years, and gave rise to almost textbook models of different forms of the struggle for democracy.

Three comments on political currents and traditions will serve to illustrate this. First, the clarity and strength of the Enlightenment project and then the 1789 Revolution is important. Crucially, it was a time when the perceived legitimate sovereign in terms of political power shifted from a tiny but supposedly divinely-inspired elite to the people themselves, a pivotal shift that has come to dominate the vast majority of the world's political regimes and notions of political legitimacy in the two centuries since this time.

Although the *philosophes* expressed notions that were to be dear to, and laid the intellectual basis for, liberal democracy, most of them stopped well short of promoting anything we might today call democracy, either liberal or otherwise, the obvious exception to this being Rousseau. Likewise, 1789 certainly drew in the people, but was modest in its democratic aims and achievements. However, the people were indeed involved in a direct way, and were in fact so involved that in France there grew up a strong tradition of direct involvement; from the *sans culottes* to twentieth-century communism and trade unionism, from the revolution of 1830 to 1968, via 1848, 1871, the strikes of 1936 and 1947, the tradition of direct democracy and popular involvement endured. Indeed, the Paris Commune of 1871 became a landmark and an inspiration for believers in direct democracy such as Marx, and Lenin admired the Commune because it was a state 'without permanent army, without police opposed to the people, without civil servants opposed to the people' (Lenin 1973: 39).

This popular involvement constantly opposed the status quo. But – and this is my second point – the impulse for direct popular participation and radicalism was sufficiently powerful that the enduring, mainstream political ideology of France became Republicanism, which put the people at the heart of its philosophy. Certainly, republicanism became the ideological framework within which social relations and formal politics became more stable and within which capitalism was able to flourish, in a country where labour, while less formally organised than in some other countries, took to the streets easily. It includes broad values such as the importance of individual rights and freedoms (despite less emphasis on this than in Britain or the U.S.), equality before the law, defence of the private sphere against encroachment by the public sphere, and the right to private ownership, all of which are characteristic of conventional liberal democracy as well. But republicanism put the rights and interests of the people centre-stage, at least notionally. It was a compromise between the formal democracy that has always manifested itself more clearly in the philosophy and socio-political practice of, for example, Britain and the U.S., on the one hand, and the radical impulse of popular movements on the other. By adopting the collective interests of the people as its central preoccupation, republicanism could serve as a way of channelling, of accommodating and containing the revolutionary urges of the people and stopping them going further.

Thirdly, compared with many other countries of Northern Europe and the U.S., what is missing in terms of both political practice and political ideology is liberalism, and this remained the case well into the late twentieth century. To continue the theme of depoliticisation and to borrow concepts from Antonio Gramsci (1971), in the nineteenth and twentieth centuries, modern bourgeois rule became established via a blend of coercion (by the ruling class) and consent (by the mass of the people), and is therefore not an order simply imposed by force from above. Certainly, the strength of the popular insurrectionary tradition in France was such that overt coercion was often used in the form of authoritarian regimes, before a more modern 'republican synthesis' tended to bring more consent, and there are plenty of examples of coercive, violent behaviour by republican regimes as well, of course. In Britain and the U.S., in particular, depoliticisation – or what Gramsci calls bourgeois hegemony – relies ideologically on liberal notions of the sanctity of the individual, the rule of law, a minimal state, and very limited participation of the people in politics.

The end of exceptionalism?

Given what has been argued above, it should make sense that, come the 1980s, the most forceful and famous 'end of exceptionalism' argument came from the 'revisionist' historian of the French Revolution, François Furet, along with co-authors Jacques Julliard and Pierre Rosanvallon. Their book *La République du centre*, published in 1988 and subtitled 'La fin de l'exception française', presented a synthesis of their ideas. Although these authors reach somewhat different conclusions, they agree, and generally applaud the fact, that France was falling into line with the more consensual politics of other West European countries and North America.

Emerging particularly strongly in the few years before the bi-centennial celebrations of 1989, Furet's other work also demonstrates his desire to theorise and, in a sense, formalise depoliticisation, and thus to create an orthodoxy of both a different view of French history and of the end of French exceptionalism (see Furet 1978 and 1988; Furet and Ozouf 1988). Furet argues that in late twentieth-century France, where modernisation and liberal democracy have succeeded in eliminating profound ideological conflicts, the notions of revolution and counter-revolution are no longer relevant. Moreover, historians have always accorded too much importance to 1789, he argues, in the mistaken assumption that social and political history is more about sudden, revolutionary breaks with the past than about a slower and less dramatic evolution. France, then, was shedding the revolutionary tradition, so turning the traditional republican or Marxist interpretations on their heads.

But Furet, Rosanvallon and Julliard were part of a broader – and quite conscious – movement that can be described in general terms as liberal, and that set out to consolidate such weak liberal tradition as there was in France. They aimed to rework areas that had hitherto been largely the preserve of left intellectuals, to import ideas from abroad and to create on the intellectual plane an ongoing, sympathetic discussion of French political liberalism that was in harmony with the dominant political and economic practices of the time (Lindenberg 2002). In addition to the authors of *La*

République du centre, this group included such writers as Marcel Gauchet, Luc Ferry and Blandine Kriegel. Significantly, it was very often the role of the 'people' and the notion of popular sovereignty that was addressed in their writings, either implicitly or explicitly, as they sought to replace Rousseau and Marx with Tocqueville and Constant, in both the realm of political philosophy and related areas of intellectual activity.

For Marcel Gauchet, for example, the real significance of French history 'does not lie in its rôle at the forefront of revolutions, as Marx suggested; it lies, rather, in the exemplary difficulty that democracy faced to establish itself and find a means of functioning peacefully' (Gauchet 1995: 14). This is what has been described here – and what Gauchet would probably not describe – as the failure to de-politicise. Rousseau is widely criticised by these writers, and Jacques Julliard, in his book *La faute à Rousseau: essai sur les conséquences historiques de l'idée de souveraineté populaire* (1985: 76–77), claims that Rousseau: 'freed the real modern Leviathan; he unleashed the most unheard of, the most incongruous concept, and also the most difficult to tame: that of the sovereignty of the people'.

Another landmark book was Luc Ferry and Alain Renaut's *La Pensée 68* (1985), which was intended as a critique of Marxist, structuralist and post-structuralist philosophy since the Second World War, and was an attempt to establish a new conceptual model. More significant in the clarity of its attempt to promote a paradigm shift than in the quality of its critique, it sought to challenge all the major French forms of non-liberal thought that retained a systematic rebelliousness, so scorned by these new liberals.

A more obviously strategic attempt to put down the roots of the new liberalism was the establishment in 1982 of the Fondation Saint-Simon think tank, with clear socio-political, and this time business, ends, involving some of the same liberal intellectuals (Laurent 1998).

At the heart of all of this, of course, and much more fundamental than the thoughts and actions of a group of intellectuals, was what has been described as the Mitterrand experiment. Books and articles about the left in France appear regularly, reminding us of the critical role of the Socialists in enabling the decline of left activism; the year of the twentieth anniversary of the first Mitterrand victory – 2001 – saw, for example, the publication of Giret and Pellegrin's *Vingt ans de pouvoir*, where they argue that 'the left … carrying the flag of progress … is today perceived as the incarnation of a certain conservatism' (2001: 228); Collin and Cotta's *L'Illusion plurielle*, meanwhile, is subtitled 'Why the left is no longer the left (*Pourquoi la gauche n'est plus la gauche*)'; and the most recent edition of Serge Halimi's book on the history of the French left is now entitled *Quand la Gauche essayait*.

Regarding this history of the left in the 1980s and 1990s, I would argue that a common theme in many of the changes was precisely the dwindling importance of political activism, the decline of the direct intervention of the *demos*: the weakening and social-democratisation of the Communist Party, the erosion of the more militant trade unions and falling-off of strike activity, the increasing rarity of the left intellectual, the decreasing interest in elections, but also the 'conservatisation' of Gaullism. All these phenomena point to a less participatory profile for France.

That *cohabitation* became possible, and even apparently went down well with the electorate, demonstrates the degree of change of political culture. The most notable exception of course was the rise of the Front National, which was arguably a reaction to the *banalisation* of the rest. The brief and uneven Fordist compromise, which enabled a certain tri-partite consensus and the decline of activism (Hewlett 1998), gave way to the sort of neoliberalism whose social tinge might distinguish it from the more extreme neoliberalism of Blair or Clinton, but its underlying motivation became intimately related with a project of harmonisation with the needs of global capital.

Globalisation is indeed highly germaine to any discussion of French exceptionalism, for if France was or is still exceptional, what happens as advanced capitalist countries become increasingly similar? Not that globalisation is anything new, contrary to what many contemporary commentators seem to believe; the concentration of capital on a global scale has been taking place for centuries, although I would argue that since the early 1970s there has, world-wide, been a substantial increase in the power of capital over labour. That *is* an important change.

One of the single most significant changes under Mitterrand was of course the economic policy *volte-face* of 1982/83, which was a watershed in that it permanently reoriented government policy in favour of capital and against labour, a process illustrated so clearly by the fact that while the value of shares on the Paris Bourse went into free-fall after the Mitterrand victory in 1981, reflecting blind terror on the part of big business, there was a slight rise in the value of shares immediately after his second presidential victory in 1988. The 1982/83 U-turn was in fact an act of submission to the trends and needs of the global economy, at the time dominated on the political stage by the policies of Reagan and Thatcher. Certainly, the modernisation and internationalisation of the French economy has been taking place steadily since the Second World War. More recently, consolidation of the neoliberal nature of international financial and trading organisations, such as the International Monetary Fund, the World Bank and the OECD, has reinforced the notion that there is no alternative to tayloring many aspects of society – and therefore its governance – to the needs of big business. The European Union, meanwhile, has done the same, through the market-driven nature of the Single European Act, the Maastricht Treaty and monetary union, despite some gestures in the direction of a 'social Europe'.

Many different currents in France today are preoccupied with what global harmonisation is doing to the country. On the one hand there is a discourse that draws on nationalism, especially anti-Americanism, and despairs for example at the anglicisation of the French language and the increasing dominance of Hollywood, not to mention the prevalence of Nike and Macdonalds in the high street. There is a significant anti-European lobby, split between right-wing nationalism and left movements against big business. There is the José Bové phenonomen, which draws on traditional left militancy and anti-capitalism, as well as a certain nationalism. Finally, there is, it seems, since 1995, a resurgence of left activism which partially taps into global movements, a point to which I return below.

Jill Lovecy (1999) suggests that during the last two decades of the twentieth century, there were two 'waves' of literature on the end of exceptionalism. The first was authored by François Furet and other, like-minded writers, who were optimistic as to the changes that were taking place. Writers of the second wave, she argues, were far less optimistic because they were reacting to (and often against) globalisation. I would agree to an extent, but would argue that this was generally speaking a right-left split, as the interests of liberal capitalism were fairly close to the interests of international capital. Gone are the days when a '*certaine idée*' of the French economy could sustain itself in competition with the global economy, as became clear in 1981/82.

New struggles, new exceptionalism?

Before concluding, I want to suggest tentatively and briefly that the global harmonisation of the way in which capital operates and the more intense exploitation of labour world-wide, which is part of the weakening of France's exceptionalism, has now led to increased militancy on the part of the labour movement and certain social groups (Brochier and Delouche 2000; Pingaud 2000; Crettiez and Sommier 2002). Especially since 1995, there has been an increased tendency for labour to strike and to take to the streets (Béroud, Mouriaux and Vakaloulis 1998; Groux 1998; Lelaube 1997). New or adapted forms of collective action have gradually evolved, including the Solidaires Unitaires Démocratiques (SUD) trade union movement, and the *coordinations* phenomenon. There are movements in defence of immigrants, the homeless, and generally *les mouvements des sans*. Also there is the anti-globalisation movement, mentioned above, which has clear links with the anti-capitalist demonstrations that have been seen in Seattle, Prague, Gothenburg, Nice, Genoa and, most recently, on the Larzac plateau, which attracted millions of mainly young people and which *Le Monde* (Dupont 2003) described as a '*carrefour de la contestation sociale* (crossroads of social revolt)'. In the more conventionally political sphere, the Arlette Laguiller phenomenon, and more generally the resurgence of the far left, is part of an expression of disillusionment with the conventional left. Finally, as far as the left intellectual movement is concerned, the Bourdieu phenomenon is well-known, as is the *Liber-Raisons d'agir* book series he was closely associated with (e.g. Bourdieu 1998; Halimi 1997). But it is also worth mentioning Alain Badiou, Daniel Bensaïd, Dominique Lecourt, Jacques Rancière and Emmanuel Terray, each of whom produces serious and increasingly influential philosophical work, all of which is strongly influenced by Marxism (also see Bourseiller et al. 1999; Actuel Marx 2000; Kouvélakis 2000). The success of *Le Monde diplomatique* in its current incarnation as a paper critiquing and campaigning strongly against the neoliberal global agenda is also central to these developments. The importance of these developments should not be exaggerated, but I would argue that the radicalism of the past has certainly not been entirely extinguished.

Conclusion

To conclude, it emerges from the above that we should treat the notion of French exceptionalism with caution, and that unless it is approached in a serious and rigorous way it is in danger of leaving us none the wiser. I have argued that, if France is (or has been) exceptional, this is because of the combination of popular involvement and radicalism, on the one hand, and the importance of France on the international stage and at the forefront of advanced capitalism, on the other. Another way of putting it is that France expresses particularly clearly the various dualisms of modernity: it is both radical and conservative; progressive and reactionary; democratic and elitist. Arguably, in most industrialised countries with which France is compared it is the latter tendencies – conservative, reactionary and elitist – that have been more dominant, while in France there has been a stronger blend of both tendencies. This chapter has attempted to illustrate this point by exploring the purported 'end of exceptionalism', which in its interpretation by intellectuals is closely bound up with an examination of the role of ordinary people in politics. Advanced capitalism – particularly the neoliberal variant with which we are now living – needs depoliticisation, which was for a long time difficult in France. But I have also suggested tentatively that, if we take what is special about France to be its radicalism, rumours of the end of exceptionalism are probably exaggerated.

Notes

1.   I would like to thank Gregory Elliott for comments on an earlier draft of this chapter.

Chapter 2

EXCEPTIONALISM AND UNIVERSALISM: THE UNEASY ALLIANCE IN THE FRENCH-SPEAKING WORLD

Margaret A. Majumdar

The notion of French exceptionalism is at the heart of French political discourse and culture. Yet it sits in an uneasy alliance with another concept, equally central to the dominant French republican ideology – that of universalism. This chapter explores the contradictions constituting the couplet exceptionalism/universalism, with particular reference to discourses articulating relations between France and its present and former colonies. It will look at the evolution of these discourses, as well as examine contemporary shifts and modifications in relation to what is known as the francophone world.

Exceptionalism and universalism: paradoxes of colonial ideology

The notion of French exceptionalism has developed on the basis of a fundamental paradox, in which universalism figures as one of its key components. It is not a simple particularism, a particular ethnocentrism, such as one finds elsewhere in almost all conceptions of national, ethnic or religious identity. *L'exception française* is signally different because it is founded on wide-ranging pretensions to universalism.

The origins of this universalising tendency can be traced back to ideas developed at the time of the Enlightenment, in the development period of modern capitalism and its expansion into a global economic system. Enlightenment universalism was initially based on the notion of the universality of human reason. It expressed itself through the belief in universal knowledge, through the advances of science, and its application, through technology, to increasing industrial production, greater economic wealth, trade and prosperity. It also expressed itself through a belief in the progress of the human race itself, on the physical, moral, political and cultural planes – in short, the idea of civilisation.

These ideas were of course not limited to France alone, but were at the core of the development of modern European thought. However, their development in the realm of political philosophy and their practical application in the French Revolution and later French Republics have given rise to a specifically French brand of political ideology, inherent in which is the contradiction between universalism and particularism. On the one hand, this political universalism is indebted to Enlightenment ideas of humanity and nature, in which the rights of man and of natural justice extend to all human beings equally. On the other hand, these ideas have found their specific application within the particular framework of the French State. The contradiction between the particular and the universal is there from the outset of the revolutionary period, when the legitimacy of the political state is derived from a universalist concept of human rights and natural justice, but incarnated in the sovereignty of the particular nation. The State needed to define itself in accordance with a particular territory, where the universal basis and aspirations of French republicanism were limited by the constraints of a territorially-based state, with the restriction of citizenship rights, to exclude those outside the nation, as well as to effect internal exclusions on the grounds of gender, wealth or property. The Other was, therefore, from the outset, closely implicated in the definition of the French nation and the jurisdiction of the French State.

The contradiction between universal concepts and national specificity was not, of course, limited to geographical considerations. It was apparent in the development of philosophies of world history, in which the French Revolution had a clear role to play in the universal history of humanity, while at the same time providing legitimacy as the founding national event of the modern French State. It was also apparent in the role assigned to the French language: on the one hand, French was instituted as the national language, the language of the Republic; yet, increasingly, its role as universal language came to be emphasised. A similar process was implicated in the development of a national culture.

Moreover, the role of the Other, upon which all particularisms are predicated, could only be intensified with the expansion of empire in the nineteenth century. Nonetheless, imperial ideology continued to rely heavily on the notion of universalism. This is none too surprising given the form that universalist ideas came to assume and the corresponding importance of history.

Following the expansion of European imperial power, alongside the development of international political movements, such as socialism and communism, founded on a universalist conception of history and inspired by the philosophy of Hegel and others, Europe increasingly arrogated to itself the driving role in world history. Whether this right to sole agency was rationalised on the grounds of greater scientific knowledge, the higher stage of civilisation that it claimed to have achieved, or military might and supposed racial superiority, it expressed itself through the notion of a historical mission. European universalism thus required the existence of the Other, whether this was articulated through the academic problematic of Orientalism, essentialising the inferiority of the non-European through the proselytising mission of universal Christianity to the heathen or through the ideological project of the *mission civilisatrice*. As Partha Chatterjee (1986: 17) has pointed out, 'Enlightenment itself, to assert its sovereignty as the universal ideal, needs its Other; if it could ever actualise itself in the real world as the truly universal, it would in fact destroy itself'.

The extent to which universalist phraseology masks what is in essence a particularist ideology promoting European domination over the colonised peoples has been amply commented upon. Indeed, Samir Amin (1989: vii) insists on the fundamentally anti-universalist character of the Eurocentric approach: 'Eurocentrism is a culturalist phenomenon in the sense that it assumes the existence of irreducibly distinct cultural invariants that shape the historical paths of different peoples. Eurocentrism is therefore anti-universalist, since it is not interested in seeking possible general laws of human evolution. But it does present itself as universalist, for it claims that imitation of the Western model by all peoples is the only solution to the challenges of our time'.

While all the above elements figure in specific expressions of French colonial ideology, there are other elements, characteristic of the phase of Third Republic colonial expansion in the last quarter of the nineteenth and early twentieth centuries, which distinguish it from that of other imperial powers, particularly that of its great rival, Britain. This is its avowed political and cultural project of *assimilation* of the colonised peoples under the banner of a supposedly universal republicanism, based on equality of political rights but equally importantly on the universality of the French language and culture.

The universalism inherent in French colonial ideology has been well documented and analysed, as has its specific link with the political values of republicanism. It is, however, worth pointing out that a great distance had already been travelled from the universalism of knowledge and human rights, characteristic of the Enlightenment philosophers. Abbé Raynal's *Histoire philosophique et politique des deux Indes*, first published in 1770, argued for a truly universal concept of knowledge, in which his particular origins, attributes and beliefs could be put aside in the search for objective truth.[1]

This may now appear a naïve assertion of the possibility of wholly objective knowledge and an ignorance of the link between knowledge and power. However, there is no doubt that there was a clear shift away from the abstract universality of this conception of knowledge to a particular association of universally valid ideas and values with France. This linkage was already evident in the earlier phases of empire, when progressive elements lent their support to French expansionism overseas. Louis Blanc, for instance, argued eloquently in *La Revue du Progrès* of 15 July 1839 for France's unique historical mission to conquer the world through the force of its ideas and values. This not only clearly indicates the exceptionalism inherent in the universalism associated with France; it also marks the beginnings of a shift away from a universalism based solely on political *rights* and scientific *knowledge* to one based on *values*, which will ultimately extend beyond the political to the linguistic and cultural domain.

In this Gallocentric vision, France was at the hub of the universe, a beacon of universal values, to use the familiar image of French *rayonnement*. These values, propounded through imperial ideology, were always closely linked to the particular qualities of the French nation. As Edward Said has said: 'For the lobbies and what today we call publicists – ranging from novelists and jingoists to mandarin philosophers – the French empire was uniquely connected to the French national identity, its brilliance, civilizational energy, special geographic, social and historical development' (Said 1993: 206).

This is not to say that there has been a monolithic vision of France's colonial role. Earlier phases of empire have to be distinguished from the brief impact of the Second Republic on the colonies, as well as the key phase of Third Republic expansionism, carried out mainly in the name of the values of the French Republic. However, even during this phase, tensions were still there, broadly speaking between, on the one hand, the doctrine of *assimilation* linked to a universalist republicanism and on the other, the doctrine of *association*, linked with more pragmatic colonial ideologues such as Lyautey.

If *assimilation* became the watchword of colonial ideology in key territories of the French Empire, notably Algeria and West African colonies such as Senegal, it is perhaps most notably through its appeal to the colonised elites, for whom its attractiveness is evident. Senghor, for instance, expressed his idealistic view of the impact of this policy, dating from the 1848 Revolution, in eloquent terms, not just for the political rights that were granted, but also for the cultural benefits that it brought to the individual.[2]

However, the granting of male political rights at this time to the Four Communes of Senegal, along with the French Caribbean territories, was the exception rather than the rule. In other territories, and throughout the period of the Third Republic, there was no concrete agenda for assimilating the subjects of the empire with the citizens of the Republic through the application of universal political rights. In contrast with the *ideological* promotion of universalism, the *practice* of French imperialism, as with that of other European powers, was to accentuate difference and divisions in the colonies, as Sartre pointed out in his preface to Fanon's *Damnés de la Terre* (Wretched of the Earth).[3]

In reality, French imperialism was not a moment in the ongoing march towards effective implementation of universal human rights, to include the colonised on the basis of equality. In spite of the importance of the notion of a universal history to European modernity, history was in fact evacuated from the French colonial sphere. This could be seen as a throwback to Hegel, who, in his *Philosophy of History*, dismissed Africa as outside history altogether:

> At this point we leave Africa never to mention it again. For it is no historical part of the world; it has no movement of development to exhibit. Historical movement in it – that is in its northern part – belongs to the Asiatic or European World ...

> What we properly understand as Africa, is the Unhistorical, Undeveloped Spirit, still involved in the *conditions of mere nature* and which had to be presented here only as on the threshold of the World's history (quoted in Ashcroft et al. 1995: 15).

Others, such as Marx and Engels, saw colonialism, in spite of its negative aspects, as nonetheless carrying the positive benefit of bringing those countries excluded from history back into the onward march of universal history. Many of those who became involved in anticolonial struggles seized on the importance of becoming fully part of this history as agents in their own right. For Fanon, in particular, this was the moment for the colonised to snatch back their human status and, at the same time, to enter history and make it truly universal for the first time.

This was also a crucial element for some proponents of *négritude*, who affirmed the particularism of race, while inscribing it in an overall historical philosophy, as a stage in the dialectical movement towards a universal synthesis of humanity, the moment of negativity, or a means to a higher end. Sartre (1948a: *XLII*) describes the black man as 'marching on a crest between the particularism of the past, which he has just surmounted, and the universalism of the future which will signal the twilight of his *négritude*'.

Of course, Sartre's universalism is based on the concept of a universal proletarian class, transcending racial particularisms, and not a liberal Enlightenment universalism, couched in terms of the Rights of Man.[4] It remains nonetheless essentially an abstract concept, in which to become universal, the 'Negro' must tear out his heart, i.e., his race, unlike that of Aimé Césaire, who describes his vision in more concrete, pluralistic terms (1957: 15):

> I'm not going to entomb myself in some strait particularism. But I don't intend either to become lost in a fleshless universalism. There are two paths to doom: by segregation, by walling yourself up in the particular; or by dilution, by thinning off into the emptiness of the 'universal'.

I have a different idea of a universal. It is a universal rich with all that is particular, rich with all the particulars there are, the deepening of each particular, the coexistence of them all.

Some argue that the contradictions in French colonial ideology can be attributed to the notion of the two Frances: on the one hand, *la France généreuse*, home of the Rights of Man and revolutionary ideals; on the other, a France characterised by reaction, colonialism and racism. We have seen the appeal of the former to some members of the colonised elites, such as Senghor, or indeed Césaire himself (Confiant 1993: 88–89). In France itself, these two Frances have been embodied in very different political traditions, which have waged an almost continuous conflict for more than two centuries. At the same time, the existence of the two Frances has also been seen as a contradiction inherent to France as a whole, across the *franco-français* divide, expressing itself, on the one hand, in an idealism advocating a universal humanism, and, on the other, in a practice of racism that particularises its Other.

Moreover, this split was reflected in quite brutal, blatant terms in the divide between the Home and the Colonial. As Sartre has pointed out, not only was the treatment of workers different, it was rationalised in terms of different ideological stances: while workers in France and Britain were portrayed, in terms of a universal humanism, as human beings who freely sell their labour power, in the colonies there was no pretence of a free contract. Forced labour and military conquest were rationalised through the dehumanisation of the colonised.[5]

It is clear that contradictions are operating on a number of levels: on the ideological level, between different conceptions of France; within colonial ideology itself; as well as between the ideology and the practice. If it is nonetheless possible to insist on the internal contradiction at the heart of the couplet, universalism/exceptionalism, it is in full recognition of the fact that both these concepts are relative and ideological in nature. As such, one would look in vain for evidence of their incarnation in any pure form in the historical reality of French colonial practice. It now remains to be seen how these concepts have fared since decolonisation.

The original francophone project

The francophone movement, generally said to be launched with the publication of an issue of *Esprit* in 1962, in the immediate aftermath of decolonisation, gave a new lease of life to the universalist discourse. *La Francophonie*, in its original form, represented an idealistic vision of a community sharing the French language and culture, based on the core universalist values of Enlightenment and republican philosophy. The founding fathers, including Senghor, Bourguiba, Diori, Sihanouk, articulated their vision of this new community in sometimes almost mystical humanist terms. Senghor, for instance, described *La Francophonie* as 'this integral humanism which is weaving its threads around the globe, this symbiosis of dormant sources of energy arising from all the continents, all the races which are awakening to their shared warmth' (quoted in Deniau 1983: 21). For Bourguiba, it was the French language that allowed the members of the Francophone community to become 'truly human beings' (Deniau 1983: 17). This new concept was thus portrayed in absolute ideal terms, a new version of the brotherhood of man, or the virtual realisation of a form of heaven on earth.

In fact, the links that might have given it a more concrete foundation, in terms of a shared history or geography, were largely evacuated from the discourse. Indeed, it was only subsequently, and gradually, that the community was to acquire an institutional basis of any kind. History, which had played an important role in the theorisation of the anticolonial struggles, was once more relegated to the shadows. The reasons for this are plain: given its origins in the process of colonisation and decolonisation, the recent history of those concerned could hardly provide the basis for the conceptualisation, nor for the legitimacy, of the francophone community, without reawakening the conflicts of the past. The absence of one of the key founding principles of modernity, that of historical progress, was nonetheless a serious flaw in the discourse and affected its credibility as an appropriate vehicle for taking the former colonies forward in a progressive way. Far from acting as a conduit for modernisation and development, the birth of *Francophonie* thus signalled the end of history, through the establishment of this virtual paradigm of the abstract universal defined in idealistic terms.

The virtual character of *Francophonie* was further accentuated by the absence of geography as a key defining concept. *Francophonie* was defined as a virtual space, not linked to particular geographical territory. Bourguiba had made this plain, by insisting that *Francophonie* was 'situated beyond politics or geography' and that its founding principles were above all 'philosophical, involving the great ideals of 1789' (quoted in Deniau 1983: 17). The notion of geographical spaces, demarcated into national or regional territories and regional groupings, as well as through hierarchical ordering into *métropole* and colonies, or, in the later terminology, of centre and periphery, is a factor of differentiation, which was at odds with the ideal universalism of this discourse.

Again, this is a clear break with one of the guiding principles of the anticolonial struggles, the reclamation of a geographical identity, the recovery of the national land that had been usurped through colonial violence. As Said has said (1993: 271):

> If there is anything that radically distinguishes the imagination of anti-imperialism, it is the primacy of the geographical element. Imperialism after all is an act of geographical violence through which virtually every space in the world is explored, charted, and finally brought under control. For the native, the history of colonial servitude is inaugurated by loss of the locality to the outsider; its geographical identity must thereafter be searched for and somehow restored.

The universalist focus was thus entirely provided by the common French language and culture. In practice, difference, sometimes described as 'special flavour', or seasoning added to the common heritage, was consigned to the exotic regions of the former colonies.[6]

However, the unifying role of the French language and culture was advocated without reference to a leading role for France itself. This was all the more surprising, given that one of the key sources often quoted in support of the universality of the French language, Antoine de Rivarol's *Discours sur l'universalité de la langue française* (1784), actually links this universality to political, geographical and cultural factors, particular to France, in other words, French exceptionalism.[7]

Indeed, the impetus for the development of *Francophonie* had come not from France itself but from former colonies, in collaboration with francophone Canadians. To a certain extent, the language and culture had become disembodied, almost Platonic ideas.

In fact, French politicians had shown considerable ambivalence towards the developing francophone movement and reluctance to associate France too closely. On the one hand, this has been interpreted as a wish to protect France against accusations of neocolonialism. On the other hand, however, there was clearly a preference for pursuing French interests through the promotion of bilateral ties with individual countries, rather than encouraging a real forum for multilateral connections and cooperation.

However, in spite of this initial reticence, there was clearly no sense in which the universal mission of France had disappeared from metropolitan political ideology of the time. This mission was implicit in the ideas of de Gaulle, who, in presenting his New Year wishes to the nation on 31 December 1967, could automatically assign universal validity to the objectives of the French State, solely on the grounds of their Frenchness. Some years later, François Mitterrand was still articulating this same belief in the role of France to guide the human race and bring enlightenment to it, as in his 1981 inauguration address.[8]

The capacity to influence the course of world history has been closely related to the sphere of ideas, rather than other more tangible factors. One may disagree with those, who, like Adda and Smouts, insist that France is not a real world power in economic, political or military terms and never has been. There is nonetheless a kernel of truth in their view that French power has had an immaterial, abstract basis, dependent upon 'prestige' and the 'quality of its message', particularly when this aspired to universal significance (Adda and Smouts 1989: 9). Or, as Edward Said (1993: 204) has put it: 'not all empires were the same. France's empire, [...] though no less interested than Britain's in profit, plantations and slaves, was energized by "prestige"'. While real material interests are certainly involved and have a major part to play in defining the nature of France's relationship with its ex-colonies, it is clear that the 'message' is an important element in defining French power. If one defines a predominantly ideological discourse through its lack of correspondence with reality, then it is certainly the case that ideology was a paramount element in the earliest phases of *Francophonie*.

The ideological nature of the discourse was evident in the promotion of the *virtual* dimension of *Francophonie*, far removed from an analysis of real geopolitical and historical considerations. It was also indirectly indicated by the absence of one of the most important former French colonies, Algeria, which had not, for a variety of reasons, felt able to join the francophone organisations. Moreover, it comes out through the shifts that the discourse subsequently underwent, in parallel with real shifts in global power relations, but which were not articulated in relation to these. It is these developments that will now be examined.

The shift to binarism

With the increasing involvement of France in the institutional life of *Francophonie* from the 1970s, culminating in 1986 with Mitterrand's hosting of the first francophone summit at Versailles, it was evident that the francophone discourse had undergone a significant change. Although universalism continued to play an important part, *Francophonie* was increasingly seen as a vehicle for the defence of French exceptionalism in the face of 'Anglo-Saxon' cultural hegemony. Once again, the tensions between universalism and exceptionalism came to prominence.

While other issues relating to French resistance to global U.S. economic, political and military power were involved, the debate was conducted predominantly on the terrain of culture. At first, the universal quality of the French language was defended, in a direct binary opposition to the global domination of English. This was supported by the French State's language policies, including repression of foreign linguistic influence at home through legislation, terminological decrees, pressures on scientists to deliver papers only in French and quotas of French-language material in the audio-visual media. Outside France, an active policy promoted the teaching and learning of French as well as the export of French culture. This was reflected in the francophone discourse by a constant reminder of the presence of the French language and culture 'on all five continents', echoing the reality of continuing French global power and influence.

However, it soon became obvious that such a direct challenge on the linguistic front was doomed to failure. French could simply not compete as a world language on the same basis as English. A new tack had to be found. It was at this point that a major shift in the discourse began to emerge, in which French exceptionalism was defined through its aptitude to promote *diversity*. Still defining itself in binary opposition to Anglo-Saxon hegemony, *Francophonie* was presented as the natural vehicle of diversity, in the face of the homogenising, steam-rolling tendencies of globalised U.S. mass culture, which was imposing Disney, MacDonalds, Coca Cola and other products and cultural phenomena on the entire planet. The enormity of this discursive shift can only be understood when measured against the centralising, homogenising tendencies of France's own cultural apparatus at home.

Increasingly throughout the 1980s, differences within the French-speaking world were not only acknowledged but also celebrated, most strikingly through the creation of the television network TV5 in 1984, to provide a media forum for this geographical and cultural diversity.

The shift was crystallised most strikingly in the 1993 GATT negotiations, when France became the champion of the defence of the *exception culturelle*, to protect the diversity of French culture against the influx of audio-visual media material from Hollywood. Moreover, the defence of French culture was soon broadened to include a defence of European cultures across the board. The *exception culturelle*, at least momentarily, acquired a general European significance and all in the name of a defence of cultural diversity.

These changes were reflected in the discourse of *Francophonie*, when the Mauritius Summit of 1993 marked a profound shift in the type of language used to define the objectives of the community – '*unité dans la diversité*'. Henceforth, *Francophonie* would have as its mission the promotion of diversity and the fight against the '*uniformisation de la planète*', in which the French language was now considered the ideal weapon, as Jacques Toubon, Minister of Culture and Francophonie, stated on the eve of the summit (*Le Monde*, 15 October 1993).

This did not imply the end of universalism, but rather its redefinition. From the abstract universal humanism that had characterised the beginnings of *Francophonie*, the new universalism was now expressed in terms of the mission to be the universal champion of diversity. This new discourse certainly came closer to recognising the importance of the notion of differential geographical and cultural spaces, and it is noticeable that, in this phase, geography came to play a more important role in the definition of *Francophonie*. It was subject to further redefinition in subsequent years, when French or francophone exceptionalism was increasingly articulated through its role as champion of pluralism and plurilingualism.

Multipolarity in the new francophone discourse

Moving away from the binary opposition between French and English and in line with its new pluralistic logic, Francophone discourse evolved quite rapidly from the mid-1990s into a defence of plurilingualism and cultural pluralism. *Francophonie* was promoted as the vehicle for the defence and promotion of all cultures and languages, struggling to survive in a globalised world.

The promotion of national languages other than French had in fact been an objective of the former ACCT (now Agence de la Francophonie) for many years. Indeed, the first programmes go back to 1975 (Judge 1999: 6). Nonetheless, the development of the French language remains a key objective for the organisation. Indeed, at the Cotonou Summit of 1995, it was proclaimed the most important objective for *Francophonie* (Judge 1999: 13). At the same time, those responsible for the organisation at the highest levels, e.g., Margie Sudre, Minister for Francophonie from 1995 to 1997, and Stélio Farandjis of the Haut Conseil de la Francophonie, insisted that their brief was much wider than the promotion of the language and involved a large measure of idealism in the definition of the organisation's goals, to include basic political values of freedom, equality, fraternity, solidarity and partnership (Judge 1999: 13).

Given the increasing scope of the francophone organisations to include members whose populations count only a minority of francophones, the common thread previously provided by the French language has assumed less importance. The most modern version of the Charte de la Francophonie does not require any language qualification. Given the centrality of the French language to the earliest definitions of the francophone community, this new position is not without its contradictions and tensions. While it may offer an appealing pluralistic vision to actual or potential members, the ties uniting these very diverse countries or regions have become very diffuse, given the theoretical dilution of the role of the French language.

The new ideology may fruitfully be compared to notions of *créolité*, developed in the French Caribbean by writers such as Glissant, Bernabé, Chamoiseau and Confiant, for the new francophone discourse is clearly dipping in the same pool for its ideas of a complex, heterogeneous diversity.

Supporters of *créolité* seek to establish a distance both from universalist notions of the *same*, as well as the monolithic notion of difference expressed through the concept of *négritude*, itself defined as a universalism. Diversity is seen not as a single substance or essence, but 'a multiplicity of relations, a constellation of forces held in place by a complex process of attraction and repulsion. In contrast to *Négritude*'s obsession with the 'pure', *Antillanité* makes of *le métissage*, understood both culturally and, presumably, racially, a supremely positive, indeed constitutive, principle' (Burton and Reno 1995: 147).

These ideas are not confined to the Caribbean context. Diana Brydon, for instance, makes a similar point about Creole texts in the Canadian context:

> these creole texts are also part of the post-colonial search for a way out of the impasse of the endless play of post-modernist difference that mirrors liberalism's cultural pluralism. These books [...] are searching for a new globalism that is neither the old universalism nor the Disney simulacrum. This new globalism simultaneously asserts local independence and global interdependencies. It seeks a way to cooperate without cooption, a way to define differences that do not depend on myths of cultural purity or authenticity but that thrive on an interaction that 'contaminates' without homogenizing. (Ashcroft et al. 1995: 141)

While much of this reflects what is being articulated in the new francophone discourse, it remains to be seen how far the idealistic vision is in fact being translated into the reality of the new institutional relations, which are being developed in tandem with this new ideological approach.

The shift to politics

A key question to be asked is whether the development of the political dimension of *Francophonie* in fact marks a shift away from ideology towards a greater realism or whether it signals a move towards a greater degree of pragmatism, modelled on the Commonwealth.

The decisive shift came at the 1997 Hanoi Summit, which created a permanent organisational structure, the Organisation Internationale de la Francophonie, and gave it political substance through the election of the former UN Secretary-General, Boutros Boutros-Ghali, to head it. There was also evidence of a new realism in the discourse of the decision-makers. Prior to the summit, Charles Josselin, then Minister for Cooperation, including Francophonie, talked in an interview on RFI on 12 November 1997 not only about the special relationship that bound France to its African partners, but also its real embeddedness in history and geography (quoted in Judge 1999: 23). This marked an attempt to link French geopolitical strategy to the further development of *Francophonie* in a way that was far removed from the idealistic vision of the founding fathers.

Boutros Boutros-Ghali certainly attempted to turn *Francophonie* into a body similar to the United Nations, capable of cooperating with organisations like the Commonwealth, the League of Arab Nations and NGOs, in a shift that could be interpreted as a move to 'normalise' the organisation and put it on a par with other international bodies. Anne Judge (1999: 3) claims that *Francophonie* now mirrors the Commonwealth in terms of political organisation, while insisting that greater idealism still provides its theoretical basis. There has been a change of focus in the matters considered pertinent to *Francophonie*, whose remit now covers the new ground of political issues (for instance, monitoring elections and organising peace missions), as well as economic cooperation and development, with the cultural and linguistic issues that previously gave it its direction figuring less prominently. The 1999 Monckton Summit set the seal on this new agenda, with the backing of the Jospin government.

It remains to be seen of course whether the real changes and the political aims that the organisation is now setting for itself, under its new Secretary-General, Abdou Diouf, will eventually produce a further shift in the discourse through which it proclaims its identity to the world. There is certainly a perceptible gap between the idealism of the present discourse and the political and economic realities that have now come to the fore. However, the universalism/ exceptionalism couplet, which has been at the heart of this discourse until the present time, has already proved its adaptability through the various shifts and may well show further resilience.

Notes

1. Cf. this section attributed to Diderot (Raynal 1981: 14–15): 'O vérité sainte! c'est toi seule que j'ai respectée. Si mon ouvrage trouve encore quelques lecteurs dans les siècles à venir, je veux qu'en voyant combien j'ai été dégagé de passions et de préjugés ils ignorent la contrée où je pris naissance ; sous quel gouvernement je vivais ; quelles fonctions j'exerçais dans mon pays ; quel culte je professais : je veux qu'ils me croient tous leur concitoyen et leur ami'.
2. 'C'est ainsi que les hommes de couleur, singulièrement les Nègres, ont pu accéder non seulement à la liberté du citoyen, mais encore et surtout à cette vie personnelle que seule donne la culture ; c'est ainsi qu'ils ont pu, malgré la régression que constituèrent le Second Empire et la Troisième République, apporter leur contribution à l'humanisme français d'aujourd'hui, qui se fait véritablement universel parce que fécondé par les sucs de toutes les races de la terre' (Senghor 1948: 1).
3. 'Ainsi l'Europe a-t-elle multiplié les divisions, les oppositions, forgé des classes et parfois des racismes, tenté par tous les expédients de provoquer et d'accroître la stratification des sociétés colonisées' (Sartre 1987: 7–8).
4. Sartre also propounds another concept of universality, which is founded on the universality of Reason. In his preface to Memmi's *Portrait du colonisé* (1966: 32), he describes Memmi's own approach thus: '… entre l'usurpation raciste des colons et la nation future que les colonisés construiront, où il « soupçonne qu'il n'aura pas de place », il essaye de vivre sa particularité en la dépassant vers l'universel. Non pas vers l'Homme, qui n'existe pas encore, mais vers une Raison rigoureuse et qui s'impose à tous'.
5. 'Nos soldats, outre-mer, repoussent l'universalisme métropolitain, appliquent au genre humain le *numerus clausus* ; puisque nul ne peut sans crime dépouiller son semblable, l'asservir ou le tuer, ils posent en principe que le colonisé n'est pas le semblable de l'homme' (Sartre 1987 : 10).
6. Cf. the criticisms attached to some Commonwealth writing 'on the grounds of a specificity which runs counter to abstract universal concerns', as in Flemming Brahms, 'Entering our own ignorance. Subject-object problems in Commonwealth literature',

(Ashcroft et al. 1995: 67). Universality is assumed to be the sole province of European or Western writing and thought, as one critic illustrates: 'Mere race and color problems never produce good literature. These problems have to be submerged in more universal themes', A. L. McLeod, *The Commonwealth Pen*, 1961 (quoted in Ashcroft et al. 1995: 67).

7. 'Cette universalité de la langue française (…) offre pourtant un grand problème: elle tient à des causes si délicates et si puissantes à la fois que, pour les démêler, il s'agit de montrer jusqu'à quel point la position de la France, sa constitution politique, l'influence de son climat, le génie de ses écrivains, le caractère de ses habitants et l'opinion qu'elle a su donner d'elle au reste du monde, jusqu'à quel point tant de causes diverses ont pu se combiner et s'unir pour faire à cette langue une fortune si prodigieuse'(quoted at http://www.france.diplomatie.fr/francophonie/citations.html).

8. 'Une France juste et solidaire qui entend vivre en paix avec tous peut éclairer la marche de l'humanité' (quoted in Adda and Smouts 1989: 9).

THE ELUSIVE FRENCH EXCEPTION

Sue Collard

What exactly is the French exception? What, if anything, makes the French claim to exceptionalism more convincing than others such as the American, the German or the British (Lipset 1996; Adams and van Minnen 1994; Madsen 1998; Gauzy 1998; Colley 1992)? Are all nations not in some respect exceptional? Here my approach is not to seek the answers through a scholarly demonstration of the ways in which French history, politics and culture have combined to produce a particular set of events and traditions that are allegedly different from those of any other country, or by means of a comparative study of policy areas intended to highlight particular aspects of divergence or convergence. For even if these methods may generate some interesting observations and conclusions, it is hard to see how any such attempt to judge or measure national uniqueness could ever escape the obvious limits inherent in a necessary but infinite set of comparisons, making the quest to define the French exception somewhat elusive. Rather, I shall seek to show that what has made the case for the French exception so much more convincing than any other is the manner and extent to which both the expression 'French exception' and the concepts that it denotes have come to pervade public discourse in France today. This has happened on a scale and with an impact extending well beyond the boundaries of the Hexagon, far surpassing that of any other potential contender and it is this that makes the French exception so exceptional. Secondly, I shall show how a group of, mainly, centrist and centre-left intellectuals, politicians and business people with a specific political agenda of their own have orchestrated and promoted the notion of the 'end of the French exception'.

Uses and origin of the expression 'the French exception'

The uses of the term 'French exception' embrace a vast range of subject areas and registers of discourse, from the trivial and weird, through the spectrum of journalese to the seriously political and academic. Indeed, academics both within and beyond the borders of the Hexagon have adopted the notion of the French exception as a useful framework for their analyses of contemporary France, usually to evaluate manifestations and degrees of change, either on the 'before and after' model of 'France then' versus 'France now', or as a means of comparing particular policy areas in France with those of other Western democracies.[1] They have largely taken their cue from the political debates that have dominated the agenda over the past twenty years and which, for reasons to which we will shortly return, have had as their underlying focus the question of whether or not the French exception still exists, if it ever did, and if so, in what form. But beyond these serious political and academic debates, and at a more general and accessible level, the French exception is clearly also being very widely used as a way of pointing to areas in which France is perceived as being different from other countries, such as road safety, gynaecology, the banking system, the constitution, culture, the teaching of mathematics and philosophy, treatment of AIDS, the success of the National Front, the blood contamination controversy, the *grandes écoles*, the shooting of migrating birds, cryptography, the fight against religious sects, and most recently the number of deaths in the summer heatwave of 2003. The use of the exception concept usually takes on connotations that are either positive (the defence of culture or gynaecology as a medical specialism), or negative (statistics for road accidents), depending on the issue and author's position. Yet the important thing to note is that the expression seems to have broken through the barriers of élite discourse to become a commonplace shortcut for raising issues or fighting battles, so that it now permeates debate at all levels, independently of its origin or intended application.

But what exactly was the origin of the expression and how did it become so popular? Curiously enough, in spite of (or perhaps because of) the very common usage of the expression, none of the academics, journalists or ordinary citizens to whom I posed the question were able to give its origin, making it appear all the more elusive. Nor apparently had any of them ever asked this question themselves, which is surely an indication of the extent to which the expression has become an accepted dimension of the political landscape. An explanation for this state of ignorance can no doubt be found in the fact that the expression 'the French exception' is naturally 'understood' by any scholar or observer of France, since it evokes a whole host of features which can easily be identified with it: the uniquely important role of the central state, the construction of a republican model which was intended to be exemplary, with a universal and civilising mission, committed to spreading the values of the Revolution, the propensity towards conflict and political turmoil rather than consensus and reform, and the traditional divide between the political right and left. Indeed, in the very extensive literature analysing France over the past couple of centuries and beyond, going back as far as Montesquieu, de Tocqueville and Michelet, France has often been described in terms that emphasise its singularity, its originality, its exemplarity and even its *'hexagonalité'* (Montesquieu 1961; de Tocqueville 1928 and 1966; Michelet 1963; Hoffman 1963; Wyplosz 2000). These rather mystical representations of France were successfully tapped into by de Gaulle in the 1960s when he set about 'restoring' French grandeur on the basis of a position of national independence that was totally at odds with the collective security policies of its neighbours. His gamble that to restore greatness necessitated an ambitious set of policies matched by bold rhetoric was clearly successful, in the sense that accounts of the Gaullist period published in recent years often emphasise that these were indeed the glorious years of the French exception, even if the analytical framework most commonly adopted to describe them in the earlier literature was usually that of modernisation rather than exceptionalism (see for example Hoffman 1963; Cerny 1980b). So the concept of French exceptionalism is familiar to all observers of France and has been much commented upon, even though the expression itself seems only to have been coined in 1988; paradoxically, this was in the context of its own alleged demise, as the subtitle of the book *La République du centre. La fin de l'exception française* by François Furet, Jacques Julliard and Pierre Rosan-vallon indicated.

The 'end of the exception' debate

La République du centre is in fact a collection of three essays, all of which contribute to the central theme that is best summed up in Furet's preface: 'we are all agreed: we are at a turning point … an era is coming to an end … What we are living through is quite simply the end of French exceptionality' (Furet et al. 1988: 11).[2] He went on to describe how France had had an unparalleled history, marked by the early development of the state and by a series of revolutions, so that until recently it occupied a unique position among other nations, which it saw as being exemplary. Indeed, it was this claim to the exemplarity of the French model that made France exceptional, rather than any differences it may have had in comparison with other nations (54). France, he explained, has traditionally had a particular way of orchestrating its national dramas, of celebrating its contradictory passions and conducting its politics that has both infuriated and fascinated foreign observers. But now, he argued, France was stepping into line, and it is this 'banalisation' of French politics that the essays all aimed to describe (11).

The timing of this publication was significant: it was the year of François Mitterrand's re-election as president on a campaign for *ouverture*, the loosening up of the left-right party divisions and an apparent attempt to move towards the centre ground. It was also the year before France was to celebrate the bicentenary of the 1789 Revolution, founding moment of the French exception. Furet's claims that the 'Revolution was over' (Furet,

1978) were not of course new, and in fact, the journal *Le Débat* had, in September 1983, launched a discussion, which continued in subsequent issues, as to the relevance of the Revolution in the context of the forthcoming bicentenary celebrations: 'to what extent did the divisions of '89 continue to pervade the national consciousness? With the Republic now definitively in place, what remained of the great antagonisms of two centuries of social and political struggles? ... What was left, if anything, of the fundamental divisions and irreconcilable sensibilities?' (Ozouf 1983; Furet 1983; Duhamel et al. 1984). While acknowledging a certain loss of identity as an inevitable consequence of the political transformations experienced, due to the blurring of the traditional reference points of French political culture, the main conclusion was that a turning point had been reached in the history of the French left, which made it possible to break out of the political tradition derived from the Revolution, and this, for them, was a cause for celebration and a certain optimism (see for example Julliard 1988). They therefore saw the bicentenary of 1789 as 'the shroud of a tradition' (Furet et al. 1988: 10) and portrayed this two-hundredth anniversary as an opportunity to bury it. There was a clear conceptual link here with the discernible new mood of political consensus underpinned by Mitterrand's attempt, albeit short-lived, at an *ouverture* to the centre under the first government of Michel Rocard, which was a significant aspect of the banalisation of politics that the essays welcomed.

This banalisation had already been masterfully described by Serge July in 1986. July's book retraced what he called the very paradoxical history of the 'normalisation' of France under Mitterrand, 'whose soul was sufficiently baroque to do France the extraordinary favour of turning it at last into an ordinary democracy' (July 1986: back cover). He saw the turning-point of March 1983 as a necessary crisis that brought about a 'rupture' that made normalisation possible. But the 1983 crisis had only taken place as a result of the Socialists' policies, which brought about a collective *prise de conscience* of the crisis and the constraints it imposed. France needed to go through this experience, he claimed, and thus Mitterrand's greatness was to have contributed to 'making us ordinary'. Roger Fauroux, former chief executive of St Gobain who became director of the Ecole Nationale d'Administration in 1986, echoed these feelings when he said in the same year that the experience of having the Left in power at least had the virtue of having brought about a change in people's mentalities and dispelled a certain number of myths as to the origin of the crisis of capitalism, which could now be seen as a global phenomenon rather than a national one (Fauroux 1986b). So the beginning of the end of the French exception can in fact be situated in the context of the Socialist experience in power, starting with the election of the first Socialist president of the Fifth Republic in 1981 and the acceptance by the left of these Gaullist institutions, despite earlier opposition, notably by Mitterrand himself (Mitterrand 1964). Contrary to common expectations and despite twenty-three years of opposition for the left, political *alternance* had shown itself to be possible after all. Together with the decline in influence of the Communist Party, this was seen by July and Fauroux as a positive move towards France becoming more like other nations.[3]

But whereas Furet and his colleagues and Serge July accepted the alleged end of the exception with some optimism, others writing at about the same time emphasised the sense of malaise and the crisis of national identity that France seemed to be experiencing during this period as people lost their political bearings. The failure of the Socialist experiment had led to a sense of gloom and doom for the many *déçus du socialisme* who found it hard to accept that there was apparently no alternative to the policies of economic austerity and the espousal of a more liberal model. If the concept of a national identity crisis is not meaningful for some, it should be noted that it did have significance for a large number of well-known authors and commentators, which indicates that it was (and arguably still is) a common preoccupation among French *élites*, if not for the ordinary citizen (see for example Espaces 89 1985; Schmitt 1986; Gauchet 1985; Lipovetsky 1983; Finkielkraut 1987; Barret-Kriegel 1989; Bruckner 1990; Duhamel 1985 and 1989; Duverger 1988; Le Roy Ladurie 1990).

This identity crisis tended to be set within the framework of the dialectic between the decline of the nation-state and the process of European integration that was beginning to erode certain traditional practices and customs (Formesyn 1984; Hayward 1988; Kramer 1994). The implicit, if gradual, abandonment of national sovereignty and loss of status in the world seemed to be hitting France harder than its neighbours. The distinctiveness of the French model meant that the introduction of change was problematic and provoked strong resistance in a number of different policy areas. Was it possible or even desirable for the French model to survive in face of increasing Europeanisation? Internal and external causes of the malaise became increasingly entwined as the integration process moved inexorably forward. Yet the signing of the Single European Act in 1986, which was to lead to the completion of the internal market by 1992, thus irreversibly opening up the French economy, was agreed upon by both left and right, and did not cause nearly as much opposition and debate as would the Maastricht debate in the early 1990s.

Thus by the mid-1980s, it was clear that an unprecedented but broad political consensus had been reached over economic policy and the need to pursue the process of European integration, rather than sticking to the pursuit of 'socialism in one country' that some Socialist Party members (and a number of government ministers) had still believed was possible before March 1983. This did not of course mean that there was total convergence between the main parties. Indeed the period of 'cohabitation' between a president of the left and a prime minister of the right from

1986/88 was largely conflictual, with both sides at pains to emphasise their political differences. Yet these differences were becoming more blurred, even if the accompanying rhetoric sought to hide this fact for reasons of electoral expediency. However, the re-election of François Mitterrand in 1988, on the famous *ni ni* campaign promise not to pursue either nationalisations or privatisations, was a clear indication of the general trend towards policy convergence and the at least partial acceptance of the idea of consensus that certain observers had been identifying and encouraging for some time (Duhamel et al. 1984; Ferenczi 1989).

Yet consensus was still a controversial issue, and many decried what they saw as the *consensus mou* ('soft consensus'), a sort of complacent 'opting out' or resignation that was often negatively (and in fact incorrectly) identified with those who welcomed the end of the French exception as an opportunity to convert the *dirigiste* model of the state into a more liberal, free-market economy more akin to the 'Anglo-Saxon' model. The publication of *La République du centre* thus came at a time when underlying trends suggested both change and continuity, convergence and divergence of ideas as to the way in which French politics was being conducted. Furet and his colleagues clearly saw the recognition of the end of the French exception as the first step towards 'opening the discussion as to the political future of France' (Furet et al. 1988: 12). In this, they were certainly successful, since the book provoked an intense controversy and numerous reviews, some of which were reproduced under the heading 'Critiques et commentaires' in a second edition published later the same year.

Reactions to the book showed that there was in fact considerable confusion about what the authors were actually saying, and many reviewers even picked up on what they saw as contradictions between the three essays. As Rosanvallon admitted: 'What has been little understood is what is fundamental to our venture: the simultaneous critique of the illusions and the dangers of a "soft consensus" and the archaism of a traditional socialist vision' (Furet et al. 1988: 183). Moreover, as Julliard pointed out, although the 'end of the exception' meant that old political habits had been broken, that politicians now had a better grasp of reality, and that this would hopefully lead to better government, nothing was guaranteed for the future, and fundamental change was still really at the embryonic stage: 'For the moment I don't see any great democratic ambition in this country'. Finally, the three authors expressed the shared hope that 'the pacification of minds', which they welcomed, should not give way to 'a complacency which would hide the resignation of politicians and the indifference of citizens' (12).

The debate initiated by *La République du centre* was in fact far from passive or consensual, even if during the initial phase – what Jill Lovecy has called the 'first wave' (Lovecy 1999) – the tone of optimism seemed to be winning the day. Claude Imbert's article in *Foreign Affairs* in 1989, expounding and espousing Furet's thesis, boldly announced to the Anglo-

Saxon world that France no longer considered that its model was unique; it had brought to an end the ideological battles between left and right, accepted new concepts of sovereignty and asserted that a strong majority consensus had now formed around the principles of a market economy and a political system similar to those of other major Western democracies. Yet very soon the journal *Esprit* was wondering whether Furet had not been too quick to assume the end of the French exception (Roman et al. 1990: 65–66). Similarly, James Hollifield concluded from his *Searching for the New France* that given all the changes of the 1980s, 'one might be tempted to jump to the conclusion that some type of non-ideological, classless pluralism [was] just around the corner. Such a conclusion not only would be premature but would be wrong' (Hollifield and Ross 1991: 292). Throughout the 1990s the debate continued, as commentators argued about whether or not, and to what extent, France could still justify its claim to exceptionalism.

There was also more than a whiff of nostalgia in the air, expressed, for example, by Raymond Soubie when discussing the theme of 'banalisation':

> So do we not have any regrets for the past? Will we not have to repent for having exchanged the banalisation of France for simple material satisfaction? To abandon these old relics and to lose a part of our soul in the process, was this really the price to pay in order to be able to exist and to succeed in the great economic game? And are we prepared to continue in this direction? ... In finally acquiring a sense of economics, have we fallen into line, after our loss of power, of our illusions, and a part of our soul? Are we condemned to be a middle-size nation like any other? Is God still French? (Soubie 1991: 14, 17)[4]

For Soubie the central issue was clear: 'The country must make a choice. Either to accept or to refuse the "end of the French exception", either to genuinely espouse the European cause or to maintain her haughty tradition ... of national independence, resign herself definitively to the market economy or pursue her dream of a path which is different to that of other Western democracies' (155). This question should be the central theme of public debate in France, he argued, in order for people to become aware of its importance. 'Europe is the reconciliation of tradition with what is new, it is the only great collective ambition left open to us. God, if he is no longer French, will certainly be European' (281).

The question of France's role in Europe had become all the more pressing as a result of the unexpected events of 1989 that led to the collapse of the Soviet bloc and the reunification of Germany, which France had always feared. These events had a significant impact on the end of exception debate for three reasons; first, because the redefining of borders in the new geopolitical map of Europe meant that France's world role, as defined by de Gaulle in the 1960s and based on a policy of claimed independence, was no longer tenable. In revising its international position, the relevance of the French exception was called into question. Secondly, because they represented the ideological triumph of liberal thought over communist ideology, making it hard to see how it could be possible for France to resist the new wave of liberalism. Finally, because they led, more or less directly, to the signing of the Maastricht Treaty, which was a way for France to ensure that the new Germany did not decide to turn eastwards and neglect her commitment to European integration. It was in the context of the debates leading up to the signing of this treaty that the French exception once again started to appear in political rhetoric. Predictably, it was the opponents of the treaty who used the notion to defend French sovereignty, and most notable in this respect was Philippe Séguin: 'I am against Maastricht because I believe in the French exception' (Séguin 1992: 49, and 1993). The extreme right also took this line, fuelling the fears expressed by many that the principal beneficiary of this debate was in fact the Front National. The main thrust of political argument however was to toe the European line, even if this was sometimes presented as being not the end of, but more modestly the 'modernisation of the French exception' that would enable the French model, which was out of step with the new international environment, to evolve (Saint-Etienne 1992a and b).

Exception culturelle and *pensée unique*

This international environment was to have a significant impact on the way France viewed her role in Europe from the early 1990s onwards, and this was articulated quite clearly through the 'end of exception' polemic as it evolved over the decade. The two main strands of the debate can be usefully referred to under the headings *exception culturelle* and *pensée unique*, and the origins of both can be located in the context of the Uruguay Round of multilateral trade negotiations that took place within the GATT framework from 1987 to 1993. For this round, new issues were added to the list of negotiable products, including cultural goods, because the U.S. felt that the EU was too protective towards its cinema and television production. France however felt strongly that cultural goods were not like other products, and that they should be excluded from (or more precisely, not included in) the negotiations. This argument became known as the *exception culturelle*, because culture was seen as being different.[5] However, not all its EU partners felt the same, and intense lobbying was necessary on the part of the French government to persuade its partners that this approach was for the general good of all non-anglophone cultures, and not simply an attempt to promote or defend French culture. Realising the need for allies in this battle, France started to emphasise the notion of cultural diversity (decried for so long within the boundaries of the Hexagon in the interests of the 'one and indivisible Republic'), which would embrace all European languages and cultures, as well as other francophone cultures (Védrine and Moïsi 2000). The French success in winning over some reluctant member-states, and in then going on to win the battle to preserve the cultural exception both in 1993 and again at Seattle in 1999 under the World Trade Organisation, demonstrated the importance of the European dimension of national policy-making, and served as a reminder that she could no longer play an independent world role, thus reinforcing the sense in which France's future lay deep at the heart of Europe.

Although space does not permit any further discussion of the *exception culturelle* here, it is nevertheless relevant to the subject of this chapter to note in passing the relationship between these two notions, of the French exception and the cultural exception, since the latter would appear to have been conceived in the conceptual framework of the former. There is a certain paradox in the fact that what originated as a defence of the French exception in the cultural domain (especially the cinema, but in fact, French culture more generally) should end up being successfully defended not at the national but at the European level. This battle over the cultural exception, perceived widely as being between France and the U.S.A., even if the European Commission was in fact the negotiator, was to take the end of exception debate into the international arena, and would make the *exception culturelle* one of its most tangible manifestations.

Indeed, during the rest of the 1990s and on into the twenty-first century a battle has been fought out, essentially in the French and American press, although supported in no mean measure by *The Economist* (see for example Pedder 1999), over cultural issues, which can be seen as a struggle for cultural supremacy in its broadest sense (Gordon and Meunier 2001; Kuisel 2001). The French accuse the U.S. of cultural imperialism, while America accuses France of living in the past by refusing to accept globalisation, which it justifies by evoking 'the French exception'. The hostility of the American press towards France is grounded in an understanding of the French exception as not just difference or uniqueness, but as a claim to superiority (Frank 1998). Moreover, the initial focus on cultural issues such as television and cinema soon widened to include lifestyle and eating habits, as José Bové took up the battle against *la malbouffe*, so that before long Franco-American relations seemed to be totally dominated by this extension of the exception debate, as acknowledged by Baudrillard: 'The old Franco-American antagonism, the almost genetic rivalry, has been aggravated ... The idea of a French exception, a French difference, is absurd, but a certain American triumphalism and our own relative decline has turned the idea into an obsession' (Cohen 1997).

The second strand of the end of exception debate was more of a continuation of the nation-state versus European integration dialectic that was rekindled after the Maastricht debate. The most striking textual example of this position was the report commissioned by Prime Minister Edouard Balladur from the Commissariat Général du Plan in 1994, under the presidency of Alain Minc (Minc 1994). Moving on from the acknowledgement that France had reached the end of an era, he argued that it needed to develop a new project (because France, being what it is, cannot do without an ongoing project), and that this project should be its integration within the new Europe. 'France can only have a powerful world role if it is part of a European plan. ... We do not have any alternative to our European choice' (10). He claimed that France had benefited from the opening of the economy and the imperatives of productivity, and that it would be less buffeted by the forces of the open market if it were well entrenched within the European entity. France needed to find a compromise between the imperatives of productivity and the desire for social cohesion to create a society based on solidarity, efficiency and equity (rather than equality). Economic and Monetary Union would be fundamental to achieving this aim, and would serve as an instrument for the necessary transformation of French society, notably in the fields of social spending, fiscal policy, and the organisation of the state and public services.

The message conveyed in this report was also being echoed in numerous different publications and press articles, to the extent that it soon appeared to some to have become oppressive and inescapable. Jean-François Kahn was the first to write about this in his news magazine *L'Événement du jeudi* in the early 1990s (see also Kahn 1995); then in 1995, *Le Monde Diplomatique* published an article by Ignacio Ramonet which was a violent diatribe against this 'new doctrine' whose key words were: market, competition, globalisation, strong currency, privatisation and liberalisation. He identified the European Commission and the Bank of France as institutions that were champions of the new dogma: 'The constant repetition, in all the media, of this catechism, by nearly all politicians, gives it such a power of intimidation that it stifles any attempt at independent thinking, and makes it very difficult to resist this new obscurantism' (Ramonet 1995: 1). The reference to the Minc report as the best example of this discourse was explicit. The two main causes for objection seemed to be both the 'blind' commitment to the euro and the sense that there was 'no alternative'. Strength of resistance to the *pensée unique* was such that in 1997–98 two different groups of opponents organised themselves into foundations in order to articulate a *pensée critique*: The Fondation Marc Bloch brought together a motley collection of mainly gaullists and *chevènementistes* such as Régis Debray, Serge Halimi, Didier Motchane, Emmanuel Todd, Pierre-André Taguieff and Jean-François Kahn, whereas the Fondation Copernic was founded by the communist historian Jacques Kergoat in order to 'put an end to the hegemony of the liberal left 'in the field of new ideas' ('*dans le champ propositionnel*') (Kergoat 1999a). However, the successful launch of the euro and the increasing liberalisation of the economy, under both left and right, have made it clear that the social-liberal discourse that grew out of the end of exception debate has won the day.

Given the significance of this outcome, and the pertinence of the end of exception debate, the reader may be forgiven at this point for feeling somewhat unsure as to how to situate in political terms the aspirations of Furet and his colleagues when they published *La République du centre*: was this the sort of transformation they had been hoping for? How can the publication of one small book have achieved such a great impact on political and economic life in France? A clue to answering these questions lies in the foreword to the book, where the astute reader will notice that these three essays were commissioned by the Fondation Saint-Simon (hereafter referred to as the FSS), in order to 'foster an initial awareness and to launch the discussion as to our political future' (Furet et al. 1988: 12) What then was this foundation, and what role did it play in the instigation and dissemination of the debate over the end of the French exception?

The Fondation Saint Simon

The Fondation Saint-Simon was founded in 1982 by a small group of men whose proclaimed objective was to provide a forum for developing analysis of the contemporary world. Significantly, the founding fathers were François Furet (historian of the French Revolution), Pierre Rosanvallon (professor and leading researcher in the field of political and social ideas, attached to both the Ecole des Hautes Etudes en Sciences Sociales and the Institut d'Etudes Politiques in Paris), Alain Minc (leading economist), Emmanuel Le Roy-Ladurie (a social historian), Pierre Nora (founder of the journal *Le Débat*), his brother Simon Nora (top civil servant), and Roger Fauroux (future Minister for Industry in Michel Rocard's government).[6] Somewhere between the model of the Anglo-Saxon think-tank and its more hexagonal version of the 'club', the originality of the FSS was to aim to bring together in fruitful discussion representatives from two worlds that hitherto had refused any type of dialogue: businessmen and intellectuals.

There were two main ideas underlying this project: the first was that greater communication between intellectuals and business people would actually be beneficial to both communities. Fauroux himself was the first to admit for example that he had made errors in his business decisions due to a failure to consult specialists regarding social and political conditions that affected his investments, and other leading entrepreneurs also began to recognise the value of seeking advice from 'experts' outside the business world. At the same time, many intellectuals and university researchers began to see the opportunity to increase their meagre salaries by engaging in studies financed by business ventures and taking on consultancies that would previously have been politically unthinkable. This was made pos-

sible by the changing political and economic climate soon after the Socialist victory in 1981: the deteriorating economic context meant that the first
steps towards a reconciliation between the left and the business world
became not only possible or desirable but essential, as even hard-liners
were increasingly forced to accept the imperatives of the market place,
although this could not yet be admitted publicly.

The traditional antipathy between these two communities of business
people and intellectuals originated of course in the long history of political cleavage established at the time of the Revolution, which placed them
quite clearly on opposing sides of the left-right divide. The persistent
intensity and rigidity of this divide, exacerbated by the bipolarising institutional arrangements of the Fifth Republic, was seen by many leading
decision-makers as being detrimental to the nation because it prevented
any real debate between the two sides. This absence of informed, constructive, 'apolitical' discussion meant that problems were always
approached from within a highly partisan agenda and any solutions proposed would inevitably be contested by the opposition, if only to make a
political point. However, the election of a Socialist president in 1981, which
made the idea of *alternance* a reality, paradoxically also paved the way for
a fresh approach to the problem; indeed, the idea that it might be possible
to move beyond this rigid right-left divide was the second big idea (albeit
less explicit) behind the founding of the FSS in 1982.

The FSS was set up officially not in fact as a *fondation* but as an *association loi 1901*, financed by a combination of private subscriptions from
members (500 francs in 1997) and business donations (120,000 francs per
year) from companies such as la Caisse des Dépôts, Suez, Publicis, Saint-
Gobain, BSN Gervais-Danone and MK2 Productions. Activities of the FFS
centred around a monthly lunch with a guest speaker and the organisation
of various *groupes de réflexion*, whose analyses of economic, social or international issues led to publications of various kinds. Pierre Rosanvallon
was particularly active in organising and supervising these research projects from his professional positions at the IEP and the EHESS in Paris.
During the 1990s, these publications became almost monthly issues and
certain studies were diffused more widely through for example *Le Nouvel
observateur, Le Débat, Politique internationale, Commentaire* and *Esprit*, with
which the FSS had close links through its members.

What the subscribers to the FSS mainly had in common was a commitment to the idea of modernisation, a programme that had its origins under
the Fourth Republic when an attempt was made to reconcile the market
with state intervention in preference to the prewar system of '*laissez-faire*
combined with protectionism' (Laurent 1998). Pierre Mendès-France had
been the main political representative of this movement, supported by top
civil servants such as François Bloch-Lainé and Simon Nora. In the early
1980s Michel Rocard was seen as the logical spokesman of the 'mod-

ernisers', opposed to the 'archaism' still strongly represented within certain *tendances* of the PS. So roughly speaking they could be classified as the 'second left' (*deuxième gauche*).

The way the FSS worked in practice was to build a system of networks or concentric circles around the central nucleus formed by the founding fathers, who used the idea of 'bridging personalities' (such as Roger Fauroux, Simon and Pierre Nora, Jacques Julliard) to establish and develop the links between the different components: civil servants, trade unionists, industrialists, intellectuals, the press and publishing. So, despite the apparent diversity of its members, the existence of a shared overarching intellectual project facilitated the bringing together of a wide range of approaches to a common cause. By deciding what issues it wanted to highlight at any given moment, it could orchestrate the dissemination of a particular line of argument through the publication of these views in different media. In addition, its members were frequently invited to participate in official commissions and working parties that gave them an ideal platform for informing discussion. A good example of this is the Minc report discussed earlier: one third of the commission members were also members of the FSS or *saint-simoniens*. Thus it was possible for the FSS to have a large measure of influence over the agenda of national debate without this being easily discernible to the outside world. Furthermore, the fact that many key members such as Roger Fauroux had connections in all of these different worlds, facilitated 'the circulation of common languages and ways of doing things, shared concerns and issues, leading to the production of common approaches' (Laurent 1998). Over time, the FSS came to represent what Alain Minc allegedly called 'the circle of reason', advocating a new pragmatic approach to solving the problems of contemporary society, and defending an 'appeased vision of social relations' outside what were seen as the pernicious ideological battles of the world of party politics.

However, as Vincent Laurent pointed out in a critical article published in 1998, this 'end of ideology' approach can also be seen as 'nothing other than an ideology that does not declare its name ... It aims to create the conditions for the implementation of a conservative project that is presented as inevitable. This is how the "narrow road" [for which, read *pensée unique*] followed by France's political leaders over the last fifteen years has emerged. In this way the democracy of the market appears as "the end of history" and social-liberalism as the only viable political project for our societies'. Thus, the FSS has been seen by its critics as 'the melting-pot in which a specific political project has been developed' (Kergoat 1999b) or as 'the cooking pot that produced the famous and woolly-minded *pensée unique*, that represents the deadening consensus of the last twenty years' (Musso 1999).

Indeed, by the mid 1990s, the quiet success of the FSS had almost become counter-productive because the sense and strength of *la pensée unique* with which it became associated meant that there seemed to be no possibility of an alternative to the new liberalism. For some, this represented a grave threat to democracy, by undermining pluralism (Chardon and Lensel 1998), and led to the creation of the 'counter-foundations' described above.

Perhaps rather paradoxically, the success of the FSS's political project led to its demise when, in 1999, a decision was taken to cease all. As Pierre Rosanvallon explained in an article in *Le Monde*, the FSS was 'a completed project' (23 June 1999), as the left had been converted to social-liberalism; 'transversality' had been created between people from different *milieux*, seventy public seminars had been held, forty books published (most of them in the 'Liberté d'esprit' collection with Calmann-Lévy), together with 110 study documents and other shorter notes, some of which had achieved great notoriety (for example Patrick Weil's paper on immigration or Emmanuel Todd's on the political malaise in France). But there was 'a risk of slipping into a routine', and since the death of Furet in 1997, the spirit of the whole venture was no longer quite the same.

Conclusion

Space does not allow any discussion of developments over the past few years, which may arguably throw a rather different light on how debate has moved on since then.[7] But the conclusions to be drawn from this analysis of the 'end of French exception' debate seem quite clear: the publication in 1988 of *La République du centre* must be understood as an important instrument used in the pursuit of an ambitious political project conceived by the *deuxième gauche*, which aimed to encourage the normalisation of French political life in its broadest sense, and more specifically, to convert the French left to social-democracy. The weight of the FSS behind this project was obviously critical to its success. It is impossible to know of course how political life would have developed had the book not been published and had the FSS not existed: to what extent would the force of events alone have coerced the recalitrant French left into some sort of compromise with the market economy? Yet the answer to this question is almost irrelevant to our initial line of enquiry into the origin and nature of the French exception, since what is more important is the demonstration of how the debate came to permeate public discourse in France over the past fifteen years in a way that was not reproduced anywhere else. The ultimate paradox is that this debate, although intended to consecrate the end of the French exception, has in fact constituted a very striking example of its survival.

Notes

1. See for example Cole 1998, Hewlett 1998 and the colloquium at the Bordeaux Institut d'Etudes Politiques Bordeaux in October 1998, 'A la recherche de l'exception française'.
2. All translations are those of the author.
3. See also Kesselman 1991 on the role of the Parti Socialiste in instigating the end of exceptionalism.
4. A reference to the book written by the German writer Friedrich Sieburg in 1930, *Is God French?* and reprinted in 1991 by Grasset & Fasquelle. The question 'Is God French?' was also taken as the central theme of the debates at the annual Festival de Radio-France organised by *Le Monde* and France-Culture in the Jardin de Pétrarque at Montpellier in July 1995.
5. Jack Lang is said to have invented this expression in the 1980s according to J. Farchy, *La fin de l'exception culturelle.*
6. It is interesting to note that the book was written 'at the request of the FSS' when one learns that two of the three authors were founding members of the organisation.
7. In particular, Rosanvallon's creation of the association 'La République des idées', and the publication of the polemical book by Daniel Lindenberg in 2002 of *Le rappel à l'ordre.*

Part II

Exceptionalism in Politics and Policy

Chapter 4

FRENCH COMMUNISM: AN EXCEPTIONAL ORTHODOXY

David S. Bell

French exceptionalism in politics comes down in many respects to French 'political culture'. 'Political culture' is used here to mean the orientation that people have towards politics and their expectations of political action. However, political culture is not a passive given. Political culture is inherited from the past but it is adapted and built on by political institutions which in this way help shape a society's attitudes to politics. In the case of the French Communist Party (Parti communiste français: PCF), it successfully picked up and used aspects of a pre-existing political culture but it also added its own components. Communism worldwide, and the French Communist Party were highly successful in this, created their own culture using a very substantial, organised and well-funded cultural apparatus.

In France this communist/marxist culture was embedded in the industrial working communities where it was sustained by the party organisation and was a 'workshop of collective identity' (Brunet 1980; Fourcaut 1986; Hastings 1991). One outcome was the integration of the working class immigrants who came to work in the new heavy industry of the interwar period (this did not work, however, with the last wave of immigrants in the 1960s).[1] Communist culture was highly influential until very recently; its half-life is long and it continues to influence French political culture as the success of 'revolutionary parties', protest groups and unions shows (Furet 1995).

As a preliminary it is important to say what is and is not 'exceptional' about the PCF. French Communism is not exceptional in its devotion to the Soviet Union, its dedication to the Leninist ideal, or in its organisation, its fronts and associations and unions or in its behaviour. It is exceptional in its sheer size, outstripping the tiny communist parties of most countries; it was a veritable behemoth in the communist movement. This size, rather than the nature of the party itself, is what needs explanation and this is to be found in the problem of French political culture and the weakness of the Socialist Party. Communist domination of the postwar left had consequences for the political culture of France in propagating philo-soviet ideas, anti-Americanism and anti-Europeanism, and criticising 'capitalism' from the standpoint of a utopian 'socialist' vision of the future.[2] Therefore the approach will be to first look at the institution and then at the political culture.

The French Communist Party

Formed from a split in the French Socialist Party (Section Française de l'Internationale Ouvrière: SFIO), the PCF was established in 1920 as the French section of the Communist International. It took with it most of its activists and its newspaper *L'Humanité* as well as its other assets like property and *locales*, although not the parliamentary leadership that remained to lead the SFIO. This Communist party, like the others in Europe, was devoted to Lenin's coup, to defending and – where possible – promoting the Soviet system, and it willingly placed itself at the disposition of Lenin's victorious 'Revolution'. (There was a brief period of relative independence before the Party was 'bolshevised' by the Komintern and a new disciplined leadership obedient to Moscow was installed.) Moscow's Third International Schools were the mill that produced Communist leaders for all the parties including the French (Lazitch 1976). This entailed the installation of Lenin's system of internal party rule known as 'democratic centralism' that was hierarchical, disciplined and militaristic. In democratic centralism nominees of the leadership held posts ratified by elections that were purely formal (Tiersky 1985). There were, of course, elections but there would be only one candidate for each post and that put the choice in the hands of the leadership.

Democratic centralism was common to all Communist parties and was not particularly French, nor was the creation of a central professional apparatus that took place under the auspices of the Komintern in the 1920s (replacing the old Socialists with steeled Bolsheviks). Communist Parties depended on their elites of 'professional revolutionaries' who were devoted to the party and who in fact owed their livelihood to the Communist Party and formed the real or inner party (referred to by Courtois and Lazar (1995) as the *'konspirazia'*). It was this Leninist core of the party that composed the central bureaucracy and advancing up this apparatus was a career in the party. Like all Communist parties the PCF had for most of its existence a much bigger central staff than its rival 'bourgeois' parties and most office holders (whether they described themselves as 'workers', 'peasants' or 'engineers') were employees – apparatchiks. The PCF, like other Communist parties, took on the aspect of a very large professional bureaucracy with many of the same recognisable characteristics. None of this, in the Communist world, can be counted as exceptional, although the size and rigidity of this apparatus made it outstanding among the badly organised and poorly funded French political parties.

By the same token the political strategies adopted by the French Communists were the same as other Communist parties and went in lockstep with the world movement's strategy as defined in Moscow (sometimes with suicidal results). There have been attempts to write the PCF's itinerary differently, but the stages of 'class against class', Popular Front, collaboration, Resistance, National Front, 'parliamentary road' and so on were the same as those of other Communist parties. Although the PCF was big it was not autonomous and had no sway in the International. Depictions of the PCF's leader Thorez as a prime motivator in Komintern strategy are not convincing. In fact the PCF was run by Komintern's delegate 'Clement' (Eugen Fried) from 1930 to 1943, and it was Fried who imposed the orders given by Moscow and built up Maurice Thorez as the Party's leader (Kriegel and Courtois 1997).

After the Second World War the French Communist Party emerged as the biggest Communist Party in the West. Within France, both in votes and in membership, it was the biggest political party under the Fourth Republic and, although reduced to 19.2 percent at the first elections of the Fifth Republic, it polled over 20 percent from 1960 to 1980. Moscow recognised its importance (particularly by lavishly funding it) but it was still low in status in the hierarchy of parties run by the Soviet Communist Party's (CPSU) international department, the Komintern having been dissolved (Kriegel 1964). 'Moscow gold' came indirectly through, for example, the purchase of the party's publications and commercial enterprises like Doumeng's Interagra and directly in cash (in reality always dollars). This finance continued and even in Gorbachev's time it was lavishly funded by the Soviets.[3] In 1964 the Western parties got over $15 million and the PCF, the Italian Communist Party and the United States Party got by far the most; in 1969 the PCF received $3.7 million (Kriegel, 1964).

At the Liberation the PCF cooperated in 'bourgeois' governments under de Gaulle and others, Stalin having decided not to promote revolution in Western Europe while consolidating communist rule in the East, where the Red Army had taken control. When the cold war started in 1947 the French, along with the Italian Communist parties and others, were trapped in 'capitalist' Western Europe outside Moscow's sphere of influence. This led, in 1947, to quasi-insurrectionary action across the west of the continent before things settled down and European economic growth started to take off in the *trente glorieuses* boom years.

French Communism's position in the Communist International was as a reliable component of the movement carrying out a particular role that required adjustments of strategy and tactics. There is, however, one episode in this history that does seem to mark the PCF as 'exceptional' within the world movement and that is the so-called 'Eurocommunist' interlude. Khrushchev's rise to power entailed a change of strategy in the West European Communist movement in 1956 from the stance of outright opposition to the 'parliamentary road to power'. Khrushchev accepted the nuclear stalemate in Europe and displaced Communist revolutionary hopes onto the decolonising Third World. Western Communists were henceforth to seek to advance electorally (not neglecting other possibilities) and that in turn meant seeking alliances with the social democratic parties. Communist parties in Western Europe adapted their messages to coalition politics and cooperation.

The implications of this strategy of seeking electoral support were not altogether clear at the time but they necessitated a disavowal of the Soviet system, a severing of links to the USSR, proof of freedom from Soviet foreign policy and the ending of the totalitarian nature of the party itself. At first French Communists reacted like the other orthodox parties and supported the Soviet Union's invasion of Hungary in 1956 and its overthrow of the new Hungarian government, while its search for an alliance on the left led it to approve the 'special measures' demanded by Guy Mollet's government to deal with the insurrection in Algeria. There was no immediate response from the SFIO.

De Gaulle's return to power, however, changed the strategic situation. On the one hand the centre, which had governed France through the Fourth Republic, was split and the political spectrum polarised into right and left, with the Gaullists dominating the coalition of the conservative right. This forced the Socialist left to contemplate seriously a realignment of the entire left and an agreement or association with the Communist Party. The PCF, in keeping with the new strategy, pressed insistently for an alliance around a joint manifesto. For electoral purposes changes were needed in the PCF's position on the USSR and for the first time criticisms were made of the treatment of dissidents. Though, if the Communists criticised the USSR, these criticisms were not deep seated and the party remained committed to 'Socialism'. As was said at the time, 'just because there are spots on the sun it does not mean there is no sun'. But things were not so simple and French exceptionalism, this time through the agency of de Gaulle, made the French Communists' position very difficult.

On the other hand Moscow's long-term objective in Western Europe was to divide the allies and to push the United States out of the continent. This was never achieved but the nearest the USSR came to a diplomatic victory was with the foreign policy of de Gaulle and the French conservative right. For Moscow the priority became the cultivation of Gaullism and not the arrival in power of the French left. Moscow seemed to regard local Communists in government as a step forward in every European country except France. In Italy, Portugal, Finland, Iceland or (possibly) Spain inroads could have been made into Western solidarity but in France the outcome would be a reverse for Soviet policy. A government of the left, under the SFIO or Mitterrand, would mean an Atlanticist and pro-European policy not in the Soviet Union's interests. In the 1960s this did not appear to matter in relations between the CPSU and the PCF as nobody seriously believed that de Gaulle could be defeated, and then in 1969 there was no likely possibility of the Socialist Defferre (or the PCF's Duclos for that matter) winning the presidential elections. In 1969, faced with the Warsaw Pact invasion of Czechoslovakia, the party's 'surprise and reprobation' of the Soviets was just enough to keep its French support and its approval of the 'normalisation' of the subject country was satisfactory to the Kremlin. However, a Socialist victory did become a real danger with Mitterrand's rise to the summit of the new Socialist Party (PS) in 1971.

Moscow's view was made abundantly clear in 1974 when, in between rounds, the Soviet ambassador visited the conservative presidential contender Giscard d'Estaing. International solidarity, said the PCF, should be a two way street. An argument started with the USSR as to the proper policy in France and the PCF adopted the hitherto reviled label 'Eurocommunist'. It is difficult, even in retrospect, to say what 'Eurocommunism' consisted of as it remained wedded to Soviet orthodoxy in most major respects, but it certainly meant a coolness in relations between the CPSU and the PCF and a willingness to criticise the USSR that in some aspects had not been evident before. Georges Marchais, the PCF leader at the time, is credited with having taken this stance, but it continued the party's line developed in the 1960s by Waldeck Rochet. French Communists may have felt that their future lay with the alliance of the left (which is what the Soviet theorists had themselves once suggested) but loyalty to the Soviet Union demanded that it be broken.

It was broken sometime after (perhaps the decision was taken before) the local elections of 1977. French Communists, subject to who knows what pressure from the USSR, had come to the conclusion that the alliance of the left which they had so ardently desired did not profit them and served only to boost their Socialist partners. Unlike the Popular Front or the Liberation when moderate policies and alliances swelled the Communist ranks, the 'Common Programme' alliance of 1972 served to make the Socialist Party the first party of France. An end to the alliance of the left enabled the PCF to swing behind the Soviet Union just as it went onto the offensive in Afghanistan and the Third World again and shortly after it had deployed its SS20 missiles in Europe. This change entailed endorsing the Soviet actions in Afghanistan and refusing to disavow the December 1981 military coup in Poland by General Jaruzelski.

Yet French Communism had always been ultra-orthodox, leading it, for example, to deny the authenticity of Khrushchev's speech in 1956 denouncing Stalin's crimes. After 1977 French Communist publications again emphasised 'revolution' and the old hard-line 'bolshevik' themes reappeared in the party's propaganda even though the pressure of opinion forced it to join the Socialist Party in government in 1981. Georges Marchais, the PCF's leader, appeared on TV in Moscow to support the USSR's intervention in Afghanistan and then threw his weight behind the coup by General Jaruzelski against Polish Solidarity.

Although what looked in 1977 like a new surge was in fact the death throes of the Soviet system, the PCF remained in orthodox mode throughout the 1980s. This put the PCF at odds with the dismantling of the Communist bloc and critical of the Gorbachev reforms in the USSR, which it believed were undermining the Communist system. At the end of the 1980s the Italian Communists were closer to Moscow than were the French and the PCF found itself, for the only time, condemning a Soviet foreign policy (on the Gulf War) and composing with the East German, North Korean, Chinese and Cuban Communists a 'Third and a Half' international deploring the absence of an aggressive world Communist movement. But it also supported the putschists in 1991 who briefly managed to overthrow Gorbachev and seemed – to the PCF – to be able to keep the Socialist system in being. It had none of the rebelliousness of the Italian or Spanish parties and to that extent was not 'exceptional'. It remained in this position of orthodox stasis for the rest of Georges Marchais' tenure as party leader until 1994.

For the most part the PCF refused to draw any lessons from the collapse of the Communist system. It ignored the demise of the Communist bloc until the end and then scarcely commented on the collapse of the USSR. It remained, it said, committed to the Communist ideal which had not been put into practice in the East but perverted. French Communism's determination not to change led it to neglect opportunities that might have saved it from humiliation, but it ignored the warning signs. The new leader Robert Hue's *'mutation'* was too little too late, and the party was mistaken in its belief that it had condemned 'stalinism' and that stalinism was not Communism and that that sufficed. Hue insisted that the idea of Communism was old and went back to the Middle Ages and that by implication the Soviet interlude was minor, though his determination that 'We must make people dream' (Il faut faire rêver) was not put into practice. But the upshot was that the PCF was until the late 1990s a recognisable Communist Party although by 2003 it no longer was. By 1992 the workers' state, the party's *raison d'être*, had ceased to exist, there was no international Communist movement and its once definite ideology had been diluted into a vague moralism. In addition the party's apparatus, which was once formidable, had also fallen apart and the party was an archipelago of isolated baronies without overall direction. Robert Hue himself was bundled out after a poor presidential election campaign and a humiliating result. He passed the leadership to Marie-Georges Buffet in 2003.

Communism and the USSR

With the exception of the brief period before the PCF's 'bolshevisation' (1920–22), its 'Eurocommunist phase (1975–77) and its lack of full support for Gorbachev, the French Party was a reliable ally of the Soviet Union and a dependable subordinate. As the political geographer André Siegfried put it '... how is it that more than five million French people ... voted 'Communist', for a party which did not hide the fact that it was a foreign party (le parti de l'étranger)' (*Le Figaro* 27 June 1951). Yet while the PCF was part of a wider world movement, it also related to its own society and culture in specific ways and those links were not shared by other communist parties. Hence the paradox of French Communism: it was a party rooted in French society, French culture and highly (not to say excessively) patriotic, while at the same time the arm of a world movement run from Moscow. This paradox nonetheless is one common to all other communist parties. There was a split between the appeal made to ordinary voters and supporters of the party and the party's inner 'bolshevik' core that was committed to the revolutionary state, to the workers' fatherland of real existing socialism that was the Soviet Union.

This commitment by the PCF was constant as long as the USSR existed. As a party, it was formed to defend the USSR and to promote its interests and one of the things that it did was to disseminate the idea of the workers' utopia under construction in the East. This usually took the form of propaganda, distributed through the Communist and 'fellow travelling' press, lauding the achievements of 'Socialism' and describing the 'advances' made in medicine, sport, science, industry and so on. This had some influence when, in the 1930s and then after the Second World War, the Soviet Union had a positive image in Western eyes. This positive attitude lasted longer in France than elsewhere but probably began to change with the publication of the Khrushchev report in 1956 and then the loss of the 'halo of proletarian sanctity' when the Communists suppressed the Hungarian uprising in the same year. However, the public mood turned quite sour in the 1970s when Solzhenitsyn's *Gulag Archipelago* was published: its three volumes sold in total 120,000 copies, proportionately probably the biggest sales in the West. On the left the PCF tried to pre-empt debate, and the Socialists avoided it, but the real nature of the 'Socialism' under construction began to become evident (Winock 2003). All the same the PCF persisted until the end in praising 'Socialism' in the Eastern bloc and it has never reassessed its views of that period, although it became able to concede the 'errors' and 'crimes' of the past. On the other side of the coin was the denunciation of the capitalist world and the description in lurid terms of the crimes of capitalism.

In addition to depicting the utopia of the Socialist USSR, the Communist Party undertook campaigns as part of the Communist movement. Of these the most notorious is the PCF's support for the Nazi-Soviet Pact in 1939; this could not be convincingly defended and undoubtedly cost the party most of its support. However there were further examples through to the 1980s in which it was able to combine defence of Soviet interests with an uninhibited nationalist rhetoric. In the first place there was an anti-Americanism that it used to combat the Marshall Plan and NATO and this continued through to its support in the 1980s for the last Soviet campaign (against the installation of Cruise and Pershing missiles in Western Europe). It also ran campaigns against the NATO bases in the 1950s and its action against the consolidation of the West was continued through opposition to the integration of Europe. Its more violent confrontations culminated in the 'Ridgway riots' of May 1952, but other campaigns expressed an opposition to the prevailing system in the name of 'proletarian' values.

Socialist weakness and the revolution

French Communism has been able to progress because of the weakness of the French social democratic parties and this failing is both conjunctural and cultural. It was because of Socialist Party weakness that the 'bolshevik graft' onto the stem of the socialist movement took in France and Communism in France occupied the space the old SFIO did not colonise. Although the PCF was less successful in the 1920s, in taking over the Confédération générale du travail (CGT) unions in 1947 and in controlling the clubs, societies and town halls the Communists took the place that would have been socialist in 'northern Europe'. In France the Communists took over the role of promoting workers from the grass roots up to the heights of authority (particularly through the CGT), as they did for Thorez and Marchais. Communism became part of a counter-culture, of a series of bastions in the Paris Red belt, the Nord Pas-de-Calais, the centre and the Mediterranean littoral, of closed, stable and hard working communities that kept their identity against encroaching 'capitalist' society over the years. There was a substantial culture reinforcing the links to the party and maintaining the counter-society as the Communist family (Derville and Croisat 1979). Being a member of this family brought psychological benefits and exclusion from it was equally painful: the threat of expulsion reinforced loyalty (Lazar 1996). French Communism sedulously maintained this identity in a large membership through its journals, texts, ceremonies and so on. This working class solidarity was also linked to the late industrialisation of France and to the rapid unstructured creation of a French working class in the new industries developed in the 1930s and 1950s (Einaudi et al. 1951).

However, the weakness of French social democracy precedes the twentieth century. French industrialisation was relatively late and lagged behind its principal European partners, with the result that a working class developed only in the few places where there was a semblance of modern industry: in the North, the Paris region and one or two isolated outliers. France remained an agricultural country with an industrial sector composed mainly of small businesses. Hence another feature of French socialism: the union movement took a different route to those in northern Europe, into that 'syndicalism' suspicious of parties and which rejected party ties. The cooperation between trade unions and the reformist wing of socialism – the structure on which social democracy could be built – was deficient in France.

This, of course, only pushes the question one stage further back and it has to be asked how the Communists came to occupy this 'social democratic' space. One answer to this is the Resistance: as Maurice Agulhon wrote, nobody who had not lived through that time could imagine the dimensions and omnipresence or the shamelessness of Communist propaganda on the subject (and added that the SFIO could not compete) (Agulhon 1987). At the end of the War Communists in most Western European societies polled well as a result of their role in internal Resistance movements and, of course, their association with the heroic ally that had defeated Hitler's armies (Kauffer 1999/2000). In addition, in Western Europe, they took a reformist line, cooperating in parliamentary institutions and putting into place the building blocks of the welfare state. Thus, for example, the Communists polled 5.1 percent in Switzerland, 12.5 percent in Denmark, 11.8 percent in Norway, 10.5 percent in Sweden and 5.75 percent in West Germany. Yet in most of these countries the voters turned away from Communists at the beginning of the Cold War, so that Communism had become a marginal phenomenon in countries like the U.K., Germany, Holland, Austria, and Belgium by the 1960s.

France was different. Along with Italy it continued to give the Communist Party a high vote. In the mid-1970s the PCI polled 9,085,927 votes (27.2 percent) to take 179 seats out of 630 and the PCF polled 5,156,619 votes (21.2 percent) in 1973 and took 73 seats out of 490. Other societies in which the Communists polled well into the mid-1970s were Cyprus (9.7 percent in 1970), Iceland (18.1 percent in 1974), Luxembourg (15.5 percent in 1968) and Finland (17.1 percent in 1972). But these, with the exception of Finland, were tiny countries, although the collapse of the dictatorships in Portugal, Spain and Greece in the decade did lead to the emergence of intermediate-size communist parties with 10 percent or so of the vote. After the 1970s the trend, with the exception of Italy, was of a saw tooth downward movement: Communism was being rejected by Western European societies when it collapsed in the Eastern bloc. By the time Gorbachev was in power, the only West European communist parties polling over one percent were in Cyprus (27.4 percent in 1985), Finland (9.5 percent in 1987), Greece (10.28 percent in 1990), Iceland (13 percent in 1987), Italy

(26.7 percent in 1987), Luxembourg (3.9 percent in 1989), Portugal (11 percent in 1987), Spain (9 percent in 1989) and Sweden (5.8 percent in 1988). In France the PCF was continuing the long slide that had seen it fall from 20.7 percent of the votes in the general elections of 1978 to 11.1 percent in 1988, but it remained one of the larger communist parties in Europe. After 1992 the world movement itself was wound up and many parties disbanded so the comparison is no longer strictly the same, but of those countries that still have a party calling itself a Communist Party in the twenty first century the PCF remains one of the largest.

Whatever the real achievements of the Resistance, and whoever undertook them, the PCF emerged from the war with an enhanced reputation (the slate of its collaboration wiped clean) and claimed the title of the 'party of the 75,000 shot' [by the nazi Occupier] le parti des fusillés). If people had got involved in the Resistance it was more than likely that they would have come into contact with, and probably joined, a Communist organisation. This was the same in Italy and, under the 1970s dictatorships, in Spain, Portugal and Greece. There was no immediate conflict between patriotism and a struggle against the occupant through the medium of the Communist Party that depicted itself in patriotic and nationalist terms as above all the party of France's resistance. This identification was sedulously maintained through the celebration of its heroes and its exploits despite the party's 1950s purge of Resistance personnel and leaders who were in the leadership's eyes too prominent.

Here, however, France was again different. French Communism's moment had been the Resistance. At the Liberation it emerged crowned with the glory of the Resistance and as patriotic. It had reconciled its commitment to the Soviet State with the highest French patriotism and it still holds, to no small extent, that position today (as the ultra-patriotic Resistance force). It was also a relatively restrained reform movement at the Liberation and benefited from the moderation of its image, so that it was seen as the victim (rather than the instigator) in May 1947 when it was evicted from government and as the defender rather than the attacker in the strikes of November 1947. It had carefully emphasised the less dictatorial period of the First Republic and periodically reminded the public about its commitment to 'the great principles of 1789' ensuring, in this way, both a revolutionary tradition and a patriotic one. But when they were in opposition Communist tactics pushed the Socialists into alliance with the centre to defend the Republic from what they perceived as a quasi-insurrection instigated by the Kremlin. But that (as in Italy) had the benefit for the PCF of exposing the SFIO to the difficulties and compromises of government while leaving the Party free to campaign on such issues as it chose.

It is the Revolution that is the key to 'exceptionalism' on the French left. France is sometimes described as the country of 'human rights' and of the

Enlightenment. This is, of course, true but the ideas of 'rights' and of the scientific and liberal Enlightenment were not the exclusive property of France and were worked out across Europe by many philosophers (including the English) and found their first statement at the American Revolution. What distinguishes France is the role the Revolution played in the idea of how progress would come about and how it would be achieved, as well as in the utopia that would be ushered in after it. Other Western societies, even Revolutionary America, did not place the 'Revolution' at the centre of the project but stressed the 'rights' dimension.

At the time of the creation of modern socialist parties there was a living memory of revolution in France: there had been the Great Revolution, of course, but also 1830, 1848 and the Commune. Jules Guesde, a journalist, an exiled supporter of the Paris Commune, and a vigorous marxist propagandist, founded the most intransigent of socialist parties in nineteenth-century France. Guesde's Parti Ouvrier Français, the first major socialist party in France, declared itself to be revolutionary, adopted a particularly rigid marxism and was designed to take the means of production into public ownership. This party had a programme based on the 'revolutionary action of the proletariat' and, however doctrinally impure it might have been, it had a big audience in the French working class, particularly in the industrial north. Guesde introduced into French socialism the revolutionary trope while at the same time using 'bourgeois' institutions (it quickly had some electoral success) as the party saw fit and where it gave them an advantage.

Guesde's revolutionary vision is usually described as blinkered and there is no direct continuity from guesdists to Communism (Guesde did not join the Communist Party and remained in the Socialist Party). But Guesde pushed out Fabianite gradualism from the French left so that the culture that was established was 'revolutionary' and in unspecified but significant respects non-reformist. And, sophisticated or not, the revolutionary vocation was consolidated and then reaffirmed at the foundation of the SFIO in 1905 (even by Jaurès) and again after the split at the Congress of Tours in 1920 (explicitly by Blum). In 1945 the Socialist Party rejected a modernised doctrine in preference to Guy Mollet's 'class struggle' strategy and at Epinay in 1971 Mitterrand's leadership spoke the same revolutionary language about a 'rupture with the capitalist system'. Thus from the origins of socialist parties in France until the 1990s there has been a revolutionary tradition expressed in marxist language on the left in general. This has been a distinctive French phenomenon as, in the rest of Europe, the Second International socialist parties abandoned their marxist heritage in the 1930s and almost all of them had by then embraced an explicitly reformist outlook.

French Communism, it need hardly be said, keyed into that tradition of the Revolution and spoke in a profoundly French manner, laying claim to the Revolutionary tradition as well as, at times, the Enlightenment. Of course, the Jacobin revolution had been a constant on the left of French politics but the Paris Commune had heightened it for the socialists. This insurrection, and current repression, became part of the left's mythology as soon as the first mass socialist parties developed. In fact the memory of the Commune served to divide the socialist left from the 'bourgeois' Republic that is still commemorated at the Mur des Fédérés every May. In Marx's account of the Commune, and that of the Socialists, the workers' revolution was against the bourgeois revolution but, of course, the central myth was still that of the Revolution. It remained the belief, however, that the Revolution would usher in liberty, equality and fraternity for all and that its socialism had a universal mission.

There was no affinity with the Bolshevik seizure of power in 1917 but the Communist Party did ally Lenin's coup with the French Revolutionary tradition. In this the ground had been well prepared as the marxism expounded by the socialist left was particularly narrow, although the Communists added the cult of Robespierre to the repertoire. Since it became the dominant mode of discourse on the French left, and since the SFIO became in 1905 the dominant socialist party, the Communist graft could be expected to take with some success (Kriegel 1964). Jaurès, among others, had made this marxist ideology into a reformist and parliamentary outlook but had left its revolutionary rhetoric unaltered. In this vision society would be transformed by a violent spasm bringing into being a new society (the so-called '*grand soir*') and this would come about through the contradictions of 'capitalism'. For many on the left, a transformation of this magnitude would not necessarily be through parliamentary means or even legal means. Thus, until very recently, an authentic socialist had to be a 'revolutionary'. In May 1968 the SFIO was to be found solemnly debating whether it was a 'revolutionary party' and deciding that it was (Guy Mollet Archives, jm: 27).

French Communism, after Robert Hue, is no longer a 'Leninist Party'. Of course the USSR no longer exists but the party has also lost its belief in the Socialism that it was set up to defend and has no project other than a vague humanism. Its internal apparatus has mostly disappeared and it is composed of a series of contending baronies with different interests and outlooks. There is no consensus on essentials. This collapse of discipline means that the party's other major asset, the 'transmission belt' of the CGT unions, are no longer tied to Communism and cannot be controlled by a party split, as it is, between warring groups. Worse, for the PCF, the spaces that post-Communists have occupied in other Western countries where the parties have been disbanded have been filled in France. There is a green party (in fact several), there are alternative anti-globalisation movements, anti-European forces exist on the right and left, there are several Trotskyite parties and, of course, the extreme right has its working class following as well. These are now competitors with the PCF for the support of workers, the marginalised and the dispossessed, but they are unburdened by the Communist Party's past and its historical inadequacies. Unlike Italy, where the former Communist Party has become social democratic and hegemonic over the left, the French Socialist Party is still a major force and is the main force on the left.

Conclusion: the continuing presence

With Robert Hue's 3.4 percent of the vote at the 2002 presidential elections and then the party's 4.8 percent of the vote at the following general elections (and 22 deputies) the party is reduced to a minor force. What remains of the Communist Party is not the institution – it is now an archipelago party – but the dedication of its activists and their devotion to 'humanitarian causes' (broadly conceived). As recently as 2002 the Communist Party claimed to have 130,000 members. This, even allowing for exaggerations, is much larger than any other political party in France and its membership is, as it always has been, a substantial asset. But the issues that currently motivate people on the French left, like anti-globalism, defence of workers' rights, suspicion of Europe and anti-American or anti-imperialist themes as well as a proclaimed hostility to 'reformism', could have been Communist campaigns not so long ago (and to some extent still are). As Robert Hue liked to maintain these ideas are older than the Communist Party, going back to Thomas More's Utopia (and why not to Plato?).[4] Hence it may be possible for other movements to exploit the opened gap, enabling the political culture of communism to continue despite the Communist Party's demise (Lavabre and Platone 2003).

There is a view – the PCF is dead, long live communism – that the space occupied by the Communist Party on the French political spectrum is still there to be exploited by other groups (Lazar 2002; Dilas-Rocherieux 1999/2000). After all, at the 2002 presidential elections the four marxist parties together (PCF, Lutte Ouvrière, Ligue Communiste Internationale and the Mouvement pour un Parti des Travailleurs) polled 15 percent. Others, like the Greens (*les Verts*) or even the Citizen's Movement, are coloured by the PCF's values in attitudes to, for example, anti-globalisation. The nationalist, anti-liberal, anti-capitalist and anti-European attitudes, once synthesised by the Communist Party in its prime, are now represented across a myriad of political groups that together have inherited the left-wing political culture of France.

Notes

1. On the failure to integrate incomers in the 1950s and 1960s see G. Maschlet (2001).
2. See for example the role of the intellectuals as detailed in J. Verdès-Leroux (1983), *Au Service du Parti.*
3. Discussed in V. Loupan and P. Lorrain (1994). See also *Libération,* 26 November 2002, which asserted that $25 million were given to the PCF in the last ten years of the USSR. The Italian Communist leader Armando Cossutta never denied receiving money from Moscow, see *Le Monde,* 14 December 1991.
4. For a communist version of this argument, see R. Martelli (1995), *Le Rouge et le bleu.*

Chapter 5

DOES IT MAKE SENSE TO TREAT THE FRONT NATIONAL AS A 'FRENCH EXCEPTION'?

Emmanuel Godin

The Front National, a 'Franco-French' exception?

What is exceptional about the French extreme right today? Pascal Perrineau (1997: 10–11) suggests that what distinguishes the Front National (FN) from previous French extreme-right parties or movements is the strength and longevity of its electoral success. From *boulangisme* in the late nineteenth century to the rise of the Leagues in the interwar period, from the Poujadist wave of the 1950s to the defence of French Algeria in the mid-1960s, the French extreme right's electoral success had always been as intense as it was ephemeral. Conversely, since its first successes in local and European elections in the early 1980s, the FN has considerably improved its electoral strength, culminating with the presence of Le Pen as a candidate for the second round of the 2002 presidential elections. Within the French electoral tradition, the FN has displayed an exceptional electoral strength and political resilience that previous French extreme-right parties clearly lacked. Recent studies have confirmed the FN's status as an established political party. Its strength can no longer be reduced to its leader's charismatic appeal, (thus ensuring its survival when the ageing Le Pen departs), nor to the expression of other parties' rejection, as it was the case in the late 1980s (Mayer and Perrineau 1992). Indeed, with a growing support for its policies among its voters, the FN's partisan identification has been reinforced. For instance, in 1997, 46 percent of the FN's voters declared their positive support for FN candidates, against 38 percent who declared that they primarily wanted to express their rejection of other candidates (Mayer 1997). A shift from a vote of rejection to a vote of conviction indicates that more

FN voters are now motivated by strong ideological reasons, even if this dynamism has been dampened somewhat by the 1999 crisis provoked by Bruno Mégret when he broke away to create his own party, the Mouvement National Républicain (Mayer 2002). Perrineau even further develops the argument: he describes the FN as '*une spécificité franco-française*' (1996: 71), insisting that this *enduring electoral* strength makes the FN an exception in Europe: 'In no other European country has an extreme-right party succeeded at such a level over such a long period' (1997: 10). Consequently, he prefers to characterise the recent successes of other European extreme-right parties as 'flashes in the pan' (*des poussées de fièvre*) (2001: 5). The recent electoral collapse of the extreme right in Austria and in the Netherlands might confirm his view. However, if the electoral strength of the FN might indeed be exceptional in the Western European context, it is less clear whether the nature of its discourse and ideology makes it a unique phenomenon.

Several contributions in this volume (see chapters by Hewlett, Collard, Kuhn and Kelly) explain the ambiguities attached to 'French exceptionalism' as a methodologically and politically loaded concept and they question its usefulness. Likewise, on the particular subject of the extreme right today, Minkenberg points out that researchers often fall into an 'ethnocentrist' trap (2001: 385). They tend to overstress the importance of national characteristics and conclude that there is something exceptional about the object they study. Thus, for instance, Markovits (2002) explains that what makes the success of the Austrian Freiheitliche Partei Österreichs (FPÖ) 'exceptional' is that it is rooted in a unique national culture which, under the cover of consocialism,[1] has consistently refused to address seriously Austria's active involvement with nazism. Conversely, Loch (2001) explains that the German extreme right's inability to capitalise on its sporadic and uneven electoral success should be treated as a 'particular case' in Europe, because it operates in an exceptional national context where the memories related to Germany's nazi past delegitimise extreme-right parties.[2] Likewise, Eatwell (2000) describes the persistent electoral failure of the British extreme right as an exception in Europe. This 'exception' is explained by the effects of the majoritarian electoral system on small parties, the ability of governing parties to manage and defuse 'racism' and the delegitimising association of the British National Party and the National Front with fascism. Finally, in the case of France, the historical weight of an authoritarian-plebiscitarian tradition within the national political culture is said to form a unique fertile ground for the extreme right's development (Taguieff 1985; Winock 1994 and 1997). All these arguments are valid and useful. However, if so many cases are exceptional, one might wonder what the norm is. Focusing too much on the specificity of national history and politics to explain the strength or weakness of extreme-right parties could reduce the argument to 'slogans such as American exceptionalism, *exception française* or *deutscher Sonder-weg'*. Rather, the extreme right should be treated as an 'international phenomenon' requiring further comparative analysis (Minkenberg 2001: 386). A growing number of comparative analyses have already highlighted, *inter alia*, the extreme right's electoral dynamics (Evans and Ivaldi 2002a), its ideological nature (Camus 1998; Mudde 2000), its political style (Taggart 1996), its relationship with the traditional right and its effects on a given polity (Kitschelt 1995; Dezé 2001).

If we are to describe a situation as exceptional this requires us to define what constitutes the norm and to test the validity of our definition in a comparative context. Researchers have been at pains to define exactly what the term extreme right should encompass (Mudde 1996a; Ignazi 1997; Merkl and Weinberg 1997; Hainsworth 2000), to test the usefulness of rival concepts, such as 'neofascism', '(national) populism' or 'radical right' (Mudde 1996b; Betz and Immerfall 1998), and to determine the degree of porosity between the extreme right and the traditional right (Kitschelt 1995; Dezé 2001; Ignazi 2001). If we accept that extreme right parties are ideologically diverse, it is nevertheless possible to extract from the literature core features that help to identify the nature of the extreme right in Europe today (Mudde 1996a).

From fascism to postmaterialism?

It has been suggested that *most* extreme-right parties that emerged as an electoral force in the 1990s are part of a *new and modern* phenomenon. They are not a simple resurgence of fascism under a new guise. Ignazi (1992, 2003) has argued that parties which have failed to sever their links with a fascist past and to develop a new ideology have been condemned to political marginality. This is true, for instance, of the unsuccessful German Deutsche Volksunion (DVU), whose obsession with the rehabilitation of Second World War German soldiers and the celebration of traditional militarist values seems to be its principal *raison d'être* (Mudde 2000). This is also the case of the various Spanish extreme-right factions, which are largely dominated by nostalgic Francoists revering the values of the Falanges (Casals 2001). The fact that some parties are trying to shed their overtly neofascist traits to increase their electoral success, such as the British National Party (BNP) under Nick Griffin (Eatwell 2000) or the Spanish Democracia Nacional under the pressure of younger generations (Casals 2001), demonstrates that neofascism cannot be the main engine of extreme-right success. Conversely, this is also confirmed by the successful transformation of the Italian neofascist party (MSI – Movimento Sociale Italiano) into a 'postfascist' party (AN – Alleanza Nazionale), now part of the Berlusconi government. Under the forceful leadership of Fini and with the acquiescence rather than active consent of most of its *cadres*, who are still imbued with Mussolinian culture, the AN has repudiated antisemitism, racism, ultra-nationalism and statism, ideas that are central to fascist ideology, and has clearly proclaimed its support for democratic principles. Those who have refused to follow Fini's postfascist agenda and prefer to defend a more orthodox line have created their own party, the Movimento Sociale-Fiamma Tricolore, which remains consigned to the margins of the Italian party system (Ignazi 1994; Gallagher 2000). Finally, and more ambiguously, the successful Vlaams Blok (VB), which still celebrates Flemish collaborators and actively promotes a blatant xenophobic discourse (Mudde 2000), has nevertheless 'polished' and diversified its message to gain respectability and to attract a new clientele: 'The leadership ... presents the VB as a "new" party... and avoids any overt association with the New Order of the 1930s, wartime collaboration, or with the extreme-right (paramilitary) organisations of the 1960s and 1970s' (Swyngedown 2000: 137). Whether this *electoral* strategy mirrors a profound change in the VB's nature or is purely opportunistic is debatable. Nevertheless, all the above examples show that neofascism is not central to the ideology of successful extreme-right parties today and in any case it would not be enough to explain their electoral success.

In this respect, the FN reveals the ambiguity of the French extreme right. From his Poujadist engagement in the late 1950s and his association with the most radical supporters of French Algeria in the 1960s, to his flirtation with openly nazi movements in the 1970s, the leader of the FN, Jean-Marie Le Pen, has a long radical past (Duprat 1972; Rollat 1985). His party still indulges in nostalgic commemorations of past ultra-nationalist figureheads, such as Marshal Pétain, entertains strong links with Catholic fundamentalists, such as the Fraternité Sacerdotale Saint Pie X (Winock 1994) and maintains tenuous, if often boisterous, links with negationist and neonazi groups (Camus 2001). For instance, in July 2002, Le Pen clearly opposed the dissolution of the neonazi Unité Radicale, after one of his members attempted to assassinate President Chirac. Likewise, antisemitism has long been an acceptable frame of reference for the FN and the party has developed good collaborative links with Eastern European antisemitic parties, such as Romania Mare (Hunter 1998). At the same time, it is often critical of other West European extreme-right parties, with the exception of the Flemish VB and the German DVU (Camus 1998). Despite recent attempts to give respectability to its discourse, (notably under the influence of a younger generation of *cadres*) the FN still has a foot in the fascist world and finds it difficult to 'complete its transformation into a modern party' (Camus 2001: 216).

The FN: a postindustrial party?

It has been argued that if the extreme right has often kept the populist style of previous Poujadist-like movements, its ideology nevertheless marks it as a different and *modern* phenomenon (Ignazi 1992 and 2003; Minkenberg 2001: 386), a response to the fears and uncertainties 'generated by the development of a postindustrial capitalism' (Perrineau 2001: 9).What is specific to postindustrial capitalism is not so much that it generates material poverty for a substantial segment of the population: blue-collar workers, the unemployed, small traders or farmers whose economic position has been eroded by global competition and unskilled young people without a stable professional future are the expected victims of any capitalist regime. What is more important is that these 'modernisation losers' feel 'alone', 'alienated' and 'powerless', and that these feelings are also shared by those whose material conditions are comfortable, but who nonetheless feel insecure, up-rooted or unable to climb any further up the social ladder (Minkenberg 2001: 394 – 98). These feelings of alienation and frustration might be unrelated to objective material conditions. For instance, it has been demonstrated that there is no mechanical relation between level of unemployment and the success of the extreme right (Knigge 1998). Therefore, Ignazi suggests that extreme-right parties are better described as postindustrial parties because they respond to and capitalise on postindustrial conflicts that are 'less centred on the redistribution of material resources than the allocation of values', such as the 'promotion and preservation of cultural values and identity' (2001: 372).

Available data usually show that in Western Europe, workers, the unemployed and young unskilled people tend to be over-represented among extreme-right voters. From the 1990s onward, there seems to have been a general trend towards a proletarianisation of the extreme-right electoral base (Evans and Ivaldi 2002a). This is particularly obvious in Austria, where 48 percent of blue-collar workers voted for the FPÖ in 2000. In this respect, the FN is no exception. For instance, the Languedoc-Roussillon region, with a high unemployment rate (12 percent against a 9 percent national average in 2002) and a high proportion of its population on income support, is fertile ground for the extreme right: in the first round of the 2002 presidential elections, Le Pen captured between 23 and 25 percent of the Languedoc-Roussillon vote (Bréchont 2002), compared to 17 percent at the national level. Moreover, at the national level, 31 percent of workers supported Le Pen in the second round of the 2002 presidential elections. Perrineau suggests that the FN is particularly good at attracting traditional left-wing voters disappointed by the programmatic orientation of the Socialist and Communist parties and their actual achievements in government ('*gaucho-lepénisme*': Perrineau 1995). Mayer, on the other hand, prefers to stress that the FN mainly mobilises workers with a low level of politicisation and a weak sense of class solidarity and professional identity (*ouvrièro-lepénisme*': Mayer 1999).

However, the FN's electoral success does not solely rest on the mobilisation of voters who have been marginalised by the 'modernisation' process. It also attracts voters who subjectively feel that their relatively comfortable social status and identity are threatened and whose hope for social promotion appears, rightly or wrongly, to be limited. For instance, 29 percent of self-employed workers supported Le Pen in 2002. The case of the Alsace region is also telling. It enjoys one of the highest living standards in France and its unemployment rate is 4 percent lower than the national average. Yet, in Alsace, the FN consistently scores higher than in the rest of the country. Squeezed between a mother country that seems to pay little attention to its particular identity and an economically dynamic German Rhineland, which seems to reduce Alsace to the status of an economic satellite, this region has become unsure about its identity and craves reassurance (Bihr 1998).

Other regions or *départements* with low precarity and unemployment levels, but which have constantly expressed serious doubt about the project of European construction, also provide strong support for the FN. In the Orne *département*, for instance, 19 percent of voters supported Le Pen (first round) in 2002. The unemployment rate is lower than the national average (7 percent), but this *département* has nevertheless consistently supported Euro-sceptic candidates since 1979, and in 1992 clearly voted against the Maastricht Treaty. Likewise *départements* with a high density of immigrants, such as the Rhône or the Vaucluse, tend to provide some 'above average' support for the extreme right. However, this is *also* the case of *départements* where the density of the immigrant population is lower than the national average, such as the Haute-Marne, Orne and Meuse.[3] The fear rather than the actual presence of immigrants here explains the good results of the extreme right. Clearly issues related to identity are as important as material ones. The FN's electoral strength rests on its ability to attract a sociologically diverse electorate, from workers, small entrepreneurs, employees and managers to the bourgeois of *les beaux quartiers*. This is not exceptional and the same trend can be found in Austria, Flanders and Scandinavia, where the extreme right is able to achieve a synthesis between groups that have traditionally been ideologically and sociologically opposed to each other (Evans and Ivaldi 2002a).

Extreme-right parties as extreme parties? Democracy reconstructed

It is debatable whether the departure from fascism to postmaterial values automatically makes extreme-right parties less extreme. It is usually accepted that such parties display a set of beliefs which undermine democracy. As such, they are an antisystem party because they reject the values and principles of the political system in which they operate (Sartori, quoted in Hainsworth 2000). If extreme-right parties pay tribute to democracy, such claims should not be taken at face value. Hainsworth, for instance, stresses the relationship between the extreme right, violence and intolerance (7), while Ignazi shows that its prevalent antiparliamentarianism, 'antipartyism' and antipluralism delegitimise democracy: 'Even if such parties do not openly advocate authoritarianism, they nevertheless undermine democratic legitimacy by expressing distrust for the parliamentary system and politics in general and by stressing the weakness of the state, the disruption of traditional communities and the unnatural equality and excessive freedom that democracy promotes' (Ignazi 1997: 52).

Yet, some authors prefer to stress that such parties are not opposed to the democratic system itself, but to the cultural (moral laxism, multiculturalism) and social (egalitarianism) programmatic elements that modern democracy promotes. As such they would be better defined as radical right-wing parties (Betz 1994) or neopopulist parties (Betz and Immerfall 1998). The main consequence of such definitions is that they tend to blur the boundaries between such parties and conservative ones. It has been argued (Kitschelt 1995) that extreme-right parties have developed and radicalised arguments that are usually found in the traditional right-wing arsenal, such as moral conservatism and tougher law and order policies. If such is the case, extreme-right ideology is an extreme form of right-wing ideology, whose visibility and appeal is proportional to the progressive ideological impoverishment of the traditional right. Finally, other authors prefer to make the point that these parties support *a kind of* democracy against the shortcomings of liberal and/or procedural democracy (Julliard 1999; Meny and Surel 2000). Far from rejecting democracy as an ideal, they castigate its 'corruption' by self-serving politicians, its bureaucratic drift that prevents the expression of popular will, or its inability to deliver effective solutions to people's daily problems (immigration, unemployment, security). As such, these parties are populist parties because they defend in the name of democracy a supposedly virtuous but victimised people against an arrogant elite.

The term 'populism,' however, is not precise enough and has little heuristic value to define such parties, for the defence of the people against the pitfalls and deviations of liberal democracy can be found in the discourse of a variety of parties from the left and the centre to the right (Taguieff 1997; Hermet 2001). What distinguishes these parties is the way they conceptualise the 'people' and the nature of the power ascribed to it. For them, the people are not the sum of critical, autonomous and equal citizens willing to debate and confront various options, informed and enlightened by experts or their representatives. Rather, the people are the undifferentiated expression of a nation, defined in exclusionary terms and incarnated in a strong state. Consequently, this justifies both a direct appeal to the people invested with an absolute power and a rejection of alien elements that might corrupt or divide the people's will. The rejection of '*les gros*' (the elite, cosmopolitan lobbies) is reinforced by a refusal of 'the other' ('*les autres*': immigrants, homosexuals) who are often '*les plus petits*' (asylum seekers) (Hermet 1997). In particular, most extreme-right parties argue that the integration into the national community of those whose values, culture and identity are markedly different is not only undesirable but also impossible. Their 'ethnopluralism' stresses that differences between ethnic groups must be respected and maintained, but to achieve this each group should live in separate communities. Some extreme-right parties, such as the VB, also insist that ethnic groups are not only defined by their shared values, but also by their blood ties. Thus extreme-right parties could be defined as 'national-populist', either because of their authoritarian-plebiscitarian preferences (Wieviorka 1993; Winock 1997) or/and because they wish to redefine democracy as an 'ethnocracy' (Taguieff 1997; Minkenberg 2001: 394), defined by cultural or biological traits. In the latter case, democracy as constructed by extreme-right parties is alien to the traditional right and sets extreme-right ideology apart (Hainsworth 2000).

This extreme right version of democracy is at the core of the FN's ideology. The FN attacks French democracy in the name of 'higher' democratic principles. If Joan of Arc is a powerful character, repeatedly mobilised by the FN to galvanise nationalist, militarist and religious feelings, Gavroche, Victor Hugo's fictional *gamin,* who died on the 1832 republican barricades fighting against the elitist, liberal and half-heartedly patriotic July Monarchy, is now also part of the FN's mythology. Le Pen argues that: '[Gavroche] symbolises a revolt against injustice and against the violations of the laws of the republic. He is the child who suffers from the poverty generated by untamed nineteenth-century *laissez-faire.* He also incarnates the spirit of revolt and freedom that defines so well the soul of our people. He represents popular patriotism' (Le Pen 1999). The mobilisation of this symbolic figure corresponds to the FN's ambition to attract potential left-wing voters in the late 1990s and the rejection of neoliberal economic policies that were far more salient in his 1980s programme. This powerful usurping of a left-wing symbol allows the FN to become the standard-bearer of democracy and to champion the virtuous but victimised people against an arrogant and decadent political class. Its hypocrisy, corruption, greed and self-interest betray the national and republican ideal in the same way as did the bourgeoisie under Louis-Philippe.

Indeed, for the FN, the French political class hides behind the mask of republican and democratic virtues, but is in fact nothing more than '*une oligarchie cosmopolite, totalitaire et corrompue*' (Le Pen 2002a). 'Oligarchy' because French democracy is in the hands of an unaccountable elite, which governs the country for its own interests. The incestuous relationship between politicians, civil servants, economic leaders and the media, mostly trained in the same *grandes écoles*, and the unofficial but effective links that the elite maintains with powerful lobbies, notably

Freemasons, contribute to the exclusion of ordinary, but deserving citizens from the decision-making process. In particular, the FN constantly denounces the alliance between all established parties to prevent the introduction of proportional representation, thus depriving the FN of any seats in the National Assembly. This is a form of 'creeping totalitarianism under the mask of democracy' (Le Pen 2002a). The FN calls for the introduction of popular referendums (*référendums d'initiative populaire*), which would give back to the people the voice that the elite has confiscated for itself: 'To break down the blockages that paralyse French society and restore true democracy, [we call for] the establishment of a national and popular republic based on the use of referendums' (Le Pen 2001). It also demands the abolition of the ENA, which ensures the social and intellectual reproduction of this oligarchy. The declared objective is to 'free the French people from the totalitarian grip of the Establishment' (Le Pen 2002a).

This oligarchy is 'cosmopolitan' because it conspires to undermine French sovereignty and dissolve the 'nation into the European *conglomérat* before it disappears into the global melting-pot' (Le Pen 2002d). Reminding its voters that the 1958 constitution stipulates that 'national sovereignty belongs to the people', the FN explains that this principle is being blatantly ignored. The political class, with the complicity of the media, the civil service, international lobbies and cosmopolitan intellectuals, skilfully avoids consulting the people about its own destiny (as was the case – it is argued – from the 1986 European Single Act to the 1998 Amsterdam Treaty) or distorts and falsifies the debate to mislead the nation (as with the 1992 Maastricht Treaty referendum). With some pathos, Le Pen asks: 'France! Will a bunch of perfidious MPs sell you out to a Europe of merchants and bankers while the pliable people look on, indifferent?' (Le Pen 1999). The FN argues that the nation is the only democratic forum where decisions can be made and asks for the primacy of French laws over European legislation to be restored. If elected, the FN would organise a referendum on EU membership which would offer people the choice of pulling out of 'Brussels' Europe' and reasserting French sovereignty. Likewise, the reduction in the president's terms of office from seven to five years – *le quinquenat* – is seen by the FN as a plot engineered by a cosmopolitan elite: 'by trivialising the role of the head of state, [the Establishment] clearly demonstrates its willingness to do away with the sovereign nation state and replace it by a federal state with at its head a mere governor who takes his orders from the Federation' (Le Pen 2001). Making good use of a long French 'Bonapartist' tradition, the FN reasserts the importance of the relation between a directly elected president and the people as a guarantee of popular democracy and state authority.

This oligarchy is also totalitarian because it rejects as 'politically incorrect' or as 'scandalous' any attempt to challenge the 'liberal' status quo (*la pensée unique*) and forbids any meaningful debate on issues that affect citizens in their daily life, such as immigration: 'The dogmas of *la pensée unique* are tyrannically imposed in this area, as in many others' (Le Pen 2002d). The increasing lack of ideological differentiation between the left and the right, the effects of three *cohabitations* between 1986 and 2002, which have smoothed over the differences between the major parties, and the acceptance by successive governments that their prerogatives were strongly circumscribed by external constraints mean that democracy has been engulfed by a consensual but indeterminate magma: 'They all belong to the same tribe, the sectarian tribe of the New World Order. The only choice we have left is between the cosmopolitanism cherished by the left and globalisation relished by the right, the common denominator being the Establishment's adulation of ultra-*laissez-faire*' (Le Pen 1997). The FN argues that it is the only party that provides a true political alternative and thus the only meaningful opposition to the established parties of the left and right: 'Do not be fooled by the outdated divisions between left and right ... For twenty years now they have lied to you about law and order, unemployment, immigration, Europe and the rest ... [I am] the only candidate who can really change things' (Le Pen 2002c).

Other extreme-right parties in Western Europe today also develop similar themes. For instance, the 1999 FPÖ manifesto stipulated that strengthening direct democracy was the best way to reduce the power of political parties, professional organisations and lobbies, which formed an unaccountable oligarchy, a 'para-government ... without democratic legitimacy'. The FPÖ argued that their ability to manipulate and subjugate the state bureaucracy through public appointments undermines the rule of law. The lack of a clear alternative between the left and right and the rise of consensual politics as an anaesthetic to democracy has also been exploited by extreme-right parties in countries where a governmental alliance between socialist and conservative parties is common, such as Austria, the Netherlands or in Scandinavia. In Western Europe 'extreme-right parties mainly succeed where monopolistic political systems tend towards inertia and reproduce *ad nauseam* identical coalition models (*Proporzdemokratie* in Austria, *consociativismo* in Italy) or weak minority governments (Denmark, Norway)' (Evans and Ivaldi 2002b).

Finally, the oligarchy is corrupt because, from Communist councillors to Gaullist MPs, from leading entrepreneurs to top civil servants, it is heavily tainted by financial corruption. Unlike ordinary citizens, the oligarchy enjoys the implicit protection of the judiciary. Denouncing the leniency of the law when it is applied to the corrupt elite, Le Pen declared: 'France's top elite is untouchable! Contrary to the virtuous declarations about the equality of all in the eye of the law, one can break the law with impunity provided that one belongs to the seraglio' (Le Pen 2002b). The corruption of the political class is a common argument used by the extreme right in

Western Europe to distinguish itself from the Establishment. The argument was certainly used by Fini in the mid-1990s when claiming to be the only leader not involved in the *mani pulite* ('clean hands') investigations that rocked the first Italian republic (Gallagher 2000). It has also been used by the VB to denounce the corruption in Antwerp generated by an unhealthy collusion between bosses, union leaders and local officials (Swyngedown 2000).

The FN's democratic ideal is a distorted representation of direct democracy, for it rests on a strong state and an exclusionary definition of the 'people'. The state should be proactive and fight against moral permissiveness (measures against 'deviant' behaviour such as homosexuality would be introduced), defend traditional family values (the legal right to abortion would be abolished) and foster strict law and order policies (tougher sentences for criminals would be properly applied). Likewise, the state has a crucial role to play in the management of the economy. The FN is highly critical of traditional French 'statism'. It recognises that the weight of bureaucracy and crippling taxation hamper entrepreneurial values and sees 'statism' as a means of using taxpayers' money to protect the established power of a 'pseudo-politico-capitalist clique': 'The elected ones get all the privileges; the electors simply pay their taxes' (Maréchal 1996: 84). Public money is wasted on dubious 'sociocultural' projects, such as the integration of young immigrants into the labour market (Le Pen: 2002d). Yet the FN also denounces the destructive forces of *laissez-faire*, which is promoted by Brussels, and calls for the introduction of protectionist measures and the development of subsidies to national companies that wish to find new markets abroad. Bilateral agreements, determined by national interest, should govern trade relations and it might become necessary for France to pull out of the European Union if Brussels' policies appear to be detrimental to the wealth of the nation. As such the FN's ambiguous economic programme is not substantially different from that of the FPÖ, which seeks to protect the national economy from foreign competition, while advocating the implementation of neoliberal policies at home. Like the Scandinavian 'radical right-wing populist parties', it is critical of state expenditures supporting 'dubious' social programmes targetting undeserving groups, such as immigrants or refugees (Andersen and Bjørklund 2000). Like the FPÖ or the VB, the FN supports a form of 'welfare chauvinism', which attributes economic and social benefits primarily if not exclusively to nationals (including access to the labour market). Indeed, the FN demands that the constitution be amended to recognise *la préférence nationale* that asserts the priority accorded to French citizens in France over foreigners in the field of political, civil and social rights (Le Pen 2002d). Thus, employment opportunities must be offered in the first instance to French citizens and companies that employ foreign workers should be subject to a special tax. Social benefits must only be given to French citizens. This ambiguous programme is well summarised by Le Pen's slogan during the 2002 presidential elections: 'I am economically on the right, socially on the left and more than ever patriotically French' (Le Pen 2002c).

Finally, for the FN the state must fight any overt or latent forms of multiculturalism. 'The rejection of a multicultural society and the preservation of French national identity are the FN's main *raison d'être*' (Le Pen 2002d). The poor performance of the French team during the 2002 football World Cup gave the FN the opportunity to deride a society based on multiculturalism: 'After the 1998 World Cup final, the *black-blanc-beur*[4] team was adulated. In 2002 it exited ignominiously in the first round. So what is left now of this cosmopolitan utopia that was eulogised by the political and media elites, which wanted to present this victory as the vindication of a multiracial France enriched by its differences? Following their defeat against Denmark, it is now clear that this supposed strength did not even get them through the first round' (Domard 2002: 26).

Against the myth of a multicultural society, the FN argues that the only solution is to promote a vigorous assimilation policy of deserving immigrants: 'To be assimilated, one needs first of all to respect and share the spiritual, moral and cultural values [of the nation]. These need to be strong and dynamic enough to make people want to abandon their own values' (Le Pen 2002d). However, the assimilation of Muslim immigrants, the FN argues, is both impossible and undesirable. Indeed, values promoted by Islam, in particular the fusion between politics and religion and the spiritual community it creates above nations, are said to be incompatible with core French values, 'our understanding of humankind, of the family (monogamy) and our secular legal tradition' (Le Pen 2000d). Whereas in the 1980s, the FN accused immigrant workers of 'stealing our jobs', Muslim immigrants today intend to 'steal our souls' and undermine French civilisation. The fact that French suburbs have become prey to a 'communitarian ghettoisation' proves the impossibility of assimilating most immigrants. The lax and generous policies pursued by all governments, from left to right, (notably '*les politiques de la ville*') have turned the nation into a series of 'settler colonies' ('*colonies de peuplement*'). Under the cover of antiracism and multiculturalism, each 'colony' insidiously diffuses its values, laws and culture into the national body and gradually modifies profoundly 'the essential nature of the French people' (Le Pen 2000d). The FN thus proposes to redefine the criteria for the acquisition of French nationality, notably through the abolition of the *jus solis*, the traditional right that confers French nationality on anyone born on French territory. Individuals who wish to acquire French nationality would have to demonstrate that they share core French spiritual, civic and moral values and that they speak the language. Furthermore, all applications would be scrutinised by the municipal council where the applicants live and they could be vetoed. If immigrants fail to assimilate, then an active state policy of repatriation should be undertaken. Thus, the FN defends a culturally homogeneous nation, but does not insist on ethnic homogeneity in the same way as the 'ethnic-nationalist' VB. As such, it is closer to 'state nationalism', defended by the Dutch CD (*Centrumdemocraten*) (Mudde 2000) or the Austrian FPÖ (Wodak and Pelinka 2002). What is original, rather than exceptional, is that the FN can tap into parts of the republican tradition (such as an instinctive allergy to any form of communitarianism) to give more strength to its argument.

Indeed, the FN argues that 'a multicultural and multi-ethnic country is inevitably multiconflictual' (Le Pen 2002d) and explictly links immigration with insecurity, which is the logical consequence of society's 'communitarianisation': 'We can now cross borders freely but we cannot go out to work freely because groups of "youths" … create ethnic borders within our own country and propagate fear and insecurity' (Le Pen 1999). The situation is made even worse by the surrender of national sovereignty to the EU. Whereas the Italian AN believes that immigration can only be solved through the definition of a common European policy, the FN, like the FPÖ, refuses this option and asserts the supreme right of the nation to define its own immigration policy. It calls for tougher law and order policies targeting the immigrant population, such as a stricter control of immigrants' associations, regular police identity checks and the expulsion of illegal immigrants. Like the VB, it also demands tougher sentences for delinquents, the expulsion of immigrant offenders and that the judiciary be purged of left-wing magistrates. Like the FPÖ, it calls for further investment in the police force and better support for the victims of crime. Like the AN, it denounces the left's soft touch on law and order and asks for tougher sentences to be applied and served in full by offenders. Like the German DVU, it is in favour of the death penalty for the most odious crimes.

Conclusions

The FN shares the broad ideological characteristics identified in the current literature on the extreme right in Western Europe. Most of the core ingredients are there: a eulogy of the nation and the strong state against the false pretences of the EU and the destructive consequences of global capitalism; a bitter attack on the existing elite and representative democracy in the name of a supposedly higher form of popular democracy; a rejection of multiculturalism in favour of an 'ethnopluralist' vision of society. It might be the case that the FN combines these broad themes in a specific way and, although there is indeed some overlap with the ideas of other extreme-right parties in Europe, there are also some differences. For example, the FN shares with the VB a 'welfare chauvinist' stance, but its attack on the EU is not shared by the Flemish party, whose attachment to the Belgian nation-state is naturally lukewarm, to say the least. Thus, the FN's 'mixture' might be original, but hardly exceptional, in the sense that all extreme-right parties are likely to develop a specific combination of the core ingredients, depending on their national environment. The originality rests on the ability to rework some traditional republican themes (most strikingly *laïcité*) to integrate them in the common language of the European extreme right. Interestingly, David Bell, in this volume, suggests that that the integration of republican traditions into a radical discourse has also been one of the most salient features of the Parti Communiste Français' ideology in its heyday.

If the ideology of the FN is not strikingly 'exceptional', its relative weight in French politics has enabled academics to argue that France has remained politically exceptional. Indeed, political polarisation is one of the defining characteristics of the so-called *exception française* (Hayward 1990; Hewlett 1998). The enduring strength of the FN is supposed to 'act as a counterweight' to the growing consensus between governmental parties and to prove that the French polity still displays strong centrifugal tendencies (Cole 1998: 185). These centrifugal tendencies have long been used to distinguish France from other European democracies with a higher level of political consensus. It is also supposed to be the surest sign of a certain French archaism, especially for American pundits (Frank 1998).

Yet, today it is argued that the growing strength of extreme-right parties in Western Europe has increased political polarisation in most Western democracies (Webb 2002; Mudde 2002), notably because parts of the traditional parties have taken on board some of the favourite themes developed by the extreme right. The vigorous law and order policies pursued by Nicolas Sarkozy, the French Minister of the Interior, are supposed to deprive the FN of one of its most effective electoral arguments against the leniency of the 'establishment' towards criminals (Ceaux 2002). The Austrian Prime Minister, Wolfram Schussels, despite the recent electoral collapse of its coalition partner, the FPÖ, indicated that he intended to continue to pursue right-wing policies, notably in the fields of European construction and immigration policy. The Berlusconi government in Italy, which comprises members of the 'postfascist' AN and of the racist Lega Nord, has also toughened its discourse against immigrants (Rouard 2001), and particularly Muslims (Osborn 2001), in the aftermath of 11 September 2001. If we are witnessing a higher degree of polarisation throughout Europe and especially a lurch towards the right, then France might prove to be the norm rather than the exception.

Notes

1. All translations are those of the author, unless otherwise noted.
   Consocialism refers to the ability of opposing partisan elites to seek consensus in order to work together.
2. Loch even argues that within Germany, the eastern Länder form a specific case.
3. In the first round of the 2002 presidential elections, Le Pen scored more than 21 percent in the Loire, 19 percent in the Rhône, two *départements* with a high immigrant density (between 5 and 10 percent of the population). He also scored just above 18 percent in the Oise, 20 percent in the Meuse and 22 percent in the Haute-Marne, three *départements* with a low immigrant density (between 1 and 2 percent of the population). See ' Le Pen IV, le retour.' (Zemmour 2002) *Le Figaro,* special issue 57,984 :'La présidentielle qui a fait trembler la Ve République'.
4. A *'beur'* is a second generation immigrant from North Africa.

Chapter 6

THE FRENCH ADMINISTRATIVE EXCEPTION: CHANGE AND RESISTANCE

Anne Stevens

In attempting to categorise administrative systems Edward Page (1995: 280) assigned the French system to a group onto itself. France is often regarded as being a particularly striking example, indeed the epitome, of a 'Napoleonic' or continental model, its features memorably summarised by Vincent Wright: '[s]tatist, powerful, hierarchically structured, ubiquitous, uniform, depoliticised, instrumental, expert and tightly controlled... a model attractive to tidy minds in untidy countries' (1994b: 116). Pierre (1995) sees it as constituting one of the two globally dominant models, the other being the 'Anglo-Saxon' model. Sabino Cassese (Cassese 1987: 12) on the other hand, identifies three models: the German model 'dominated by legalism, rigidity and administrative planning', the French characterised by 'the rigidity of the structures and the flexibility of the bureaucracy, and the English model by the flexibility of both'.

The notion that the uniqueness and distinctiveness of the social and political evolution of France were in certain crucial ways linked to the patterns and practices of the administrative system was reinforced during the first two decades of the Fifth Republic by a number of key academic studies. Perhaps the most influential was the study undertaken in the 1960s Michel Crozier, *Le Phénomène bureaucratique*, in which he identifies the isolation of individuals, the predominance of formal rather than informal activities, and in particular hierarchical separation, with a struggle between various levels for the maintenance of vested interests, as the dominant characteristics in the two large administrative bodies studied (1971: 262). He points out (364) that the 'French model', which had claimed to be exceptional as a universal example for others to follow, was, even by the 1960s, beginning to look inferior. But change would depend on the preservation of advantages for civil servants comparable to those that motivated the strong attachment of individuals to the existing system. He made a strong plea for the retention of what he saw as most valuable: the personal independence, protection from the vicissitudes of changing circumstances, and scope for intellectual freedom and clarity enjoyed by officials (1971: 368).

The autonomy and independence of the administrative system and its particular relationship to its political masters was a key theme of two other seminal studies, Pierre Grémion's work on local-central relations, *Le Pouvoir périphérique* (1976), and Ezra Suleiman's study of central administrators, *Politics, Power and Bureaucracy in France* (1974). Both identified the particular complexity of the relationships involved. For Grémion the prefect was at one and the same time the local representative of a highly centralised national level and deeply complicit in the course of local affairs. Suleiman revealed the extent to which a discourse of general interest and administrative autonomy were weapons in an institutionalised struggle between politicians, supported by their private offices (*cabinets*) and senior officials in the ministerial divisions. Alongside Pierre Birnbaum (1977) he denounced the subordination of the top civil service to party political control, and revealed clearly the paradox of a 'myth' of 'depoliticised' technocracy – and the 'technical' aptitude, training and capacity of the top civil service in France was and is no myth – and the reality of political direction, including some elements of a political 'spoils system' at the top. While such paradoxes are by no means peculiar to the French system, that system was perhaps exceptional in the clarity with which they emerged under the Fifth Republic.[1]

Both Crozier and Suleiman were concerned with the extent to which the nature of the French administration made it receptive to the possibility of reform. This chapter looks at those reforms that have related specifically to the procedures and structures of the central administration. It does not seek to consider the whole gamut of 'reform of the state' (Machin 2001: 137), where the pressures of Europeanisation and of local politics feature strongly. There is inevitably throughout an element of implicit comparison with experiences elsewhere: the conclusion returns to the issue of French exceptionalism.

The context of change

Since the emergence of the modern state, administrative reform has never been absent from the agenda of politicians and governments (Dreyfus 1999). However, in the early 1990s there was, worldwide, 'an almost frenetic quality about the reform programmes' (Wright 1994b: 103; Kickert 1997: 15). Economic pressures provided one explanation. 'It was the economic climate … that focused the attention of politicians on reform proposals in a way that critics alone could not have achieved' (Ridley 1996: 16). The consequence was a wave of reform, of a type succinctly described by the phrase 'the new public management', which appeared to be sweeping ineluctably across the Western world (Kickert 1997: 17; Dunleavy and Hood 1994).

Economic pressures and growing consumer demand are, however, not the only factors accounting for the increased salience of administrative reform in the 1990s. Ridley (1996: 17) identifies the role played by the ideological stance of the New Right but, crucially, adds that this is 'something of an Anglophone phenomenon'.[2] France was not, however, immune to what Wright (1994a) called 'convergent and interconnected pressures for change' on the state and hence on public administration, even if French specificity was demonstrated by a very distinctive reception of the neoliberal ideas that underpinned many reform programmes (Guyomarch 1999; Jobert 1994). As this chapter seeks to map the scope of administrative change in France and consider where its boundaries lie we need first to turn to the national context of the reform programmes.

Administrative reform in France potentially occurs within a very large arena. The number of persons subject to the *statut général* in the mid-1990s in France was some 4.8 million (Ministère de la Fonction Publique 1999; Meininger 2000: 198).[3] Indeed, including those working in the public services somewhat more broadly defined (though excluding nationalised industry) and retired public servants, some 9 million people in France draw their remuneration from public-service employment. However, the main impact of administrative reform falls upon approximately 600,000 central officials (Ministère de la Fonction Publique 1999: 203). The contrast with the U.K. is thus slightly less stark than is sometimes alleged (Anon 1996: 97). Civil service reform in the U.K. affects just under half a million officials.

In France administrative law concerns itself not only with the relationship of the citizen to the state, but also with 'the state administration as inhabiting an autonomous domain apart from civil society' (D. Clark 1998: 100). The principles and provision that apply to officials are specified in law (the *statut général de la fonction publique*) and seen as a crucial guarantee of the integrity and above all the independence of the civil service. This has had a profound influence on the deployment and management of human resources within the civil service and on expectations about, and the nature of, the careers it offers since 'many crucial aspects of public service management … fall within the jurisdiction of the administrative courts' (100). The consequence is that reform is frequently equated with the continual refinement of the structure and of the texts that formally describe it.

The importance of career structures derives in part from factors identified by Luc Rouban. He points out (1998a: 16–17) that the civil service, over some two centuries, constituted a social safety valve – a promise that social mobility was possible and families would see reasonably diligent sons safely settled with a certainty of progress to economic security and respectability. Michelet observed in 1846 that families would make immense sacrifices to place their son as an official, seeking for him a secure, stable and regular life, before going on to point out that in fact official life was frequently no such thing (reprinted in Gallouédec-Genuys 1998: 53). But the aspiration has persisted. In 1996 86 percent of respondents in an opinion poll said they would be happy for their child to become a civil servant (Rouban 1998b: 196).

The arrival in power in 1981 of a president and government who represented a complete replacement of party orientation and ministerial personnel was expected to herald an era of administrative reform (Stevens 1988; D. Clark 1998). The two decades since then can be divided into three periods. First, in the 1980s the *statut*, which had survived since 1946 with only minor amendment at the advent of the Fifth Republic in 1958, was completely overhauled. At a period in the early 1980s when Mrs Thatcher in the U.K. was energetically pursuing the 'de-privileging' of the civil service the French Socialists responded to the demands of an important part of their electoral constituency by extending to local and health service officials the principles and guarantees of the central officials. The economic U-turn of 1983 introduced a discourse of modernisation that centred on increasing the effectiveness of civil servants through the adoption of new technology and training in its use, and improvements in working methods (D. Clark 1998: 102; Stevens 1987). The policy of 'rigour' meant the end of the accent on the civil service as a location for job creation and the de-indexation of civil service pay, i.e. the removal of the automatic link between rises in the cost of living index and rises in pay rates. It also lowered some of the civil service's defences against familiar criticisms of remoteness, unconcern, complexity and lazy insistence upon the preservation of procedures and positions (Closets 1982; Gonod 1998: 205–6).

Much more crucial for the long term was the policy of decentralisation embodied in the *lois Defferre*. Some of its effects were paradoxical. The enhancement of the status of local officials symbolised a stronger role for local authorities, but they lost some aspects of control of local councillors over the personnel management of their officials (Stevens 1988: 149). For the field services of some central ministries, particularly those that lost functions to the local executive, the potential impact was more serious, so the period also saw the development of a number of modernisation programmes involving some devolution of responsibilities in ministries particularly closely affected by decentralisation, notably Agriculture and Infrastructure (*Equipement*) (Jones 2003).

A second period of administrative reform began in 1989 when Michel Rocard, appointed Prime Minister in 1988, launched a programme of public-service renewal (*renouveau du service public*). David Clark (1998: 104) characterises the administrative reform programme after 1989 as 'a key element in the Left's response to the neoliberal critique of the State'.

Rocard, whose own political career had been punctuated by returns to his administrative functions as a Finance Inspector, sought mechanisms that would make the state more efficient and its officials more creative and cost-conscious, without undermining its key role as the architect of social and economic development (Bezès 2001: 48).

Guyomarch (1999) emphasises the role of political competition as one of the institutional factors that shape the conjunctural context of reform. Michel Rocard's high-profile programme of renewal was launched under the slogan 'the state is back'. This rhetoric enabled him to build a consensus that was large enough to support his minority, coalition government (Elgie 1991). Rocard was rejecting the neoliberal discourse of the Chirac government that had been defeated in 1988, and opposing what could be seen as the denigration of the state prevalent in the English-speaking world. Bezès argues that he was also responding to social unrest amongst public service workers, who were agitating for higher wages after the freezes imposed in response to the 1980s recession (Bezès 2001: 49). The programme was partly built upon themes that had already begun to be developed, in particular accessibility and evaluation, and partly upon a rhetoric of consensus, participation and empowerment.

The Socialist defeat in 1993 brought the right into power and initiated a third period of administrative modernisation. In 1995 Chirac's and Juppé's RPR government returned to high-profile administrative reform, with the issuing of a major circular. The argument that this constitutes an overlapping but clearly different programme from its predecessor (Guyomarch 1999; Bezès 2001: 50–51) is based, first, on political style; Juppé's 'top-down' approach helped, however, to trigger the strikes and demonstrations of 1995–6. Second, it is argued that the sources and approaches of the reforms were rather different from those of Rocard. David Clark (1998), on the other hand, asserts that there has been a great deal of continuity. There were signs of a fight-back by senior administrators against the unaccustomed and uncomfortable impact of increased political competition, and hence policy change, over the 1980s and early 1990s, and a plea for more autonomy in policy-making at official level (Bezès 2001: 56). Jospin's arrival in 1997 and Raffarin's in 2002 produced some change of rhetoric, but substantial continuity in substance.

The shape and scope of change

'A situation for which the word "prudence" is a euphemism' (Dupuy 1999: 3): this verdict on the French administrative reform process over the last two decades is a harsh one given the apparent proliferation throughout the 1990s of programmes, laws, decrees, circulars and a kaleidoscope of evolving bodies – from the Commissariat à la Réforme de l'Etat to the Délégation Interministérielle à la Réforme de l'Etat, the Conseil Scientifique de l'Evaluation followed by the Conseil National de l'Evaluation. But how much has changed? Ridley's analysis (1996: 19–21) suggests that there may be three major aspects to administrative change: systems, structures and culture, and these provide a useful framework for a response.

Systems

Defined as 'techniques or procedure', systems have begun to change if only rather slowly. Several types of system have been affected, including systems for relationships with members of the general public and evaluation systems.

A first area for reform has been the accessibility of the administration whose unfriendliness, remoteness and inaccessibility has been a constant theme of attack under the Fifth Republic. The impetus for improvements has come essentially from the modernising and essentially democratic pressure to avert what Wright calls 'generalised disgruntlement at the performance of the public sector' (Wright 1994b: 106). The 1980s saw attempts to end the traditional anonymity of officials behind the *guichet* or despatching letters, and the development of 'one stop shops' – *administration à votre service* points – in prefectures and subprefectures. This theme was taken forward by the Rocard *renouveau*. It was at this period that the term *usager* (user) came generally to replace the untranslatable term *administré* (a person subject to administration) in official parlance. Implementation was largely dependent on exhortation.

Reinforcement was provided by the issuing of a Public Service Charter (*Charte des Services Publics*) in 1992. This picked up the public-service values traditionally entrenched in French administrative law (equality, continuity and impartiality) and added transparency, simplification and accessibility – understood in a geographical (*proximité*) as well as individual sense (Jones 2003; Ministère de la Fonction Publique 1998). Juppé's version was entitled 'Charter for Citizens and Public Services' (*Charte des Citoyens et des Services Publics*). Juppé placed more importance than Rocard on good relationships between administration and citizen, but in general there is considerable continuity (Jones 2003).

New information and communications technologies are also playing a larger part, with the development of user-friendly internet portals. The website http://www.service.public.fr/ provides a wealth of information from the weather forecast to how to apply for a passport, as well as allowing, for example, for the electronic filing of income tax returns. At the turn of the century over 60 percent of official forms were available on line. All government departments and seventy-five prefectures maintain their own web sites.

Simplification and speed are closely related to all the other aspects of modernisation, and in particular to both accessibility and the devolution of decision-making. Ongoing efforts have been made to simplify procedures and improve the accessibility and legibility of official forms and documents. Increased devolution of decision-making is intended to tackle the slow and difficult process of extracting decisions from the administration. One means has been an effort to reduce the number of cases in which prior official authorisation is required, to extend (by the law of 12 April 2000) the number of cases in which absence of response within two months may be taken to imply consent, and to shorten to two months the period – in all other cases – after which absence of response means refusal. However, compensation for poor performance still has to be sought by damages through the administrative courts. Nor has there been any suggestion that service may be improved by way of competition, 'naming and shaming' or market-testing (Guyomarch 1999: 177; D. Clark 2000; Cole and John 2000).

A third element of systems reform, evaluation, was not as such a new concept and procedure when it was highlighted in Rocard's *renouveau* programme, since both the local and the central audit bodies and the various state inspectorates have traditionally been concerned with monitoring and assessing the nature and propriety of policy implementation. The French approach has largely eschewed specific performance indicators in favour of a '"positivist" or "scientist" epistemology ... in keeping with the traditional linear model of decision-making' (D. Clark 1998: 110). A decree in 1990 set up elaborate arrangements for the commissioning and undertaking of interministerial policy evaluation.[4] Juppé's 1995 circular identified evaluation as one of the core roles of the central administration and attempted to revivify it by linking it to devolved decision-making and ministerial modernisation plans. However, the area is a potentially fraught one. Evaluation of policy formulation and performance is liable to question the merits of policy decisions that have been made which may suit the technocrats who are trying to preserve their positions, but is likely to prove uncomfortable for politicians in a context of continuous political competition. It is scarcely surprising that ministers were not interested in encouraging studies and those that were carried out produced largely inconclusive results. Rouban (1998a: 113) goes so far as to call evaluation a long series of failures. The failure of evaluation may also in part be explained by considerable resistance to notions of the monitoring of performance (Bezès 2001: 54). There is a surprising absence in France of internal financial management and information systems. As they expand their role into some elements of value for money audit – still a barely translatable concept – some of the regional courts of accounts are trying to develop such systems, but they will inevitably be difficult to graft onto already very cumbersome accounting procedures.

Fourthly Rocard intended that the reshaping of systems of decision-making should include the empowerment of local offices and services. Devolution to them of the authority to define their objectives and achievement indicators should increase the participation and morale of staff, and improve the effectiveness of the services. Since the earlier projects in Infrastructure and Agriculture served as a model, there was an implication that this would ensure that the central administration maintained its status in the localities, in the face of the increased role of the local authorities. By the mid-1990s, some 700 devolved projects existed in the Infrastructure Ministry, and also in the Ministries of Culture, of Youth and Sports, and of Justice (Rouban 1998a: 106), largely in the field services. Budgetary devolution, which has been one of the most marked elements of administrative modernisation in other countries, took the form of 'devolved budget centres' (*centres de responsabilité*). By the mid-1990s there were just over 200 of these, mainly in the Infrastructure Ministry, and other field services. They incorporate welcome freedom from constraining financial procedures but their impact on the overall operation of the administration has been quite limited.[5]

Many of the constraints on real devolution of responsibility for financial management stem from the *ordonnance du 4 janvier 1959 relative aux lois de finances*. This much-criticised *ordonnance*, finally reformed by the organic law of 26 July 2001 following thirty-five unsuccessful attempts at amendment over the preceding four decades, was one of the bastions of the Budget Division's system of expenditure control (Dreyfus 2002). Philippe Bezès' interviews with officials in this division revealed their hostility to structural change (Bezès 2001: 54). The consequence of reform should, however, be the association of expenditure with specific programmes with defined outcomes, much greater freedom of manoeuvre for those authorising expenditure and reinforced parliamentary scrutiny.

If this reform turns out to enable the overturning of very long-standing habits to the extent that some commentators predict, it will be at least as important as the second element of responsabilisation embodied in the law of 6 February 1992 which laid down the general principle – linked to the Maastricht concept of subsidiarity – that decisions should always be taken as closely as possible to the citizen, company or other body affected. This was followed up by a decree of July 1992 setting out what was called the Deconcentration Charter. The logical consequence – that the role of the central administration was not to make implementing decisions itself but to confer the power to do so on services at local level – was explicitly spelt out. Coordination and coherence were to be assured by the prefect. However, the local services were, and are, in fact rather autonomous (Montricher 1995: 2) and likely to be deeply involved with a local clientele and the preservation of good local relationships (Dupuy and Thoenig 1985). The initial impact of the Deconcentration Charter was almost imperceptible. Juppé's modernisation programme repeated the theme in a more robust way, and the Jospin government filled in the details in December 1997. The central administrations were to be confined to 'the tasks of forecasting, analysis, policy formulation, drafting legislation and evaluation. These regulatory functions must be clearly distinguished from the operational tasks of managing, applying regulations and providing benefits' (translation from Rouban 1998a: 111). Normally all decisions involving individual persons or firms are now taken locally, mostly by the prefect.

Juppé's plans (expressed in a circular of July 1996) involved the conclusion of service-agreement contracts between the central ministries and the deconcentrated services. The implementation of this has not been a success: three years after the circular only three such agreements had been concluded and by 2001 such 'contracts' were still confined to the Ministry of Education (Ministère de la Fonction Publique 2001: 14).

The rhetoric surrounding developments in the decision-making system is substantial. Progress, even where it has grown out of the initiatives of entrepreneurial officials (Guyomarch 1999: 190), has been slower and less generalised than the hype suggests. However, these slow developments, and especially the increased powers placed in the hands of the prefect, may, when viewed retrospectively, emerge as a major contribution to an eventual, long-term reshaping of centre-periphery relations.

Structural reform

The overhaul of the *statut* at the beginning of the 1990s produced substantial change to the legal position of administrators in the service of local government or the health services, but rather little to central government civil servants. In general human-resource management is still tightly corseted by the provisions of the *statut*. At the beginning of the 1990s it seemed that this rigidity might be beginning to soften. While Rocard's emphasis on dialogue with the staff representatives and consensual change served to mollify civil servants faced with reform, Michel Durafour, his Minister for the Civil Service, negotiated a number of structural changes that are embodied in the Durafour agreements of 1990. At the same time a major departure saw the transfer of the PTT (posts and telecommunications) out of the scope of the *statut*. This might have served as a model for other movements of services, such as have occurred in other countries, but no further restructuring has happened.

It may be the way that the *statut* has been interpreted rather than its actual provisions that has limited the development of human-resources management (Cieutat and Tenzer 2000) and it has proved possible to move forward in some areas. There has been some attempt to open up the very closed circuits, so dependent on networks and connections, by which some senior posts have traditionally been filled. A 1997 decree stated that no new graduates from the Ecole Nationale d'Administration (ENA) or the Ecole Polytechnique may be promoted to a post at middle level in the senior civil service (*sous-directeur* or *chef de service*) unless they have spent at least two of their first five years at operational level in a field service. Unsurprisingly, this was not well received, but is still in operation. A prime ministerial circular of February 2000 provided that senior officials may not stay in any one post for more than two three-year terms. All vacancies at this level are to be announced on the Civil Service Ministry's website, with the intention that eligible officials from a range of backgrounds shall apply and may be asked to attend an interview (*audition*). Increased competition for senior posts and the reform of recruitment to the *grands corps* were also themes in the debate on the continued existence of the ENA in Autumn 2002 and Spring 2003 (Cieutat and Tenzer 2000; de Silguy 2003). Given the ingrained hierarchies and habits of senior French civil service it is hard to be other than sceptical about the impact of these measures.

Some progress has been made in decreasing the staffing of central ministries to reflect their reduced tasks, though this of course means redeployment or the freezing of vacancies, not compulsory retirement or redundancy. Internal restructuring has included the (long overdue) merger of the War Veterans Ministry (*Anciens Combattants*) with the Ministry of Defence, and the fusion of several overseas aid directorates with those of the Ministry of Foreign Affairs. But other restructuring attempts have not prospered, including the attempt to reduce the very large number – some 900 – of separate *corps*, each with their own terms and conditions. Finance Minister Christian Sautter's not unrelated proposal to restructure the tax assessment and collection structures brought about his downfall in April 2000. After twenty years of tinkering, the main contours of the French administration remain remarkably unchanged.

Cultural change

Since 'cultural change' involves ways of thinking and ways of behaving – values, strategies and priorities – it is particularly difficult to discern and measure. In 1994 Luc Rouban published the results of a survey of the attitudes of senior officials to the modernisation programme. He found that what had resulted was better internal procedures and fewer appeals against administrative decisions by members of the public, and a change in mentality, producing better standards of service without 'the traumatisation of civil servants, as was the case in America and the United Kingdom, where they were forced to toe the private management line' (Rouban 1998a: 107). However, Juppé's much more top-down approach did produce a good deal more resistance, which influenced the nature and pace of subsequent reforms. Despite Jospin's conciliatory style, efforts at structural and organisational reform within the Ministries of Education and Finances resulted in the departure of the ministers concerned in the spring of 2000.

If cultural change is to be effected, winning the hearts and minds of those concerned may be crucial. A major element of Rocard's modernisation programme was the attempt at all stages to involve the civil service trade unions and portray the renewal of 'social dialogue' as an integral part of the modernisation programme. The Durafour agreements were part of this. The emphasis on dialogue, alongside that on *responsabilisation*, was expected to result in raised morale and improved working relationships. Substantial publicity efforts were made, including the issuing of brochures and booklets and, since 1992, a magazine, *Service Public*, and the organisation of a number of meetings.

After the conflicts of the Juppé period the Jospin government took a non-confrontational stance. There has been no attempt to undermine the *statut* (Cieutat and Tenzer 2000). The regulation of the civil service continues to involve a substantial consultative element: at the highest level the Conseil Supérieur de la Fonction Publique de l'Etat involves management and unions, and its Modernisation Subcommittee, which now includes representatives of the *usagers*, keeps an oversight over the whole modernisation programme. At every level the cumbersome union-management structure for personnel management has been maintained, although at the level of the *département* the increase in the management role of the prefect is resulting in the merger of some of the committees and reducing fragmentation.

The relatively limited extent of systemic change and the very cautious nature of structural change have been accepted, especially since, when change seems likely to go beyond the limits of a broad, if not total, consensus, it has been modified; the proposed transfer of the ENA to Strasbourg resulted in an expensive and cumbersome compromise, condemned by the Review Committee in 2003 (de Silguy 2003) and the reforms of the local Ministry of Finance structures were shelved. Senior officials have, on the basis of their own prestige and their *corps* networks, a substantial potential capacity for resistance (Fabre Guillemant 1998: 59) and change has largely kept pace with what they have been willing to accept.

This is not to imply that all senior officials share the same mentality and interests, or have the same stake in the extent and limits of modernisation (Elgie 2001: 39). Officials who found themselves needing to face up to challenges from the private sector in order to maintain their position – as the local level heads of the Ministry of Agriculture and Infrastructure Ministry did – embraced the greater flexibility which, for example, the development of *centres de responsabilité* gave them (Jones 2003). But they faced considerable difficulties (Ministère de la Fonction Publique 1999: 95; Ministère de la Fonction Publique 2001: 6).

Cultural change has, despite some attempts at propagandising, and some change at local level, been very limited. At senior level officials continue to rely upon their provenance and allegiance (especially *corps* membership, but also in some cases political connections) for their legitimacy and the possibility of shaping an interesting career. As a consequence, the ENA has largely retained its prominence as an important, if contested, mechanism of validation. Senior officials have been largely successful in their fight to retain their claim to expertise and their control of their role. The apparently important redefinition of the roles of central and local government specified by Juppé, and the internal re-organisations that have followed (which have now affected fourteen ministries with more in the pipeline) have had rather little impact on the role and functions of senior staff in those ministries. 'Modernisation champions' in each ministry, linked in a network supported by the Civil Service Ministry, and multi-annual modernisation plans (*plans pluriannuels de modernisation*) – each ministry now has one – do not seem to have altered the fundamental orientations.

Indeed, the process may be seen as conforming rather closely to Patrick Dunleavy's bureau-shaping model. He contends that senior officials will measure their satisfaction and welfare by their ability to be central to the strategic and policy-shaping functions of government, and will seek to increase these aspects of their role and decrease extensive, routine and 'managerial' decision-making and resource management aspects (Dunleavy 1991). The intellectual roles of *conception*, forecasting, control (rather than management) and strategy have always been those most highly valued, and in attempting to concentrate and refine the central ministerial structures those are the aspects highlighted in Juppé's circular. Not only has the role of senior officials changed very little since the end of the 1970s (Elgie 2001: 14) or even the 1960s but the discourse surrounding it has also changed very little. So a *directeur d'administration centrale* emphasises that his position is influential because of the incumbent's ability to influence policies 'in the sense that if he's permanently putting forward proposals, then he ends up by adding to the minister's policy' but saw little administrative change. 'In terms of its organisation ... it hasn't really, really changed. By contrast, what's in the process of changing a lot is the way of working ... We are using the new technologies, internet, intranet, paging ...' (Interview with a *directeur d'administration centrale*, quoted in Elgie 2001: 35).

Incentives to change can be provided by 'leadership', or by material rewards or improved working conditions that value responsiveness to change. For example, it was intended that the savings effected by more effective working through a *projet de service* could be ploughed back into better conditions for the staff concerned. In practice constraints upon public spending have limited the extent to which this has proved possible.

However, the extent to which levers of this kind can be used to induce cultural change is very limited.

It is not so much the *statut* that limits such change as the mentality underlying the nature and operation of the *statut*. Crozier argues that one of the benefits of the civil-service system is not only secure employment, but the guarantee of a career, an essential safety valve in an unstable and volatile society (see also Rouban 1998a). It is an essential channel of upward social mobility, within which aspiration can be securely contained. If it is to operate like this, then steady upward movement must not be dependent upon individual striving, nor even – once the original threshold has been passed – upon performance, for that would remove the safety-valve effect. Still less can it be dependent upon the whims, arbitrary decisions, favour or patronage of a leader or boss, for that would be to encourage desertion of the public good for the pursuit of personal interest. So civil servants need the protection of a legal framework, both against arbitrary decisions from above and against competition and conflict with colleagues. The need to introduce incentives for change without jeopardising the fundamental guarantees of 'independence' explains the preference for 'hearts and minds' approaches described above. But a good deal of the process of reform involves maintaining a delicate equilibrium between the necessary maintenance of legal and procedural frameworks and the equally necessary requirement for user-friendly, successful outcomes.

Conclusion

Unlike its counterpart in Whitehall or (to a lesser extent) the Netherlands, the French civil service has experienced no more than mild and incremental change. The structural factors identified by Crozier and the complex elite relationships explored by Suleiman both contribute to making the French pattern exceptional and the pace and nature of change within it distinctive. The change should neither be underestimated nor overestimated. A decade and more of steady insistence on the need to pay some attention to the needs and convenience of the general public, and especially of those at risk of social exclusion, is gradually bearing fruit. More significantly, changes in administrative relationships at local level and the introduction of more integrated project-based methods of coordination have also had some effect.

Nevertheless change has been slow and often relatively peripheral. The contours of the local landscapes are changing; but France still has a highly distinctive system, and the features of both centre–periphery and political-administrative relationships described by Grémion and Suleiman are still readily discernible. Moreover France is exceptional in:

- The extent to which change has impinged upon the frontier between central and local.
- The extent to which change has been – or has been perceived as having to be – negotiated and accepted (rather than imposed and endured).
- The extent to which the two traditional roles of the civil service – as the servants of the general interest and as a crucial means of upward social mobility – remain uncontested.
- The extent to which change has not been the result of the development of a new, alternative or competing set of ideas to which the politico-administrative elite could appeal. Even under governments of the right there is in France no presumption that the private sector is more efficient or competent than the state sector: indeed, the state's crucial role in watching over business is, at least implicitly, justified by the need to defend the citizen against the nefarious effects of private sector greed or incompetence, just as in centre-periphery relations state tutelage developed and has not been wholly abandoned because of fears of secession.[6]

The exceptional history of the emergence of the French State and nation makes the protection of the public sphere and its personnel by a specific legal framework seem crucial (Cieutat and Tenzer 2000). If the possibilities for change that exist within this framework are exploited too brutally then resistance is the inevitable outcome. It may well be that in this context much of the reform programme, modest though it may seem, has at last become intelligent (Crozier 1991: 293).

Notes

1.   These issues are further explored in Stevens (2003: ch. 5) and Knapp and Wright (2001: ch. 10). I am grateful to Philippe Bezès for discussion of these themes and for allowing me to see the paper on 'How to Characterize and Explain the French Pattern of Administrative Reforms?' which he presented at a conference on Civil Service Research at the University of Leiden in September 2002.
2.   The French administration took up the fashion for quality circles (*cercles de qualité*) in the 1980s, for example, but has never found an adequate translation for, let alone adopted, the discourse of cost-benefit analysis, value for money or performance-related pay (see also Meininger 2000: 207)
3.   Though it is worth noting that the accuracy of the figures is far from certain and the publication of figures always lags: those published in late 2000 related to 31 December 1997.
4.   I owe much of the information and ideas in this paragraph to the paper presented by Dr David Clark to the joint meeting of the Political Studies Association Public Administration and French Policy and Politics specialist groups in September 2000, and the discus-

sion that ensued.
5. The curator from a museum that had constituted itself a *centre de responsabilité* rejoiced in the ability to take a local decision to procure a new display case (personal communication 1994).
6. I owe this formulation to Vivien Schmidt's intervention in the Political Studies Association Standing Group on French Politics conference on The Fifth Republic at Forty, Institut Français, London, 16 May 1998 and to Lucien Jaume's paper on 'The Paradoxes of French Liberalism' to the Midlands Political Thought Seminar, University of Birmingham, 11 May 1998.

Chapter 7

FRENCH INDUSTRIAL RELATIONS – STILL EXCEPTIONAL?

Nick Parsons[1]

In the 1990s, there was much debate among observers of the 'normalisation' of French industrial relations (Freyssinet 1993; Ruysseveldt and Visser 1996; Goetschy 1998). Broadly, the argument is that there has been a shift from an under-institutionalised system in which state intervention was needed to mediate a more or less naked class conflict between capital and labour to one based upon regular decentralised compromise bargaining between 'social partners'. From this perspective, the system of labour regulation in France – the 'rules of the game' by which wages and working conditions are established – is coming to resemble more closely that of other advanced industrial democracies, as the conflict of interest between capital and labour is no longer seen in ideological terms but now relies upon the give and take of compromise bargaining. This chapter will examine the veracity of such a hypothesis in order to ascertain the extent to which the French system of industrial relations can still be considered exceptional. In order to do this, we shall examine the pressures for convergence affecting all industrial relations systems in advanced industrial societies and the effect that these have had on the French case in particular.

Convergence and specificity

When comparing the industrial relations systems in advanced capitalist societies at a macro-economic level, the characteristics they have in common and the trends towards convergence are immediately apparent. These characteristics and trends concern the political economy, economic and social policies, institutions and labour markets. Thus, across Europe in the postwar period, welfare state institutions were created to protect workers from the risks of unemployment, accident, illness and old age; Keynesian economic policies aimed to maintain high employment levels and demand in order to sustain mass production industries oriented primarily towards national markets; and wage rises were granted to workers in exchange for the productivity gains afforded by their acceptance of Taylorist work practices. In effect, what has now become commonly known as the 'Fordist compromise' ensured that increased productivity led to increased wealth for wage earners and sustained a generous social welfare system. This benefited industry in a virtuous cycle through the provision of mass consumer markets as an outlet – and therefore source of profits – for the increased output and productivity of industry. Within this, trade unions played an essential mediatory role between workers, the state and the interests of capital, ensuring that wage growth was tied to productivity gains. Since the mid-1970s, this 'European model of society' (Ross and Martin 1999) has come under strain for several reasons, but notably due to economic crises, globalisation and, to use Aglietta's (1998) term, the 'financialisation' of the economy.[2]

The results of these processes have been, firstly, an increase in the severity of international economic competition. Secondly, the increasing investment role of (particularly U.S. and British) financial institutions has led to the need for high profit margins in order to maintain shareholder value.[3] In addition, as the markets for the standardised goods typical of Taylorist production were becoming saturated from the late 1960s onwards, more sophisticated consumer demand required differentiated products.

As far as labour regulation is concerned, these trends have affected advanced capitalist societies in broadly similar ways. At the micro-economic level, the consequences have been an emphasis on quality and innovation in production while reducing production costs. Taylorist production lines have been replaced by forms of work organisation that allow for flexible production through the use of computerised machinery and that rely increasingly on a worker's responsibility and initiative.

At the macro-economic level, the economic role of the state has been called into question. The postwar commitment to full employment has been abandoned in favour of neoliberal economic policies that are supposed to ensure price and wage stability, stimulate investment (and attract investment from abroad) and restore growth by boosting company profit margins. Welfare systems in many countries have been reformed in order to reduce their financial burden on the state. Labour markets have become increasingly tertiarised, as national production systems have moved into high value added areas and abandoned traditional industries under the challenge of cheaper production in developing economies. They have also become increasingly casualised through the growth in part-time and temporary employment. As employers seek greater control over production costs and greater flexibility from their workforces, the decentralisation (often centrally coordinated) of industrial relations has occurred, resulting in trends towards 'microcorporatism' (Ferner and Hyman 1998). The above developments have been harmful to trade union movements, which have lost members in many countries, and this shift in the balance of power away from labour towards capital has been accompanied by a marked decline in strike levels across all European countries (Ferner and Hyman 1998).[4]

Thus, in the postwar years up until the late 1970s at least, a 'European social model', based upon the notion of the 'Fordist compromise', can be identified. However, an examination of *how* this regulation takes places reveals considerable national variation in institutions, levels of bargaining, legal regulations and so on (Boyer 1988). In effect, all countries in some way or another deviated from the 'ideal' Fordist model, that is to say that all countries were 'exceptional' in some way. Thus, it is perhaps more accurate to talk of national specificity rather than 'exceptionalism'.

Since the late 1970s, however, advanced capitalist societies have faced common problems associated with the maintenance of national competitiveness, and balancing this with the imperatives of social cohesion, in the face of economic globalisation. Although changes in the world economy may pose common problems, however, this does not mean that different countries will react in the same way. Thus, as for the postwar period, although common trends can be discerned at a fairly abstract level, closer examination again reveals considerable national variation in responses (Boyer 1988; Lipietz 1995). This should not surprise us as current responses will depend, to some extent at least, on pre-existing institutional structures and the former compromises they embody, as well as upon pre-existing actors, all with their own attitudes and values that inform their past, present and future choices and strategies.

French 'exceptionalism' in the postwar period

As has been suggested above, France broadly conformed to the 'European social model' as it evolved in the postwar period. A generalised welfare state was introduced in 1946 in the aftermath of the Second World War. Throughout the '30 glorious years' of sustained high economic growth from 1945 to 1975, a broadly Keynesian economic strategy was followed, ensuring that unemployment remained a marginal phenomenon. Throughout the period, Taylorised production processes resulted in rapid productivity gains and high rates of economic growth that fed through into improving standards of living for French wage earners.[5] In order to provide mechanisms through which the fruits of production could be bargained over, the state recognised trade unions as the legitimate representatives of wage earners, with five confederations being accorded 'nationally representative' status.[6]

Nevertheless, the idea that the French system of industrial relations was 'exceptional' over the post-war period was based on three main observations. Firstly, the domination of the communist-oriented CGT over a weak trade union movement ensured that industrial relations were seen in terms of class conflict, with no mutual recognition of legitimacy between employers and organised labour. Secondly, and as a result, the system was under-institutionalised with, in particular, no regularised collective bargaining to distribute the fruits of Fordist production. Where it occurred, bargaining was generally sporadic, took place at the level of the industrial branch, and mainly dealt with job classifications and set wage minima for the industry. Moreover, it was often associated with conflict, as trade unions mobilised workers to create a 'balance of power' that would force reluctant employers into negotiation. As they were the result of a struggle, and therefore reflected the balance of power at the time, collective agreements had little legitimacy and would be denounced by either side once they felt that the balance of power permitted them to do so.

Finally, the consequence of this was that conflict and state intervention acted as substitutes for collective bargaining. As Michelle Perrot (1974) has shown, strikes in France have had a political dimension since their legalisation in 1864 – even when ostensibly over wage levels – as they were often accompanied by a rhetoric emphasising the emancipation of the working classes through political change. Into the postwar period, a lack of local bargaining meant that conflict inevitably became generalised, and pushed up to the national level as both employers and trade unions pressured the government of the day to legislate in their favour. In this sense, as Shorter and Tilly (1974) have argued, French strikes represented a political rather than economic mobilisation of the working classes, as wage concerns were articulated with wider questions of access to power. Whereas in other European countries (with the exception of Italy), workers had achieved national level political representation or constitutional arrangements that gave them a voice in their national polity, in France this was not the case until 1981. Their collective exclusion from power in France therefore led to short but widespread stoppages, important not only because they put pressure on decision-making elites to act, but also for their symbolic displays of strength and impact upon the public consciousness, as working-class organisations attempted to force open the doors to the corridors of power.

The above situation has led some to claim that there was no 'Fordist compromise' in France (Hewlett 1998: 56–59). While it is true that there is no French equivalent of the 1932 Historic Compromise in Sweden, for example, it should be seen as a tacit rather than explicit compromise in the French case. In effect, workers gave up any claims to control of the workplace when they accepted Taylorised production processes in exchange for the continually increasing wages and improving standards of living that these promised. What is striking in the French case is that such a compromise found no institutional expression that would permit the peaceful redistribution of the fruits of production, but relied upon continual conflict – which expressed itself in terms of a class struggle – and state intervention to achieve this. Nevertheless, as in other advanced capitalist countries, this French version of the Fordist compromise was to come under strain and eventually collapse in the changing economic environment of the late 1970s onwards.

Globalisation and change?

Trends towards convergence

If France has faced the same problems as its European neighbours of maintaining national economic competitiveness in a more competitive global environment since the late 1970s, the country has also responded in similar ways. The state has accepted that it cannot play the *dirigiste* role that it did in the past, and privatisations and financial deregulation have taken place under governments of both left and right, allowing the market to play a far greater role in investment, production and employment decisions. Low inflation rather than full employment has been the priority of government economic policy from the mid-1980s onwards, a priority linked to the creation of the single European currency. Welfare state provision in France has been cut and recent reforms represent a shift towards the social-liberal idea of 'welfare to work'.[7] The national labour market and production system are now based upon a dominant tertiary sector, as traditional blue-collar industries such as coal, shipbuilding and steel have been allowed to decline. Finally, flexibility has increased as employers have sought to render their workplaces reactive to fluctuations in demand in their product markets, notably through the use of fixed-term and temporary contracts.

Within this macro-economic and labour market context, there are signs of change in the regulation of labour in France that point to a convergence with other European countries. Firstly, company level collective bargaining has increased exponentially over the last twenty years. From 1,600 at the start of the 1980s, the number of company-level agreements continued to steadily rise in the following decades to reach 13,328 in 1998, and, following the introduction of the Aubry Laws on the reduction of working time, more than doubled in the following year to reach 30,965 (Ruyssevdldt and Visser 1996: 110; Ministère de l'Emploi et de la Solidarité 2000: 40). Furthermore, the fact that all 'representative' trade unions show a marked propensity to sign agreements where they are present suggests that negotiation and contractual agreement are replacing conflict and state intervention as the primary means of resolving differences of interest between employers and employees. The other trade unions (CFDT, CFTC, CFE-CGC and FO) have signed in around 90 percent of cases and the CGT in over 75 percent since the start of the 1990s (MES 2000: 45).

Along with the development of collective bargaining there has been a significant decline in the level of conflict in France. The period 1971–1980 saw an average of 3.5 million days lost to strikes per annum, 1981–1990, 1.9 million and 1991–1998, 1.5 million.[8] In the 1990s nearly half of the days lost are accounted for by the single year 1995. Qualitatively, too, there has been change. Gone are the grand 'days of action' orchestrated by the CGT-Parti Communiste Français (PCF) tandem, which aimed to pressure governments into reform and secure support for a left electoral victory in the hope that this would lead to a transformation to socialism. In decline, also, are generalised strikes based on calls to class solidarity. Strikes nowadays are more localised and centred on concrete objectives, without any relationship between them. In 1999, almost all of the disputes occurred at local level, mainly in large companies, while 'generalised' industrial action accounted for only 1 percent of the 573,561 days lost, compared to 2 percent in 1998 and 14 percent in 1997 (*European Industrial Relations Review* 2001a: 6).

Thirdly, since the 1970s, the CGT's quasi-monopoly of employee representation has ended under the impact of industrial change and the consequent fragmentation of the working class. Moreover, the CGT has been weakened by political changes that have seen the disintegration of its system of reference – Soviet-style communism – and the French left's acceptance of capitalism. In 1945, the CGT could claim 93.4 percent of trade union members in France, and still over half in 1960. Although this figure fell to 46.8 percent in 1970, it was still the largest trade union by far. By 1995, however, it could only claim 23 percent of French trade unionists, and had been overtaken by the CFDT (Visser 2000: 269).[9] Thus, the CGT no longer dominates the French labour movement in the way that it once did. Furthermore, since 1995, it appears to be converging towards the reformist path sketched out by the CFDT (Vacquin 1999; Andolfatto 2000).

Finally, several recent disputes have thrown into stark relief the state's decreasing capacity to influence the employment and investment decisions of French multinationals and foreign-owned companies operating in France. In March and April 2001 a series of announcements were made by companies to the effect that they would be laying off employees (Girard 2001; *European Industrial Relations Review* 2001b: 7). In one of the most publicised cases, that of Danone, the government was powerless to prevent the closure of factories in France despite the fact that they were highly profitable.[10] Its response was to legislate on stricter conditions for collective redundancies, making such plans more expensive, particularly for large companies. Such are the objectives of the 'Law on Social Modernisation', adopted by the National Assembly on 19 December 2001 (Mandraud

2001). However, it shied away from outlawing redundancies by profitable companies, called for by the PCF and the CGT among others (Eeckout 2001). Laurent Fabius, the then Finance Minister, revealed that the reason for such circumspection lay in a fear of the judgement of the markets and he admitted to having 'serious reservations' about the new legislation, which he saw as a disincentive for investment and recruitment in a modern economy (*European Industrial Relations Review* 2001c: 5–6).

The above, then, would seem to indicate an evolution away from conflict and state intervention towards a system of labour regulation based upon autonomous decentralised collective bargaining involving employers and reformist trade unions in a more flexible labour market and production system. In this sense, France would seem to be heading towards a 'microcorporatist' model of industrial relations, with negotiated flexibility responding to market needs, and the state limited to a role of welfare management to correct the social deficiencies of the market. However, despite the pressures towards convergence from European integration and economic globalisation, a closer examination of the French industrial relations system reveals the opacity of certain elements of French specificity.

Continuing specificity

While the role of the state in French industrial relations may have changed, it remains central to the regulation of labour and the mediation of capital-labour conflict in France. Although the state can no longer intervene to block economic decisions such as those taken by Danone, as it may have done in the past, it has reinforced the legislative regulation of relations between employers and their workforces. Indeed, a series of laws, from the Auroux Laws in 1982 through to the Aubry Laws of 1998 and 2000, have attempted to decentralise the conduct of industrial relations to enable companies to be more reactive to their economic environment while taking into account the needs of their workforces. Since the 1982 Collective Bargaining Act first obliged firms with a trade union branch to negotiate annually over hours and pay at company level, legislation has reinforced the incentives for employers to engage in company-level bargaining, particularly in the area of working time. Notably, it has allowed local agreements to derogate from labour law and to be signed in the absence of union representation. The second Aubry Law also attempted to reinforce the legitimacy of local agreements by introducing the notion of majority support. Thus, state financial aid for the reduction of working time requires either the signature of unions or employee delegates amassing a majority of votes in workplace elections, or a company referendum where agreements are signed by 'mandated' employees or minority unions (Vincent 2001).[11]

However, despite the increase in local collective bargaining, only 27 percent of employees were covered by a company – or establishment – level collective agreement in 1999 (MES 2000: 49), although this figure may well rise with the conclusion of agreements on the reduction of working time in small- and medium-sized companies in the next few years. Coverage is much higher at branch level, with 93 percent of employees covered at the end of 1997 (Combault 1999). However, once again, state voluntarism and labour law exert considerable influence at this level: 'The political wish to extend coverage has led to the growth of small branches with little life and where the content of agreements does nothing more than reproduce the Labour Code, with hardly any improvement' (Vincent 2001: 529). Furthermore, although they still play a pivotal role in some areas (such as job classifications), the capacity of branch agreements to regulate the laws of the trade is being seriously undermined as company-level bargaining can derogate from higher-level agreements in some areas, notably working time (Jacquier 1998: 82; Jobert 2000: 47).

It should also be remembered that this negotiation often takes place under legal compulsion. In other words, the state, through legislative enactment and exhortation, still plays a central role in the French system of collective bargaining. Furthermore, doubt has also been cast over the quality of local agreements as they are seen as benefiting only employers due to the imbalances of power involved (Howell 1992; Coutrot and Boulin 1994; Mériaux and Trompette 1997; Mériaux 1999 and 2000; Jobert 2000). Finally, as the saga of the thirty-five hour week has shown, decentralised collective bargaining may also be associated with conflict (see below), and where it has the potential to lead to substantial gains for employees it is likely to be met with resistance by employers. In effect, the failure of the social partners to negotiate an effective reduction in working time clearly demonstrates that state intervention is still necessary in order to force the social partners to negotiate over social advances.[12] The reaction of employers to Jospin's announcement of legislation on the question on 10 October 1997 was predictably hostile, and led to the announcement by the MEDEF (Mouvement des Entreprises de France), on 2 November 1999, of plans for a wholesale reform of social relations through a *'refondation sociale'* (new social constitution) to be negotiated with the unions.

Although it involves national inter-professional negotiations, this should not be seen as an acceptance of any form of neocorporatist regulation. In essence, the MEDEF argued that the state was increasing its intervention in the social sphere, thereby stifling entrepreneurial activity through excessive regulation and high social charges and taxes. For the employers' organisation, in order for companies to be able to survive and prosper in a globalised economy, the regulation of social relations, including of the welfare system, should be a matter for the social partners, and local collective bargaining should take precedence over centralised agreements or the law. In a profoundly neoliberal project, the state would be marginalised in a decentralised and flexible system, with the company at the heart of social relations. Negotiations were proposed to the trade unions around eight themes, three of which had led to agreements by 2003.[13]

Rather than the break with the past that it was intended to be, however, this process of negotiation has revealed several continuities. Firstly, the agreements have been signed by unions that cannot claim to represent a majority of employees (the CGT or FO have not signed any), as the employers' organisation has been able to play divided unions off against each other in its traditional manner. Secondly, the negotiations have been accompanied by ultimatums and threats from the MEDEF to stop its contributions to social welfare institutions unless an agreement was forthcoming. Agreements still, therefore, appear to be the result of a trial of strength between two antagonistic forces, rather than the reconciliation of divergent interests through compromise. Finally, although the MEDEF has undoubtedly achieved some of its objectives, such as reducing employer social contributions, as the debates over unemployment insurance and pensions have shown, the state cannot easily be marginalised from the process of social regulation but retains a central place in it. Two versions of the UNEDIC agreement were rejected by the state before the 19 October 2000 agreement was ratified. The state imposed its view of the general interest by refusing to link the payment of benefits to the signing of a PARE (return to work action plan), on the grounds that the state, through legal regulation, and not the social partners through the UNEDIC, should decide who was and was not eligible for unemployment benefit. Likewise, the 10 February 2001 agreement over supplementary pensions signed between the employers and the CFDT and CFTC, renewed the arrangements for financing supplementary pensions until 31 December 2002, but required further negotiations with the state in order to bring about a wholesale reform of the pensions system. The MEDEF has thus failed in its attempt to define a sphere of social regulation based upon compromise bargaining autonomous of the state.

In any case, genuine autonomous bargaining requires strong independent trade unions, and any discussion of French exceptionalism in the sphere of industrial relations cannot avoid the question of trade union strength. French unions confronted the onset of economic crisis in the 1970s already in a weak position compared to their European counterparts, with only one in five wage earners unionised (Ebbinghaus and Visser 2000: 63). While economic, social and industrial change and new forms of work organisation have had negative effects on trade union movements in many countries over the last twenty to twenty-five years, nowhere has this been felt more seriously than in France. The rate of unionisation is the lowest of any OECD country and is estimated at 8 percent by INSEE (Andolfatto 2001: 484). As 60 percent of union members are concentrated in the public sector, whole branches in the private sector are 'veritable trade union deserts' (484).

In addition, despite the CGT's abandonment of the aim of social transformation, radicalism persists and feeds another enduring trait of French specificity: that of the ideological and strategic division of French trade unions. A feeling among employees, particularly in the public sector, that their unions were unwilling or unable to negotiate effectively on their behalf and were granting concessions to their employers too readily, led to the emergence of *coordination* movements in the 1980s, and to the growth of autonomous organisations in the 1990s. The CFDT has suffered most in this respect. As it has moved towards the political centre and accepted the market economy and the need for economic and social modernisation, the CFDT has seen internal division, culminating in some of its activists in the public sector setting up a rival organisation, Solidaires, Unitaires Démocratiques (SUD).[14] As a member of the Groupe des dix (G-10) autonomous unions – which claims 65,000 members, mainly in the public sector – SUD has been influential in giving this group a 'contestatory' identity (Andolfatto and Labbé 2000: 43). Meanwhile, the 1993 break-up of the FEN teaching union has led to the establishment of rival umbrella groups of autonomous unions, the social-democratic Union Nationale des Syndicats Autonomes (UNSA), of which the Fédération de l'Education Nationale became a member, and the left-wing Fédération Syndicale Unitaire (FSU). The former now claims 360,000 members, with 60,000 of them in the private sector. The FSU has become the largest education trade union organisation in France, claiming 190,000 members,[15] and is now seeking to expand recruitment in the private sector.

These autonomous organisations are challenging the supremacy of the 'representative' organisations in the public sector, particularly in the *fonction publique d'Etat*, where the FSU and UNSA arrive in first and second place respectively in professional elections (Adam 2000: 213), and may increasingly challenge them in the private sector. While there is a possibility that the UNSA may in the future constitute a reformist pole with the CFDT (and possibly the CGT), other trade unions in the FSU and G-10 generally base their actions on very sectional interests, and adopt hard-line positions in strike movements.[16] French trade unions therefore now appear more divided along ideological, professional and strategic lines than ever, just at a time when some form of *rapprochement* between the CFDT and CGT around a reformist orientation appears possible. An enduring source of trade union weakness in France is thus perpetuated.

It is not surprising, given the declining union strength and the high rates of unemployment of the 1980s and 1990s, that the level of conflicts has also fallen.[17] Conflict, however, has not disappeared, and may resurface with improving labour market conditions. Indeed, evidence of increased combativeness can be seen at the local level. In 1999, negotiations over the reduction in working time contributed to a 60 percent rise in strike activity in the private and semi-public sector, while in a context of economic growth and falling unemployment, the beginning of 2001 saw widespread strikes over pay in many sectors, after years of wage restraint linked to the implementation of the thirty-five hour week (*European Industrial Relations Review* 2001a: 6; Lemaître 2001b). The 'hot summer' of 2003 also saw many national protests against the Raffarin government's reform of pensions, announced in April, while throughout the summer many prestigious festivals, such as at Avignon, were cancelled as contract workers in the showbusiness industry struck over the reform of their entitlement to unemployment benefit while out of work, following an agreement between the MEDEF and the CFDT. The regulation of labour is still, therefore, a divisive and explosive issue as the state attempts to cut back on social expenditure.

'National days of action' are not totally a thing of the past, then, as the 1995 strike movement also showed. At the beginning of the twenty-first century, when they have attempted to mobilise on a national level, unions have met with varying levels of success. Thus, the demonstration against the Danone redundancies, called only by the CGT (and PCF) among the major trade unions, in Calais on 21 April 2001, attracted paltry numbers (14,000 according to the police) (*Le Monde*, 24 April 2001). On the other hand, MEDEF proposals to reform the supplementary pensions system, which would have threatened the right to retire at sixty on a full pension, led to large-scale demonstrations on 25 January 2001, involving 300,000 people in many large French cities, including an estimated 80,000 in Paris (Monnot 2001a). As we have seen, the new right-wing administration's announcement of pension reform in April 2003 was likewise greeted with mass rallies and symbolic shows of unity as workers attempted to pressure decision-makers.

Furthermore, although mobilisation for the 'days of action' was disappointing for the unions in the Danone dispute, this and other conflicts have shown that French unions still have the capacity to articulate strike movements with wider questions such as developments in global capitalism. In both this and other disputes, unions have been highly successful in gaining media coverage for the question of shareholder value and the treatment of employees in multinational companies, and have also managed to gain widespread support for their actions through their impact on the public consciousness. In the case of Danone this led to a well-publicised, although ultimately ineffective, boycott of the company's products. As the 1995 strikes also showed – when questions of the future of pensions and the welfare state were articulated with the neoliberal focus of European integration – French unions still have the capacity to bring many people out onto the streets in political protest, despite their weakness, through the articulation of particular and collective interests. Even the contract workers in showbusiness were able to gain much public sympathy, despite the obvious deficit in their unemployment benefit fund and stories of widespread abuse of the system, through an articulation of their concerns with the issue of the necessity of public support for the arts for social well-being and the preservation of French culture.

Conclusion

Over the last three decades, economic, political and social change has certainly had a major impact upon the conduct of industrial relations in France, and several trends mirror those that can be observed in other countries. Along with the decrease in the organisational strength of labour, there has been a decline in strike levels, and these are less couched in terms of a class struggle engendered by capitalist relations of production. Collective bargaining, particularly at the local level, has now become widespread. The withdrawal of the state from economic management now gives greater reign to market forces in regulating capital-labour relations.

However, this convergence towards a 'European model' of decentralised regulation and 'microcorporatism' should not be exaggerated. Firstly, the extent and forms of decentralisation vary considerably across European countries anyway, while some (Austria, Spain, Portugal, Ireland, the Netherlands) have seen the maintenance or resurgence of national-level neocorporatist structures (Ferner and Hyman 1998: xx). While decentralisation in France has, in common with other European countries, been 'centrally coordinated' (xvi), it can be seen that the pre-existing configuration of institutions and actors has greatly influenced the adaptation of the French industrial relations system to global economic imperatives. Collective bargaining has certainly been decentralised, but it is still very state-dependent.

Furthermore, trade union weakness, especially in the private sector, and exacerbated division mean that developments towards labour regulation through autonomous local bargaining may well continue to be problematic. Recent improvements in trade union presence[18] will have to continue and prove to be durable for a new mode of regulation based upon autonomous decentralised bargaining and 'legitimate' agreements to develop. Nothing is less certain. These improvements and the recent spate of collective agreements are largely due to the implementation of the thirty-five hour week. Once this question is resolved in small- and medium-sized companies, collective bargaining and trade union presence may well decline again. Under such circumstances, it is more than likely that the state will continue to substitute itself for strong labour organisations in order to force employers to negotiate any social progress that transcends their narrowly defined interests. Indeed, as it can no longer direct economic management as before, the role of the state in establishing a framework for the resolution of differences of interest between capital and labour may well be reinforced as it attempts to protect its view of the 'general interest'.

Likewise, agreements signed as part of MEDEF's *refondation sociale* should not be seen as a developing neocorporatism either. They have been signed by weak, generally minority, unions after conflictual negotiating processes, and the whole programme has been aimed at sidelining the state rather than negotiating with it. Again, failure in this points to the state's continuing central role in social regulation in France.

Conflict and mobilisation may no longer be based around class struggle, and an acceptance of capitalist relations of production may mean that France has moved closer to other advanced liberal democracies. However, as recent debates have shown, the building-up of favourable power relations through demonstrations and symbolic shows of strength is still an important part of the negotiating process, and the articulation of local disputes to wider societal issues is still seen as an effective means of gaining media coverage and mobilising people. Conflicts over welfare state reform and the shedding of labour in multinational companies operating in France also suggest that there may be space for a renewal of ideological conflict based around opposition to the globalisation of a form of capitalism obeying a purely financial logic. This, however, is still in its infancy and will require better international coordination among trade union movements and their articulation with other social movements.

These speculations apart, two of the defining elements of French specificity – a chronically weak and divided trade union movement and the consequent need for state intervention in the area of industrial relations – remain. Thus, while the forces for convergence and change unleashed by economic globalisation are strong, France has reacted to them in its own specific way, and in accordance with the pre-existing institutional structures and actors of its industrial relations system. Beneath apparent convergence, and restraining it, lies French specificity, even if it is getting more difficult to talk of exceptionalism.

Notes

1. I would like to gratefully acknowledge funding through a Research Fellowship from The Leverhulme Trust that enabled the research that lies behind this chapter.
2. All translations in this chapter are those of the author.
3. In France, 36 percent of the value of the stocks and shares on the Paris stock exchange were in the hands of foreign investors, who accounted for 80 percent of transactions, in

2000 (Duval 2000: 40). A commonly quoted figure is that these investors require a 10 to 15 percent annual return on their investments (Sauviat and Pernot 2000: 423–4).

4.   Exceptions to declining union strength are Spain and Finland. Unions in other Scandinavian countries have also managed to limit their losses (Ebbinghaus and Visser 2000: 63).

5.   During the height of Fordist growth in France, from 1960–1973, GDP growth averaged 5.6 percent per annum, productivity growth averaged 4.9 percent per annum, real wages rose by 5.0 percent per annum and unemployment averaged 1.0 percent of the active population (Boyer 1988: 20).

6.   These were the Confédération Générale du Travail (CGT), the Confédération Française des Travailleurs Chrétiens (CFTC) – and later the Confédération Française Démocratique du Travail (CFDT), Force Ouvrière (FO), the Confédération Générale des Cadres (CGC) – later the Confédération Française de l'Encadrement-Confédération Générale des Cadres (CFE-CGC) and the Fédération de l'Education Nationale (FEN).

7.   In the 1980s and 1990s, levels, conditions of access to and coverage of unemployment benefit, for example, continually deteriorated (Tuchszirer 2000: 543–45). In December 2000, the government ratified an agreement signed on 19 October, by the employers' organisations and the CFDT, CFTC and CFE-CGC, reforming the UNEDIC unemployment insurance scheme. This introduced the PARE (*plan d'aide au retour à l'emploi*) in which jobseekers will be asked to sign up for a 'personalised action plan' aimed at facilitating their return to employment. The plan is not obligatory, however, and a refusal to sign will not lead to a loss of benefits (as had been the case in earlier proposals rejected by the government). See *European Industrial Relations Review* (2001a: 5–6); Monnot (2001b).

8.   Source: Adam (2000). This decline is all the more striking as before 1982, statistics did not include the *fonction publique* (public sector).

9.   The CFDT now claims 830,000 members and the CGT 650,000 members on their respective websites. Nevertheless at the end of the 1990s, both confederations were neck and neck in works committee elections, with the CGT gaining 23 percent of votes and the CFDT 22.3 percent in 1997/98 (*Liaisons sociales* 2001: 1).

10.   On 29 March 2001, Danone announced that the LU biscuit factories in Calais and Ris-Orangis were to close, with the loss of 570 jobs, after the group had made a profit of four billion francs the previous year. According to Lemaître, the management of Danone saw this as 'indispensable' because the operating profit of the biscuits operation was 'only' 7.9 percent compared to 10.5 percent for the group as a whole, and this was seen to affect share prices (Lemaître 2001a). The figure of 1,700 jobs was later reduced to 570 when the official announcement was made on 29 March.

11.   The Aubry Laws of 1998 and 2000 took up the idea of a system of employees elected by the whole workforce or 'mandated' by an external trade union organisation to conclude agreements in the absence of trade union representatives. For full details of the second Aubry Law, see *Liaisons sociales quotidien* (2000).

12.   Employers and unions were first invited by the state to negotiate on the issue in 1978. For details, see Freyssinet (1997).

13.   So far agreements have been signed on the unemployment benefit system, workplace health and supplementary pensions. On 31 July 2001 a 'common position' on collective bargaining was signed but will require legislation in order to be implemented as it gives precedence to local agreements over the law. In 2003, talks on training encountered difficulties. The other themes are equality at work, the role of managers, and social security.

14.   The first SUD union appeared in the post and telecommunications sector in 1988. This development is not confined to the public sector, however. The latest notable split occurred at Michelin, where activists left the CFDT to set up SUD Michelin in January

2001 following disagreement over the holding of a referendum on the thirty-five hour week. See Lauer 2001.

15. According to Andolfatto (2000), UNSA is the third largest union organisation in France, and the FSU the fourth largest, ahead of FO (300,000) and the CFE-CGC and CFTC (80,000 each).

16. Such was the case in the March–April 2001 railway strike, when SUD-Rail was at the forefront of the movement, along with the autonomous train drivers' union, the FGAAC. Both continued with the strike movement long after the CGT had called for a return to work on April 7 following ten days of strike action. See Bostnavaron 2001a and 2001b. *Coordination* movements also continue to appear from time to time: in March–April 2001, midwives created a *coordination* during a five-week strike to prevent a political recuperation of their strike.

17. Unemployment averaged 4.2 percent between 1971 and 1980, 9.3 percent between 1981 and 1990 and 11.4 percent between 1991 and 2000. Source: OFCE 2001: 117.

18. A recent study by the Ministry of Employment and Solidarity shows an increase in union presence, with 72 percent of companies employing over fifty people having a trade union presence in 1999, compared to 63 percent in 1993. See *European Industrial Relations Review* 2001a: 6–7.

Chapter 8

THE FRENCH SOCIALISTS, *DIRIGISME* AND THE TROUBLED EUROPEANISATION OF EMPLOYMENT POLICY

Ben Clift

The case for French exceptionalism in the field of state-economy relations centres on the distinctive French State tradition of *dirigisme*. *Dirigisme* has been succinctly defined as 'a set of interventionist policies and directive policy-making processes' (Schmidt 1997: 229). Traditions of state direction of, and intervention in, economic activity in France have a long heritage, traceable at least as far back as Jean-Baptiste Colbert, minister under Louis XIV between 1661 and 1683. His bent for state interventionism in economic affairs reached a zenith when, in 1666, he issued a *règlement* to the effect that the fabrics of Dijon and Selangey were to contain 1,408 threads (no more, no less), and those of Auxerre and Avalon 1, 376 (Heilbroner 1992: 24). French State traditions of interventionism have remained powerful, if at times less pedantic, ever since.

This chapter begins by defining *dirigisme* and situating it within the context of French political economy in the postwar era. It outlines challenges to, and the partial undermining of, French *dirigiste* traditions, and then proceeds to explore enduring *dirigiste* tendencies through the case study of the French Socialists' *dirigiste* employment policy aspirations at both national and European levels. French Socialist aspirations for the 'Europeanisation' of a *dirigiste* macro-economic and supply-side employment strategy are placed in comparative context by briefly comparing employment strategies pursued at the national and European level in France to those of British and German Social Democrats. The argument presented here suggests that, in relation to employment policy, the French, British, and German social democrats sought different goals from Europeanisation. Thus French Socialists' desires for a 'rearticulation' of employment strategy at the European level were undermined by

French *dirigiste* exceptionalism regarding the EU's role in securing full employment.

The French *dirigiste* model

Dirigisme was an important dimension of French postwar reconstruction, and was widely credited as the reason behind France's *trente glorieuses* of economic growth and widening prosperity and affluence. The traditional postwar French model was captured in Zysman's account of France's state-led industrial development (Zysman 1983), portraying an actively interventionist, *dirigiste*, 'player' state using its key agencies to steer the nation's economic development (Shonfield 1969: ch. 5; Hall 1986). The French *dirigiste* model, underpinned by the Republican *étatiste* tradition (see Hazareesingh 1994: chs 3 and 6), was predicated upon a set of coordinating and steering mechanisms in the postwar era. The policy mechanisms included, firstly, price, credit and exchange controls. Secondly there were norms of *tutelle* (or hands-on supervision) over key (public and private) industries, involving 'an intricate network of commitments on the part of private firms … all in return for favours from the state … [and] the habit of the exercise of power by public officials over the private sector of the economy' (Shonfield 1969: 86 and 128). The final element was state orchestration of industrial finance through the plan.

Central to France's *dirigiste* interventionism was the state's role in providing funds for industrial investment (Zysman 1983). The state's centrality to the system of 'institutionally allocated credit' (as opposed to 'asset-based credit') from private and public banks gave the French State extraordinary leverage, acting as 'gatekeeper' to 'strategic', cheap capital. The degree of dependence of industrial and financial capital on the state was highly distinctive. State loans tended to be conditional upon meeting specific restructuring targets, incorporating subsidiaries into parent companies, or merging with other big firms. In addition to the 'economy of administered finance', a further characteristic of the French model was the 'inflationist social compromise' (Cohen 1995). The state's inability to control the inflationary growth of credit was compounded by 'the consensual refusal of the state, the trade unions, and the employers to control nominal changes in incomes and prices' (Cohen 1995: 26).

France's exceptional 'meritocratic' elitism was of central importance to the *dirigiste* model. The coordinating role played by 'an interpenetration of state and business elites' (Maclean 1999: 101), whose schooling within the *grandes écoles* creates a relatively homogenous elite, has long been noted as a distinctive characteristic of French capitalism. Top civil servants, politicians, and bosses follow a similar educational path in France and become part of the French *grands corps*, an informal community that operates as a coordinating mechanism of French capitalism, in part through *pantouflage,* or the smooth passage, from higher civil service to the boards of major enterprises – public or private (Hancké 2001: 313–14). These coordinating networks found institutional expression in the *noyaux durs,* or 'hard cores' of cross-shareholdings and overlapping board memberships of large French firms, which provided stability and coherence at various stages in the development and evolution of France's 'financial network economy' (Morin 2000).

An extensive literature questions the coherence of the picture advanced by Zysman, and a debate remains as to how much 'glorious' growth was really due to indicative economic planning and strategic interventionism in industry creating 'national champions' (see for example Hancké 2001: 309–12; Guyomarch et al. 1998: 161–68). After 1971, the French government's complex credit rationing scheme (*encadrement du crédit*) controlled the direction of financial flows, but did not always display the logic and virtues highlighted by Zysman, left many areas of the French economy undercapitalised, and hindered the development of capital markets. Often state funds did not feed a dynamic industrial core, but delayed lay-offs and restructuring in industries whose collapse was deemed too politically costly in the short term – such as steel. For example, in 1978, a handful of firms, most of them uncompetitive and many in declining sectors, were receiving more than 75 percent of all public aid to industry (Levy 2000: 321). The French State was picking losers! The problem became acute in the wake of the 1974 industrial crisis, when the chronic lack of investment in many areas led the French economy to be caricatured as 'capitalism without capital' (Stoffaes 1989: 122). These problems were compounded by a growing fiscal crisis of the French State, leading many to question whether the French state could afford to play its traditional role, *even if* it were to be done effectively.

Nevertheless, what flowed from this model and these state traditions was a presumption on the part of administrative, economic and political elites, and on the part of the wider populace, that the French State could and should actively intervene in economic activity to deliver such public goods and economic growth, full employment, and, in accordance with Republican values of equality and social cohesion, limited redistribution of wealth. This presupposition in favour of *dirigiste* interventionism has come under increasing threat in the last twenty-five years from structural changes in global financial markets, from the European Union, and from the ideological ascendancy of neoliberalism. The size of the French public sector was, and indeed remains large by comparative standards. France has the highest share of government expenditure and employment among European countries outside of the Nordic ones (OECD 2000: 62), and the public sector enjoys a peculiar importance within the French constitutional nexus (Cole 1999).

Dirigisme undermined

France's postwar *dirigiste* 'model' was predicated upon 'embedded liberalism' (Ruggie 1982), a regulated exchange rate international economic order, involving fairly extensive capital controls, codified at Bretton Woods. This context, and the 'competitive devaluations' and levels of state spending and state debt it permitted, were a necessary condition of the success of France's 'inflationist social compromise' (Cohen 1995). As that system unravelled amidst the Nixon shock, oil crises, and advancing liberalisation and deregulation in the 1970s, France's *dirigiste* policy paradigm came under increasing strain. International financial liberalisation, for example, rendered the *dirigiste* 'credit rationing' approach to monetary policy (*encadrement du crédit*) increasingly unworkable (Cohen 1996: 351).

The Mitterrand era began in 1981–1983 with an ambitious contra-cyclical demand-boost and a dash for growth in the context of a world slump. Such policies were termed by Hall, 'redistributive Keynesianism' (1986). The Mauroy Government was initially strongly committed to *dirigisme* in a wide range of industrial, economic, and social policy areas. However, within two years, financial crises and external pressures, perhaps most importantly in the form of commitments involved in staying in the European Monetary System (EMS), proved incompatible with this stance (see for example Muet and Fonteneau 1985; Cameron 1996). The so-called *autre politique* offered a protectionist and *dirigiste* 'solution' that remained within the established referential of French economic policy-making. It was rejected in favour of an 'ordo-liberal' (Dyson 1999a: 34–35), anti-inflationary and market-conforming solution, accepting EMS conditions for revaluation, and a distinctly German-influenced conception of what constituted sound macro-economic policy, and indeed macro-policy making institutions.

This engendered a paradigm shift of priorities in macro-economic policy, relegating full employment to a distant future aspiration, and promoting tackling inflation to priority number one (Lordon 2001; Blanchard and Muet 1993). Although the initial 1983 decision was confined to the hierarchy of priorities of macro-economic policy, and a shift of emphasis from redistribution and employment to a strong currency, tackling inflation and budgetary austerity, this formed the springboard for an 'across-the-board assault on the *dirigiste* model, with reforms extending to policies and practices that had little or no bearing on the value of the franc' (Levy 2000: 324).

The process of European integration, which gathered momentum after the 1984 Fontainebleau Summit, was built upon decidedly non-*dirigiste* economic foundations. The creation of a single market through the 1986 Single European Act, and the neoliberal understanding of state-economy relations that underpinned it, had wide-ranging implications for French industrial and economic policy. Drawing heavily on U.S. anti-trust regulation, the new competition regulation framework saw state industrial subsidies, protected sectors, and preferential public procurement – all key weapons in the *dirigiste* arsenal – as trade-distorting practices. The acquisition of subsidiaries, another arm of traditional *dirigisme*, was also curtailed, as evidenced when Aerospatiale was prevented from buying De Havilland (Schmidt 1996: 182). High profile cases such as Renault – forced to pay back 4 million francs of state aid in 1990, after a four-year dispute with the European Commission – demonstrated that state subsidies were similarly threatened. Thus *dirigiste* industrial policy was decreasingly viable, given the weakening of traditional policy instruments, advancing Europeanisation, and a Commission policing competition with increasing vigour.

However, one should not generalise too widely from the above cases. Scratch the surface and one sees that 'certain nationalised industries continued to receive large infusions of capital while others were encouraged to merge, regardless of their anti-competitive effects and despite the possibility of censure by the European Community' (Schmidt 1996: 176). As for French public procurement norms, despite a directive stating that bids from companies from any member state for French State contracts must be treated equally, by 1996, 90 percent of state contracts *still* went to French firms. Furthermore, Air France and Crédit Lyonnais continued to receive sizeable state subsidies. As Guyomarch et al. note, 'theory has changed more than practice' (1998: 176).

These European developments interacted with domestic policy change. Perhaps the most significant shift was the reform to the French financial system. As Cohen notes, 'until 1984, France's financial system was almost wholly nationalised, protected, and centrally controlled. The state was simultaneous regulator, owner, and interventionist' (1995: 42). Beginning with banking reform in 1984, the French State set about deregulating and liberalising, and to an extent creating the French financial market, the aim being to generate alternative sources of financing for industry (Coleman 1997: 280–84). Banks were encouraged to raise capital beyond their deposit base, new instruments for interest rate, stock market and currency hedging (copied from international markets) were introduced, and new institutions created. The development of a commercial paper market allowed companies to raise capital directly from the public through private bond issues. Further deregulation involved the freeing up of the securities and foreign exchange markets and facilitating the decompartmentalisation of markets (Cerny 1989: 183). This was due to an increasingly cash-strapped French State realising it could no longer afford the role of *dirigiste* player it had enjoyed for much of the postwar era. With reduced reliance on state finance came reduced leverage over industry, and decreasing *tutelage* or directive capacities of how French industry tackled the painful adjustment programme.

This requires some qualification. The privatisation process, for example, although reducing the size of the French public sector since the mid-1980s, has been pursued in a *dirigiste* manner, with state actors exploiting elitist networks to ensure that controlling holdings end up in safe hands, where influence can endure (Schmidt 1996: 147–62). With later privatisation, Schmidt argues, 'the *dirigisme* has moderated, and although state interventionism has not disappeared entirely, it is more circumscribed and market oriented' (1999: 446).

Dirigisme in the context of Economic and Monetary Union (EMU)

Given our focus on employment policy, what is most striking about the evolution undergone by the French *dirigiste* model in the 1980s is the abandonment of the Keynesian paradigm as the dominant referential through which French Socialists analysed unemployment and macro-economic policy and the relationship between the two. The new hierarchy of priorities owed a good deal more to neoliberalism than it did to Keynesian insights into the role of the state in maximising the level of employment within the economy.

EMU was entirely consistent with the ordo-liberal frame of reference that had set the parameters for the macro-economic dimension of employment policy in France. German cooperation was contingent upon the anti-inflationary 'German model' forming the basis for discussion, but this was by no means antithetic to a 'conservative liberal' advocacy coalition within the French state. As Howarth notes, one reason why EMU bore the imprint in particular of the Trésor and the Banque de France was that this group was empowered within the French State by the EMS, and then the European Exchange Rate Mechanism (2002). This hindered the Socialist politicians' attempts to attenuate the influence of central bankers and introduce more *dirigiste*, growth- and employment- oriented concerns into the policy mix, and shift away from an exclusive focus on price stability and budget deficit reduction. Mitterrand and Bérégovoy's desire for an 'economic government', designed to provide a 'political counterweight' to the powers of the European Central Bank (ECB), was sacrificed in the face of unstinting German hostility in the Maastricht negotiations.

The enduring 'asymmetric dependency' of Franco-German relations was graphically demonstrated in the post reunification period. Germany decided to finance reunification through European borrowing, and accordingly set very high interest rates. French interest rates were constrained to shadow sky-high German rates despite such a move further crippling France's already sluggish growth. Employment priorities suggested the urgent need for a reduction in interest rates, and a devaluation of the franc vis-à-vis the Deutschmark. However, employment was so low on the macro-economic hierarchy of priorities that when the Germans proposed a realignment of parities within the EMS, revaluing the mark, Bérégovoy refused. In 1993, his Government suffered a crushing defeat at the polls, in part as a result of the abject failure to bring down France's high and rising structural unemployment levels.

Jospin's dual-level strategy: reinventing *dirigisme* on a European scale?

However, French Socialists' *dirigiste* aspirations endured, and indeed revived in the mid-to-late 1990s, particularly in the field of employment policy where the *laissez-faire* approach failed so miserably in the 1980s and early 1990s (Lordon 2001). French Socialists recognise the constraining context of the post-Bretton Woods international political economy. However, in the face of macro-economic constraints at the national level, they sought to transcend these by creating a new *dirigiste* policy space at the European level: 'As Prime Minister [Jospin was] often saying, the problems of growth and unemployment are also European problems ... that is why the strategy for fighting unemployment has two facets: a national dimension, and a European one seeking to reorient European construction in favour of jobs and growth' (Muet 1998: 85).

For the Socialists, European economic integration and EMU is a long run 'game'. The necessary accommodation to the German model was accepted on the understanding that increased influence once European integration advanced, and EMU was in place, would offer more scope for moving the goalposts and recovering Keynesian economic sovereignty (Clift 2003a and b). In this vein, the Jospin Government's 'dual-level' approach to employment strategy emphasised expanding 'room to manoeuvre' through European economic policy coordination in tandem with domestic *volontarisme*. This was part of an attempt to rebalance the German 'ordo-liberal' emphasis on 'sound money' and low inflation with more familiar, French *dirigiste* emphasis on the state's role in delivering full employment. Dyson notes that the French Socialists 'sought to draw a line between embracing rules of "sound" public finance and money and taking on the whole apparatus of neoliberal and monetarist policy discourse' (1999b: 202).

Macro-economic coordination: Euro-Keynesian *dirigisme*?

The EU is conceived as a political and economic 'space' (potentially) conducive to Keynesian and *dirigiste* employment policies. Jospin advocated, 'a Europe of employment, in which the priorities are growth, the development of new technologies and targeted assistance at those most affected by unemployment' (1999: 3). There are two main strands to this agenda. The maximalist position involves EU-level fiscal activism including multibillion pound 'Euro-Keynesian' public works programmes and a coordinated demand stimulus. The minimalist position calls for monetary coordination and activism through an 'economic government' – a counterweight to the European Central Bank (ECB). Jospin advocated a political role in the determination of exchange rates, and a balancing of stability with other economic priorities, most notably employment and growth, quite alien to German monetary arrangements. Here we see a re-emergence of much of the French agenda from the Maastricht discussions. The aim was for a negotiated rebalancing of the policy mix, hoping to generate coordinated fiscal, monetary and structural policies across the EU which would be geared towards jobs and growth.

While hostility remained the dominant register for German consideration of Socialist aspirations to cement the marriage of '*l'Europe sociale*' to 'monetarist' EMU through coordinated fiscal activism, dissident voices were occasionally heard, sometimes in high places. The frosty reception for Euro-Keynesianism briefly thawed when Oscar Lafontaine became finance minister. This, according to Dyson, offered a 'window of opportunity' in 1998, coinciding as it did with fears of a global recession in the wake of the Asian and Russian financial crises, thus creating scope for challenging the predominant neoliberal approach to economic policy in the EU. Jospin articulated ambitious plans for European-level coordinated action on employment and growth, combining interest rate cuts to foster growth, large-scale public investment in infrastructural programmes to boost demand and reduce unemployment. The centre-piece was a multibillion pound development loan raised on Europe's financial markets (Dyson 1999b: 203–4).

Lafontaine and French Finance Minister Strauss-Kahn formed an axis crucial to sustaining this reorientation process, and their departures undermined this agenda. The neoliberal bias of the institutions remains, and the extent to which EMU has conformed to certain social democratic aspirations (low interest rates, 'soft' currency encouraging exports) owed more to accident than any reorientation by institutional design. The Socialists' 'maximalist' aspirations to reinvent *dirigisme* on a European scale through employment-oriented macro-economic policy coordination remained unrealised.

It is thus at the minimalist end of the scale that we must look for progress. As a 1996 Socialist Party (PS) conference text argued, a political structure as a counterweight to the European Central Bank was essential to avoid the single currency being 'sacrificed to monetarism' (Parti Socialiste 1996). The deflationary bias of the EMU foundations, institutionalised at Maastricht and re-asserted with the stability pact agreed at Dublin, needed to be countered by neo-Keynesian inspired measures bolstering economic policy coordination and permitting governments under certain circum-

stances to reflate the economy to restore confidence. The rules of convergence and stability are in this reading conceived as 'hedging', not 'binding'
mechanisms (Dyson 1999b: 206).

Given that a quite different model had already been set in marble at
Maastricht, the Jospin Government (at the time only in office for a few
weeks) had no realistic prospect at the 1997 Amsterdam Summit of fully
achieving such ambitions. The 'economic government' was not established. However, some steps were taken towards institutionalising a
degree of macro-economic coordination. The Euro-11 (subsequently Euro-
12) Group, established after the Dublin European Council meeting in 1996,
was presented to French audiences as the first step towards an 'economic
government'. The Jospin Government saw the monetary committee, and
then the Cologne macro-economic dialogue, as further evidence of the
Euro-Group's nascent 'economic government' status (Howarth 2002).

Jospin's advisor Pisani-Ferry, in his report on paths to full employment,
talked of the need for 'a suitable policy mix for the euro zone through coordination and dialogue, as regards both the balance between monetary and
budgetary policies and between macro-economic and structural policies',
in the context of a 'macro-economic policy that can take risks in favour of
growth and employment' (2000: 23–24). The aim of 'economic government'
is, as Vandenbroucke notes, 'to create the institutional conditions for a sustainable mix of demand and supply policies, more precisely for the necessary flexibility in monetary management, *à la* Greenspan' (1999: 42). Yet
even the establishment of such a prudent body remains a distant prospect.
Thus the 'ordo-liberal' exigencies of budget balancing and inflation control
shape the process of European construction, and constrained the Jospin
government's more ambitious *dirigiste* and Keynesian aspirations.

Competing visions of supranational activism: Jospin's exceptional 'Euro-Keynesianism'

This dilemma is by no means unique to the French Socialists, reflecting as
it does the difficulty all social democratic governments have in reconciling
national and supranational goals. However, the degree to which the
dilemma affected the Jospin Government was distinctive, given the more
ambitious aspirations his party harbours for EU-level social democratic
activism. The problems faced by coordinated social democratic activism at
the European scale can be traced to different visions of what that activism
should entail. French aspirations for a *dirigiste* macro-economic policy at
the European level are hindered by dissent within the European social
democratic party family over the viability of such a plan.

From the German side, in the wake of Lafontaine's departure and the
closing of the 'window of opportunity', there is little or no support for

'Euro-Keynesian' demand-side activism. After the brief dalliance, the German 'ordo-liberal' scepticism about French visions of macro-economic activism returned, even within the ranks of the Social Democratic Party (SPD). One recent commentary observed, 'the Germans are reluctant to agree to more institutionalised economic coordination, critical about more active European economic (or industrial) policies, and frankly hostile to social harmonisation and cooperation in employment policy' (Trouille and Uterwedde 2001: 343–34). Schröder's advisor Hombach gives short shrift to the demand-side/supply-side debate, overwhelmingly prioritising the latter. He dismissively observes, 'most people have long since turned away from the idea of Keynesian panaceas that will work overnight' (2000: 103), from which he concludes that attention should focus entirely upon 'a supply-side economics of the left'.

New Labour is deeply sceptical of the feasibility of supranational macro-economic activism. Once committed to European contra-cyclical public spending (Brown 1996), Gordon Brown no longer retains any such aspirations. Such supranational strategies presume a very different role for the state in the economy than the Third Way suggests, and are quite simply anathema to New Labour. As Gamble and Kelly have argued, 'there is little prospect of Labour pursuing any such social democratic agenda. Even those within the government thought to be sympathetic to the traditional Keynesian social democratic agenda have gone out of their way to distance themselves from these positions' (2000: 21).

Critics both inside and outside the party exploited the inconsistencies between the Jospin Government's aspirations for European-level employment policy activism, and the nature of the actual process of European construction. The fault lines over Europeanisation emerged along the lines that Jospin had failed to sufficiently renegotiate the process of European construction away from its neoliberal bias. This critique laid bare the difficulty that the French Socialist Party continues to have living with global capitalism. The *Gauche Socialiste* faction attacked Jospin on the grounds that the 'room to manoeuvre' to which he often referred had been inaccurately conceived, and that actually there was considerably more 'slack' in terms of scope for reformist activism than the Jospin Government chose to take up. The *Gauche Socialiste* perhaps overstated the room for manoeuvre and *dirigiste* possibilities, and underestimated the constraints, but the most important point made by the *Gauche Socialiste* is entirely valid. Namely, that commitment to the single currency, and the stringent public spending and public deficit limits that it demands, hamstrings any Socialist government's aspirations to use macro-economic policy in a bid to achieve full employment. Even with sympathetic governments in most of the member states, Euro-Keynesianism did not become a reality.

Supply-side coordination – and *dirigisme*?

As the constraints on demand management have become more manifest, there has been a concomitant increase in the possibilities of pursuing full employment policies by other means, particularly supply-side policies. Here too, there was a desire to 'Europeanise' French proposals, on the assumption that coordinated European action offers greater room to manoeuvre. Furthermore, unlike the Euro-Keynesian demand-side agenda, on the supply-side front, elements of France's eclectic approach, such as subsidising low-skilled workers, find echoes elsewhere, particularly in the U.K. European social democrats by and large agree on pursuing an 'employment-centred social policy' agenda. Vandenbroucke (1999) identifies a convergence of general views on employment and employment-centred welfare reform among social democrats. The existence of a broadly common agenda in this field has informed the concentration of the institutionalisation of an EU-level job-creating agenda in the wake of the Luxembourg summit on these 'supply-side' issues.

This facilitated a process of 'Europeanisation' of employment policy first institutionalised at the Amsterdam Summit at Jospin's behest. There, the Jospin Government succeeded in inserting an employment clause, thus making employment a new 'priority' on the EU agenda. This paved the way for the growth and employment resolution and the formulation of the European employment strategy. What followed as a result were the Luxembourg and Cardiff jobs Summits, and the 1999 Cologne Summit, which codified National Action Plans for employment. These were part of the Common Strategy for National Employment Policies (CSNEP), a surveillance and benchmarking process that emphasises supply-side 'best practice' measures to promote *employability* (European Council 1997: 1).

The 'benchmarking' process undertaken since Luxembourg suggests a degree of policy transfer and an overarching commonality of approach to the 'supply-side' aspects of employment policy. Indeed, some have identified the benchmarking process as a straw in the wind of declining French exceptionalism. Milner rightly identifies emulative policy transfer undertones in Aubry's '*Nouveau Départ*' employment drive, which has created 'personalised pathways for those most vulnerable (youth and long-term unemployed) ... [and] adheres to EU targets of proportions of younger people leaving unemployment before the twelfth month' (Milner 2001: 333).

A further similarity can be found in the emphasis on 'in-work benefits', subsidies and financial incentives to employers who hire extra low-skill workers. Subsidising cheap labour by such means is seen as a highly effective job creating mechanism and is the inspiration behind the Working Family Tax Credit and the Jospin Government's *Prime pour l'emploi*. Similarly, the New Deal is predicated on offering incentives to both claimants and employers, and is intended to work in close harmony with the tax and benefit system, thus, 'side-by-side with the New Deal there will be new guarantees that work will pay more than benefits' (Brown 1998). Jospin's Government aimed to facilitate the hiring of new employees by small- and medium- sized firms and to increase low-wage employment, in part by bringing down non-wage employers' costs. One measure has been the reduction of employers' contributions on low earners (Gutman and Lefebvre 1999: 9). The onus on job creation through removing the obstacles placed upon hiring by labour market conditions and the view that small and medium-sized businesses are the best job creators, warranting tax breaks and incentives, are common to the PS and New Labour.

However, the degree of apparent similarity is a little deceptive. As Ryner notes in his examination of the Swedish Social Democrats approach to the CSNEP process, there is an absence of sanctions ensuring job creation targets are met, and 'the documents are vague about the mix of different elements of policy. This gives ample space for the member states to interpret CSNEP in many ways. National policy mixes may emphasise neoliberal or social democratic elements' (2000: 342). There is agreement about some aspects of employment creation strategy, involving both increasing flexibility and active labour market policies. Yet the commonality applies to only *some* aspects, the more market-oriented, and less *dirigiste* dimensions, of French employment strategy. It should be recalled that the full coherence of the French approach is dependent upon activism at *both* demand-side (macro-economic), and supply-side (micro-economic) levels within the PS's eclectic, multipronged employment strategy. Furthermore, the French Socialists embrace a more *dirigiste* approach to some supply-side policies, such as the thirty-five-hour week and the Youth employment plan, involving a *dirigiste* role for the state in directing adjustment and tackling unemployment (see below).

This eclecticism is not reflected elsewhere. Within New Labour's strategy, overwhelming primacy is afforded to supply-side or structural adjustment policies, with little or no emphasis placed on demand-side macro policy. As Westergaard notes, New Labour assumes that 'supply-side measures more or less on their own will prove enough to provide full work opportunities for all able to take them up: complementary emphasis on demand management takes a back-seat as one of the discarded legacies of failure' (1999: 430). New Labour's strategy departs from French active labour market policy in its degree of emphasis on the private sector, notably in the provision of training. Furthermore, except for the group of eighteen- to twenty-four-year-olds, there is no state-provided training, nor any state involvement in employment creation in areas where high unemployment and low skills are concentrated (Huber and Stephens 2001: 308).

From the German side, Hombach, as noted above, argues that attention should focus entirely upon 'a supply-side economics of the left' – which centres on issues of education and gearing regional subsidies towards encouraging innovation and business start-ups (2000: 104–21). Schröder hopes that 'Europe's social democrats will come to learn from each other, complement each other and stimulate each other' (2000: 156), but there is little enthusiasm for the PS's *dirigiste* supply-side agenda.

Enduring *dirigiste* exceptionalism

The French Socialists' enduring *dirigiste* notion of the role of the state in securing the highest possible employment levels in society leads to more emphasis on the demand side. As Muet is quick to insist, 'structural policies are only efficient in a context of rising demand … growth is a pre-requisite'; this, he argues, explains the Jospin Government's course of action after 1997: 'we wanted to simultaneously stimulate demand and to ensure that the subsequent growth favoured employment and we chose an ambitious job creation policy' (2000: 11). The role of *dirigiste* macro-economic policies affecting demand retains an important role within the French analytical framework, although macro-economic scope to redress a perceived structural insufficiency of demand is partially constrained by the framework of the euro.

As well as a different take on the optimal policy mix, the PS *dirigiste* approach informed distinctive 'structural' or supply-side policies. The PS's approach reflected a 'new alliance' between state and market, a 'cooperative balance' less heavily predicated on the role of the market (Jospin 1999: 11). This combines the 'employment-centred social policy' approach noted above with an enduringly significant state role – both as employer and orchestrator – of a more eclectic approach to an overall employment creation strategy. For example, state spending devoted to employment policy increased markedly between 1997 and 2002, reaching 4.5 percent of GDP in 2000 (Ministère de l'économie 2001: 15). The PS continued to insist upon the role of public-sector job creation in tackling unemployment. State-led employment creation schemes have become a structuring feature of the French model (OFCE 1999: 58). The state's role as employer within an active employment policy remained central to the Socialists' approach. The results of the *plan Aubry* were encouraging, with 274,900 jobs created in the public sector by March 2001, and a total of 308,000 private sector jobs under the *plan Aubry* framework.[1] In the 2002 budget, Jospin planned to expand public sector recruitment to offset possible unemployment increases that a slow-down of the French economy heralded, again indicating the *dirigiste* impulse to use the state actively in employment policy.

Nowhere was the state's enduring role in the job creating strategy more in evidence than in the Jospin Government's state orchestrated shift to a thirty-five hour week. The French law emphasised job creation, with state aid in the form of reductions in social security contributions offered to firms creating new jobs as a result of the reduction of the working week. The fixed levels of these state financial aids were relatively more generous for lower earners (Gubian 1998: 20–21). In terms reminiscent of Scharpf (1991), the thirty-five hour week involves negotiated redistribution among workers as a means of furthering social democratic egalitarian employment policy. As Fitoussi puts it, 'workers have to agree to share both their jobs and their salaries with the unemployed' (1998: 81). The thirty-five hour week, which illustrates enduring *dirigiste* exceptionalism, was seen as an integral part of its own 'model' of capitalism, in which the state prioritises employment and continues to be of central importance to France's economic development (Parti Socialiste 1996).

Conclusion

French Social democracy has attempted to rediscover *dirigisme* at the European level, most recently through Jospin's dual-level employment strategy. In part as a result of the tighter constraints that undermined national *dirigiste* and Keynesian solutions to burgeoning unemployment problems, efforts intensified to find ways of delivering the public good of full employment through coordinated European macro-economic steering. Thus there was an attempt to 'Europeanise' solutions to employment.

Such efforts, which had both macro-economic and supply-side dimensions, were at best only partially successful. PS enthusiasm for achieving full employment at the European scale, and more importantly their understanding of how that can be achieved, was not shared among social democratic policy elites in Britain and Germany. This illustrates the problems faced by the French Socialists in pursuing and 'Europeanising' *dirigiste* employment strategies. PS desires for 'rearticulation' of employment strategy at the European level were undermined by a degree of French exceptionalism regarding what constitutes an optimum 'Europeanised' employment strategy.

This was most glaringly apparent on the macro-economic front, where French calls for bold fiscal activism went unanswered, and even their more circumspect aspirations for increased growth and jobs oriented macro-economic coordination through an 'economic government' were not realised. There were some increasing similarities on the supply-side front, reflecting perhaps a nascent common agenda on some areas of employment policy. However, here too the French Socialists exhibited *dirigiste* distinctiveness, with active public-sector employment drives and the thirty-five hour week not finding equivalents elsewhere.

Note

1. For Labour Ministry figures, see the website: www.nsej.travail.gouv.fr/actualite/bilan. Such results, however, must be placed in the context of a wider economic upturn, making the precise impact of the *plan Aubry* difficult to discern.

Chapter 9

FRENCH FOREIGN AND DEFENCE POLICY: EXCEPTIONAL IN METHODS AND RHETORIC?

Janet Bryant

This chapter examines the notion of exceptionalism in the context of French foreign and defence policy in the Fifth Republic. The idea that France is exceptional in this area of policy has been characterised by the plethora of adjectives such as different, unusual, unconventional, distinctive and sometimes even maverick, that are often used when describing French actions. To what extent does it really make sense to talk about French exceptionalism in foreign and defence policy? Might it be argued, rather, that this term is particularly difficult to apply to an area of 'high' policy where every state will be seeking to pursue foreign and defence policies, independently or in concert with others and within the constraints of the international system, which are by definition designed to maintain that state's independence and power? France is not exceptional in this sense, then, although an enormous amount has been written about the French emphasis on both independence and the maintenance of French power. And, if we consider the notion of exceptionalism a little further, we are faced with another dilemma: if exceptionalism is discernable in foreign and defence policy, then this can be 'proven', presumably, by way of some understanding of what is 'normal' in the external policies of different states. But where is the yardstick against which different levels of exceptionalism might be measured? When one ponders the international system, might it not be possible to argue that there are several other states that might be more deserving of the label of exceptionalism? Is the neutrality of states like Sweden, Switzerland or Ireland not as exceptional – indeed, more exceptional – than anything that France might be able to offer? And, at the other end of the spectrum of engagement where, on this ticklishly difficult line between normalcy and exceptionalism, does the U.S. penchant for post-11 September unilateralism lie? This chapter does not claim to advance definitive answers to any of these questions, but the preceding discussion is nevertheless useful in raising questions about the very appropriateness of a term like exceptionalism to characterise foreign and defence policy.

Instead, it will examine, firstly, the reasons why French foreign and defence policy has been identified as an example of exceptionalism and why France has often been described as an exceptional partner. The review of some of the main directions of French external policy in the period since 1958 will lead us to suggest that it is in fact some of the methods and the accompanying rhetoric that France has adopted to further its ambitions which might be considered exceptional, rather than the policies themselves. Secondly, the chapter will investigate whether or not in recent years France has been experiencing a normalisation in this area of policy. This second theme will be explored through two illustrations. One will support the contention that France is less exceptional than it once was by investigating post-1990 France-NATO relations. The other illustration looks at France's position on Iraq in 2002/3, notably how French rhetoric placed it in the familiar position of leading European critic of U.S. policy, thus questioning the extent of the normalisation thesis.

Features of French foreign and defence policy since 1958

If we review the period from 1958 until the present time, we might contend that French foreign and defence policy in the Fifth Republic has been characterised by a surprisingly high degree of continuity. This continuity has been manifested in several different ways. In the first place, French policy has been underpinned by a number of objectives which have remained consistent across the years. France has tried to increase its standing in the world and to guarantee a vital minimum of independence for itself and in its international relationships. French external policy since 1958 has also sought to protect France's drive for domestic and economic progress, to reinforce the legitimacy of the post-1958 constitutional arrangements (which gave a new importance to the president in this area), and to inculcate a sense of national identity and national interest in the body politic (Cerny 1984: 52). Equally, continuity has also been present in some of the key ideas that have shaped French policy.

Many of the positions that have been favoured by France since 1958 can be traced back to the years between 1958 and 1969 when de Gaulle was in power. This is why many authors have acknowledged the significance of the Gaullist legacy – or a Gaullist 'orthodoxy' – in foreign and defence policy which, it is argued, has continued to mould French actions well beyond the Gaullist period proper (Howorth and Chilton 1984).

One of the most obvious themes that has run through policy down the years has been the belief that France has a global role to play in international politics irrespective of the changing climate, which has moved on from the cold war years to the altered, yet hardly less challenging, post-1989 environment (Gregory 2000). The emphasis on the need for France to maintain its presence at the very forefront of international affairs has led some commentators to posit a second characteristic trait of French external policy: the notion of 'mission'. This has grown from the belief in the country's historic duty, or destiny – its right, even – to fulfil such a global role. This notion, and the manner in which France has chosen to promote its interests, is rooted in the legacy of France's imperial past and stems from its position on the continent. Although France has inevitably seen its status challenged, and in some areas like Africa considerably reduced, it still enjoys important influence outside the borders of the hexagon (metropolitan France): it is a permanent member of the United Nations Security Council; it is one of the world's nuclear powers; its large arms and defence industries have traditionally acted as useful adjuncts to 'regular' policy; its overseas territories and departments in the Caribbean, the South Pacific and the Indian Oceans – as well as its considerable remaining commitments in Africa – continue to project the image of France as a power with global pretensions and responsibilities.

A third feature of French external policy since 1958, which is linked to the first two, is its 'activism'. This trait might be demonstrated by the readiness of successive administrations to sanction military intervention beyond French borders. The arena for this intervention has often been Africa, where French forces intervened on at least nine occasions during the Gaullist years and a further six times under the presidencies of Pompidou and Giscard d'Estaing. Subsequently, Mitterrand sent troops to Chad several times between 1983 and 1988, and among other places to Togo in 1986, to Comoros in 1989, to Gabon in 1990 and to Rwanda between 1990 and 1993 and again in 1994 (Cumming 2001: 410). Most recently, Chirac has authorised the use of French troops in an attempt to restore order in Côte d'Ivoire in 2002/3. France has also become increasingly involved in international peace keeping – or peace enforcement – missions closer to home in Europe in the 1980s and 1990s (Utley 2000: 179–98).

A readiness to act can be linked to a fourth characteristic of French foreign and defence policy in the Fifth Republic, namely the consistent concern to promote French rank – or, as de Gaulle expressed it – French 'grandeur' (Gregory 2000: 21). Grandeur can partly be understood as a picture that de Gaulle carried in his mind of what France – weak and the source of ridicule because of the ineptitude of the Fourth Republic – *ought* to be. It was a vision of that he articulated with great clarity and passion: 'My mind assures me that France is not really itself unless it is in the front rank. In short, to my mind, France cannot be France without greatness'. Linked to this was the notion of France's destiny: 'All of my life I have thought of France in a certain way … dedicated to an exalted and exceptional destiny' (de Gaulle 1954: 1–2). The other way in which grandeur might be understood is to see it as a discourse that de Gaulle hoped would help to 'cement' French society back together. As Cerny (1980b: 18) remarks, '[t]he concept of grandeur was to create a new and deeper sense of national unity that would enable the traditional cleavages in French political life to be overcome by reinforcing the consensus around a strengthened and dynamic state that incarnated the general will within a stable political system'. Although not all of de Gaulle's successors have employed the term 'grandeur', the central emphasis on the need to maintain France as a global player has persisted.

The other dimension of grandeur has been to do with raising the international rank and standing of France. In this vein, the constant emphasis has been on two additional linked requirements: independence and autonomy. These were key considerations in the decision to develop an independent nuclear deterrent. Not only was the *force de frappe*, as it was called, seen as central to any meaningful international strategy, it also had a political value as it was presented as a means of allowing France access to the prestige and status afforded to the members of the (still reasonably) exclusive nuclear club. Another claimed advantage of the deterrent was that it allowed France to take more control over its own defence and, in theory at least, made France less dependent upon other states for protection. This, as discussed below, is important in terms of how de Gaulle and other French leaders have traditionally viewed NATO (the North Atlantic Treaty Organisation) and the United States.

On a more constructive footing, a penultimate element of French policy which merits attention is Europe, which has been another fundamental area of interest in its foreign policy since 1958. A founding member of the EEC in 1957, France has grown to recognise that Europe is of immense significance to its international clout as well as its image of itself. This does not imply that French political leaders have always shared a common vision of what Europe should be, however. De Gaulle was hostile to federal designs (Gordon 1993: 9–14), while Giscard d'Estaing, on the other hand, was far more of a committed Europeanist. Despite these differences in perspective, Europe has nevertheless developed as an increasingly important theme in French policy. From the 1960s onwards, when de Gaulle was underlining the need for Europe to galvanise itself into a credible third 'bloc' in global politics between the superpowers, to Mitterrand's 1980s–1990s stress on the need to further the scope of integration, Europe has provided a stage upon which the French voice might be heard. France has also tried to safeguard and protect French interests – agricultural and other – *through* Europe.

A final important feature of French foreign policy in the Fifth Republic, which can also be linked to the previous one, is the forging of a new relationship with the old enemy, Germany. Against the backdrop of long-standing Franco-German rivalry and animosity – the roots of which stretch back to before 1870 – the speed and extent of the reconciliation must be considered as one of the major triumphs of postwar European diplomacy. This is not to say that the Franco-German relationship has been tension free. West Germany had serious concerns over the targeting of the French deterrent and repeatedly sought a dual key arrangement for its implementation – a request that France always refused, citing as a reason the need for complete autonomy over decision making. France has fretted about German economic potential, the possibility of a German drift towards the East, and about the dangers implicit in a resurgence of German nationalism both before and after unification (Trouille 1996). And France and Germany have not always seen eye-to-eye over the speed and depth of European integration in the 1990s and beyond. Yet, despite these stresses and strains, the significance of and the value attached to the relationship by both partners, means that relations with Germany have remained high on the agenda of French policy (Friend 1991).

A French exceptionalism?

The consistent features presented above, which have characterised French policy in the Fifth Republic, do not in themselves mean that French policy is necessarily exceptional. Most states demonstrate continuity in the broad lines of their foreign and defence policies, as they seek to defend their perceived national interests. Having said this, however, it may be possible to argue that some of the *methods and the rhetoric* that France has used to advance these interests have been rather individual and distinctive. This section therefore investigates several examples of what might be considered as French exceptionalism in operation. This is best seen in France's attitude to the superpowers, especially the U.S., in its relationship with NATO, and in aspects of its nuclear policy.

It is necessary to return to the Gaullist years if we are to appreciate the nature of the French exception in these areas. As we have already established, de Gaulle placed great emphasis on the need to reassert French independence and improve the international standing of the country. In this context, it is the readiness of France to be openly and frequently critical of American policy designs that has done most to set France apart from other members of the Atlantic Alliance during the cold war years. De Gaulle, of course, would not have considered his actions to have been 'anti-American' *per se*. He saw Europe's client status to the U.S. and the unequal nature of the transatlantic partnership as detrimental to the advancement of both French *and* European interests; the French focus on the need to build Europe from a simple trading bloc into something greater was presented as a way of loosening the grip of the bloc-versus-bloc nature of global politics, and as a way of reducing tensions between the superpowers. Similarly, the French dialogue with the USSR and the Eastern bloc, supported by trade agreements, was also designed to foster détente. Other French moves like, for instance, its 1964 recognition of Communist China, its withdrawal from SEATO (the South East Asia Treaty Organisation) in 1965, its staunch refusal to allow its nuclear forces to be part of any arms control talks or the articulation of critical views on American involvement in Vietnam, may have had the effect of exasperating Washington but were explained by Paris in terms of its right to safeguard its autonomy and interests and make its opinions known. Thus it is France, more than any of the U.S' other European allies, that has shown itself in its actions and its rhetoric to be the latter's most 'critical friend'. Moreover, the French approach has often been at odds with the approach favoured by Washington. Examples of this are the French penchant for negotiating with individual oil producing countries rather than with OPEC en bloc, as preferred by the U.S., during the oil crises in the 1970s; the refusal of France to allow American jets to overfly French airspace on their way to bomb the Libyan capital, Tripoli, in the 1980s; Mitterrand's eleventh-hour negotiations with Saddam Hussein just before Desert Storm (Gregory 2000: 43); or the mantle that France has assumed in spearheading European nervousness concerning the unilateralism of George W. Bush's 'war on terrorism'.

Another manifestation of the French exception has been its unique position regarding NATO. By the time he returned to power in 1958, de Gaulle had for years deplored the way the Anglo-American nuclear directorship of NATO effectively excluded France from a position of real influence. By the late 1950s, France had begun to develop its nuclear deterrent and de Gaulle was convinced that this ought to be taken into consideration by the U.S., and the attitude of the latter modified in the light of this new fact. Thus, in 1959 he proposed a tripartite (U.K.-U.S.-France) directorate to break this 'monopoly'. However, the proposal fell on deaf Anglo-Saxon ears: Eisenhower rejected out of hand the French proposition for tripartite consultations over the direction of strategy, control of NATO's nuclear weapons and tripartite commands in various areas of the world (Laird 1971). This helped to confirm de Gaulle's view that being part of NATO was increasingly undesirable: it crippled expressions of French autonomy, institutionalised its inferior position with regard to the U.S., and robbed it of any real protection. Thus, in order to make French defence policy properly its own, de Gaulle moved to progressively withdraw France from the integrated military command structure, once it became clear to him that he could neither bully nor cajole the U.S. into a reorganisation that would better suit France. This process of withdrawal began in March 1959 when the French Government notified NATO's permanent council of its intention to remove its Mediterranean fleet from NATO command in time of war (Gordon 1993: 29) and culminated in February 1966, when France announced the withdrawal of all its units from NATO's integrated command and the closing of all foreign bases that still remained on French soil. In July, French representatives left the military organs of NATO.

The withdrawal from NATO's command structures undoubtedly added to the feelings held by some of France's Alliance partners that France was something of a maverick whose reliability as an ally was open to question, although France and NATO did reach some behind the scenes agreements concerning the role of French forces in any future assault on Western Europe (Menon 1995: 26). Nevertheless, successive French presidents continued to reason that the benefits of continued non-membership outweighed any that might have accrued from rejoining the organisation. In these ways, therefore, France's relationship with NATO after 1966 has been quite unique. Certain changes in the French position on NATO in the 1980s and 1990s which arguably make it less distinctive will be explored in the last section of the chapter.

A final example of French exceptionalism in defence policy in the Fifth Republic concerns aspects of nuclear policy. Here again, French positions were often in marked contrast to those of NATO. The explanations for this are both practical and doctrinal. During the 1960s, NATO moved from a strategy of massive retaliation (strikes with strategic nuclear weapons against enemy cities) to a new strategy called 'flexible response' (which would in theory keep any conflict contained to nuclear exchanges at tactical – i.e., battlefield – level 'only'). While the U.S. was anxious to promote the change in strategy now that the USSR also had the capability to threaten American cities, the Europeans were less convinced. For the French, in particular, flexible response seemed to suggest that the U.S. was prepared to contemplate a limited nuclear war in Europe. Furthermore, French doctrine continued to favour massive retaliation for its own nuclear forces. In the first place, France did not have the necessary sophistication in its weaponry to allow for what was entailed by flexible response. But even if it had, the way that France conceived of its deterrent mitigated against its acceptance of the new posture, as the French rejected the very notion of limited nuclear war and the idea that tactical nuclear weapons could acquire a battlefield role. Rather, France argued that the threat of massive retaliation against 'soft' targets like cities would be taken far more seriously by an enemy, and hence would be far more likely to perpetuate deterrence.

The final way in which France differed in its approach to nuclear weapons can be illustrated by the French notion of the sanctuary. In French thinking about nuclear weapons, France's independent deterrent is seen as an important way to protect the 'sanctuary' (mainland France) because French doctrine argued that only nuclear weapons belonging to France could credibly fulfil such a role in the eyes of a potential aggressor. In this way, France rejected the nuclear pledges that came via NATO (where American systems were used to protect Europe as well as the U.S.). The French suggested that deterrence could not be credibly shared in this way. Another difference was that NATO gave a war fighting role to its tactical nuclear forces whereas the French, by contrast, saw its tactical systems as intrinsically linked to its strategic forces. This suggested a French readiness to contemplate a rapid escalation to strategic level if the warning shot role ascribed to France's tactical systems failed to halt an enemy advance.

This section of the chapter has identified a number of distinctive traits in French foreign and defence policy in the Fifth Republic, and has tried to show how they may be considered as exceptional. But what allowed France to develop and persist with these traits? One answer is that the cold war and the security apparatus that accompanied it afforded France the luxury of taking many of the controversial positions that it did in the knowledge that if or when push came to shove, France would still be privy to the protection offered by the NATO umbrella, thanks to its geographical position. Given this certainty, it was possible for France to dance to its own and different tune, and to do so for political ends. The French message played well to a varied audience, which was domestic (French public opinion) as well as international (parts of the Third World, parts of the Eastern bloc, parts of South East Asia and Latin America). The latter was important as it enabled France to project itself as an autonomous player on the global stage. In the next section, however, we will continue to suggest that in more recent years, the French exception might increasingly be to do with *rhetoric* rather than *substance*.

'Normalisation': evidence of declining French exceptionalism ?

The final section of the chapter examines whether or not the French exception in foreign and defence policy is now in decline. Has there been a discernable normalisation in some of the French positions which, earlier in the Fifth Republic, served to differentiate France from its partners? To reach some understanding about these questions, we will revisit France-NATO relations, then conclude with a section that investigates France's position on the 2002/3 Iraq crisis. But we first need to look at the notion of normalisation in a broader context.

It might be argued that French exceptionalism has indeed been in retreat in the 1980s and 1990s. A combination of two issues serve as explanations for this: one relates to what might be called the 'internal logic' – or lack of it – inside French policy; the other relates to changes in the strategic environment, particularly after 1989. We saw earlier that French policy, especially French defence policy, had developed a distinctly nationalistic bent from the 1960s on. Over the years, this position and the way policy was framed, although still of some use domestically, was becoming increasingly untenable in the wider arena. Put another way, the ethos of 'France for France and for France alone', the concept of the sanctuary as it pertained to the *force de dissuasion*, and the controversy that ensued if there was an attempt to extend French security pledges to other states (as Giscard had tried to do in the 1970s), all served to underline a growing tension at the heart of French policy. On the one hand, France was becoming more focused on Europe (substantial remaining interests in Africa notwithstanding, although, as Chafer (2002: 343–63) details, even the nature of French exceptionalism in African policy has been changing in the mid-1990s). On the other hand, France's relationships with its closest European partners were complicated by this rhetoric and by the absence of anything really constructive coming from the French in the area of European security. This rhetoric, coupled with French *immobilisme*, also sat awkwardly with other areas of French involvement in the European sphere where French ideas for continuing European economic and political development were relatively plentiful. During the 1980s and into the 1990s, however, important changes have occurred. For example, French nuclear doctrine was updated, official security guarantees were extended to West Germany in 1985, and France evolved into a far more constructive proponent of a credible European defence supplied by the Europeans themselves. France also made some moves to indicate to nervous allies that it was now ready to shoulder more responsibilities in the military defence of the continent. The creation of the Forces d'Action Rapide (FAR) in 1983 with their overtly European role, as well as the development of the Franco-German axis in defence matters, were elements in this process. In some ways it is easy to understand the rationale behind the changes because, at its core, French motivation had not really altered. What France continued to seek was a strong, stable and autonomous Europe that would act as a platform for French ambitions. To this end, the new more positive approach of France to European security in the 1980s had two roots. Firstly, France was concerned that without such overtures its key ally, West Germany, might drift towards neutralism or towards the East. This was best countered by the promotion of the Franco-German axis in particular, and a more involved French message on European security in general. Secondly, in the years before the 1989 watershed, fears that the oft repeated French message 'Yankee go home'might actually come to pass as Washington looked to reign back defence expenditure led France into a far more assiduous concern for the need – the requirement, indeed – that Europe do something to bolster its own defence provisions (Carr and Infantis 1996: 27–54; Menon 1995).

The year 1989 and the changes in the strategic environment which it represented (Carr 1998) naturally provoked a major defence rethink for all the major powers. For France, however, these events if anything reinforced the belief that the direction which France was trying to take was the correct one. The process of Europeanisation of French defence and security policy continued and intensified: France became the champion of the need to build defence and security into the European vision, it supported the Common Foreign and Security Policy (CFSP) and the European Security and Defence Identity (ESDI), and it was a chief promoter of the undeniable need for more effective European capabilities to move all this forward. France's active role, alongside Britain, in the planned creation of the 60,000 strong European Rapid Reaction Force is an example of this.

France and NATO

This overview helps us understand the background to the warmer France-NATO relationship that developed in the 1990s. This is one area that has been held up as an example of 'normalisation'. During the 1980s, France continued to reject reintegration and focused instead on the best way to develop European answers to the continent's security requirements. This position was best illustrated by France's sponsorship of the WEU (Western European Union) as a vehicle for developing a European defence persona after 1983, as well as by its policy of accelerated European economic and political integration. France was however forced to reassess its view of the importance of transatlantic links in the late 1980s and early 1990s, which led in turn to a reassessment of NATO, its functions and the future role of the Europeans within it. Put at its most simple, the French were well aware that even before the collapse of the old order in the late 1980s, the embryonic European defence structures were too weak, both in the political and military sense, to stand alone. These weaknesses were compounded by the raft of problems that arose in the post-1989 environment. In such circumstances, a troubling paradox arose for the French, given its usual stance: it began to worry far *less* about American domination and far *more* about the alarming consequences of additional American disengagement, especially in the light of U.S. foot dragging over involvement in Bosnia. Indeed, Menon argues that the experience of the Yugoslav crisis was significant in driving the French reassessment of its security requirements (1995: 30). The conclusion was obvious: more rather than less involvement with NATO was called for. Thus, the French position that 'in order to be more European tomorrow, it is necessary to be more Atlanticist today' (Casanova 1995: 26), together with its more constructive approach to NATO, were presented as part of French designs to upgrade the role of the Europeans inside the alliance.

France-NATO relations began to change from 1992 onwards, and contacts between them increased in 1993 and 1994 (Vernet 1993). The 1994 American proposal for the creation of Combined Joint Task Forces was warmly welcomed by France as a mechanism for the further development of a role for the Europeans in operations (Buchan 1994) and France's defence White Paper the same year was positive about the contribution of NATO to European security (Bryant 1996). The French defence minister also began to attend NATO meetings 'if questions concerning French forces are taken up or when the agenda of the meeting places France in a position to intervene' (Léotard 1994: 5). From October 1995, the French chief of staff attended meetings of NATO's Military Committee for the first time since 1966 – a move described by the French foreign minister as 'an important initiative to facilitate the renovation of the Alliance, and to develop the European pillar of defence' (de Charette in Palmer 1996: 15). Throughout this period, France was also gratified by all of the decisions taken to improve the capabilities and competences of the WEU, and by the endorsement that U.S. President Clinton seemed to be giving to ESDI.

The rapprochement was not absolute, however. By 1997, it seemed that the next logical step for France would be to fully reintegrate itself back into NATO – and this, indeed, was what the French desired, since it was coming to understand that the best way of promoting the continued Europeanisation of NATO structures was from the inside (Bryant 2000). But this did not happen. Instead, France and NATO became embroiled in a bitter row over the distribution of responsibilities between the U.S. and its European allies. In the run up to the July 1997 NATO Summit in Madrid, France had been working hard towards a reweighting of responsibilities within the organisation, arguing that a European commander should be given control of NATO's Southern Command Allied Forces Southern Europe (AFSOUTH), based in Naples (Menon 2002). The U.S. was reluctant to allow this because the American Sixth Fleet (vital for any operations in the Mediterranean, the Middle East and the Gulf) came under the control of AFSOUTH. The U.S. did not give way, and France, which put much store by what by what the Naples debacle *represented*, did not rejoin NATO in 1997 as had been expected. This does not mean that France and the Alliance are not speaking to each other. In fact, there is plenty of evidence that France's ad hoc integration is moved forward by operational circumstances thrown up by conflicts. Since the war in Bosnia, French operational integration with NATO has improved dramatically, and during the Kosovo campaign France was one of the Alliance's most 'participatory' members. Indeed, a demonstration of just how far things have progressed can be taken from the same Kosovan example: not only did France make a major contribution to the air campaign, but a French general, General Valentin, was also operating on the ground, under a NATO flag, against France's traditional allies, the Serbs. And surprisingly, this provoked no reaction from French public opinion (Bryant 2000).

So are France-NATO relations still exceptional? On the one hand, there are several ways in which French ties with the organisation are now less exceptional and distinctive than they once were. From the operational point of view, the 'half in-half out' quality (although it is more 'in' than ever before) of France's links hardly seems to make a difference. Yet, political tensions still remain, the nature of which are not that new. France's traditional 'agenda' for Europe persists, although the circumstances surrounding its promotion have changed.

France, the UN and Iraq

In this last illustration, by contrast, we will argue that the French position on the approach of the conflict in Iraq in 2002/3 is a useful example of continuing traits of French exceptionalism, particularly with regard to its attitude towards the U.S. In this sense, France, with its antiwar stance, became the key focus for, and mouthpiece of, European dissent on the Iraq question. The mantle of acting as the leading critic of American policy – part of the French exception, as we have already discussed – was once again adopted by France. In particular, Chirac accused the U.S. of an arrogance and high-handedness which was likely to further destabilise the Middle East; U.S. actions were characterised as dangerous adventurism, especially alarming given the declared U.S. policy shift towards pre-emption to deal with international terrorism and weapons of mass destruction (WMD).

The French position on Iraq in the run-up to the war was reasonably straightforward. In its desire to curb what it saw as the dangers implicit in excessive American unilateralism, France argued from the beginning of the crisis that all actions must pass through the UN. It was thus a key player in championing the need to pass Resolution 1441 in early November 2002, giving the UN weapons inspectors their mandate to return to Iraq in search of WMD. Thereafter, France became a galvanising force behind a growing consensus of opinion which argued that solid and irrefutable evidence of Iraq's transgression, its links with international terrorism and the threat that it posed to the West, had to be firmly established before the sanctioning of any action which *might be* authorised following the passing of a *second* UN resolution. France pleaded the case that Hans Blix and his team be given more time to complete their inspections (which, the French suggested, had begun to produce results), arguing that the number of inspectors should be tripled and that they be helped in their task by increased aerial surveillance. From late January onwards, as U.S. troops continued to assemble in the Gulf region, France made it clear that it would use its veto at the UN over any new resolution that sanctioned war. It was joined by two other permanent members, Russia and China, so that ultimately no second resolution was ever engineered.

On the European front, diplomatic activity was equally frantic. Following the rejuvenation of its partnership with Germany in the wake of the celebrations of the fortieth anniversary of the Elysée Treaty in January 2003, Chirac and Schröder seemed to suggest that their antiwar stance was shared across other European capitals. This prompted a London-led initiative in February, which resulted in the U.K., Italy, Spain and more than ten countries from Eastern and South Eastern Europe publicly affirming their backing for the U.S. U.S. Defence Secretary Donald Rumsfeld's description of France and Germany as 'old Europe' and Chirac's subsequent labelling of those former communist states who wished to join the EU but who had supported the U.S. over Iraq as 'reckless' and 'infantile' only served to increase European disunity (Parks 2003: 3).

Chirac justified his antiwar stance on various grounds. His first argument was that war is always the worst solution to a crisis. In this way, France suggested that the conflict was likely to have unforeseeable (and highly disagreeable) consequences for the long suffering Iraqi population. Second, Chirac argued that another American-led conflict in Iraq would inflame Arab world opinion. This was dangerous as it carried with it the risk of alienating moderate Arab opinion and increasing levels of militancy. Third, Chirac suggested that regional stability in the whole of the Middle East would be compromised in the event of war (especially given the added criticism from the Elysée that the Bush administration had seriously neglected the Arab-Israeli dispute). Fourth, Chirac defended his antiwar stance on the basis that the war was very likely to result in even more anti-Western terrorism. Finally, Islamic opinion in France was not an unimportant consideration to the president (Parks 2003: 2). To this list of justifications, one might add rather less publicised economic imperatives. France and Russia had substantial economic interests in Iraq and both countries had lucrative oil deals in place when UN sanctions were lifted (*The Economist* 2003b: 23–25). Whatever the true nature of French motivations, Chirac's position certainly found favour with European public opinion (McAllister 2003a: 18–25; 2003b: 18–21). The popularity of the antiwar position of France went beyond Europe, as Chirac's three-day visit to Algeria in March 2003 testified (Henley 2003). Chirac also benefited from extremely high levels of public endorsement in France. In late March 2003, his antiwar stance achieved an approval rating of 90 percent, which is the highest recorded for any French government programme since surveys began in 1938 (Webster 2003a).

During the conflict itself, Chirac had no direct contact with Bush, but after the fall of Baghdad in April 2003, France again began to work for the acceptance of a central role for the UN in postwar Iraq. In the weeks following the formal end of the war, a rudimentary Franco-American and Anglo-French dialogue was reconstituted, but both France and Germany continued to say that the war was a mistake (Webster 2003b; Black and Smith 2003: 1–2). The subsequent linked controversies over the nature and quality of British and American intelligence (at best, sloppy; at worst, deceitful), the justification for the war in the absence of a second UN resolution (that Iraq's WMD posed an urgent and imminent threat) and the continuing absence of any evidence of such weapons, means that this view is unlikely to be modified in the near future. And, at the time of writing, the jury is still out on the two other French concerns: the question of whether the U.S. really has the stomach for the peace, and precisely what the quality and nature of that peace will be.

So what further, if anything, can be said of this episode? We have seen that the rhetoric and position of France on Iraq seem to emphasise France's tradition as the U. S.' most critical European ally. We have also seen that in other quarters, French action is simply viewed as the latest illustration of habitual French grandstanding and a French desire to 'box above its weight'. But the events of late 2002 and early 2003 are not as simple as that. They must be seen in the light of other traits of French policy discussed in this chapter. This can best be done by considering the differences between the French and British positions over Iraq. Guided by two different approaches, Blair's argument has been that Europe and the U.S. can (and must) work together to shape international events: the worst scenario imaginable is a Europe divided from the U.S. For Chirac, Europe must balance American power and this may mean, on occasion, confronting American power. Hence, the old French emphasis on the requirement for an EU that is strong enough to face down Washington if need be, or which, at the very least, is robust enough in its own right to defend its own corner in a multipolar world. Like many French politicians, Chirac remains fundamentally nervous about the American 'hyperpower' that has, in French eyes, neither the need nor the inclination to heed the advice of smaller powers (*The Economist* 2003(a): 35–36).

The irony is that divisions that were exposed by the French handling of the Iraq question may militate against the realisation of France's long-term goal. Firstly, the manner in which the crisis unfolded will have added weight to the hawks led by Donald Rumsfeld inside the Bush administration who have long argued that the UN (and even NATO) limit American action. This increases the likelihood of future American unilateralism – one of Chirac's main concerns – since French actions at the UN eventually undercut the key U.S. 'multilateraliser', Secretary of State Colin Powell. Secondly, the realisation of a robust and unified European persona has been set back by the presumptuousness of Chirac and Schröder in seeking to speak on behalf of Europe during the crisis. The obstacles to the achievement of any meaningful (but necessary) European foreign and defence policy have once again been starkly revealed. In the final analysis, however, for France there is no realistic substitute for the EU and, for the majority of the EU at the present time, the consensus seems to be that there is no future whatsoever in a prolonged confrontation with the U.S. Thus even if, for some, France may have captured the moral high ground over Iraq, the wider ramifications may not, eventually, be to French liking.

Conclusion

Although it is difficult to draw any conclusive lessons about French exceptionalism in foreign and defence policy, this chapter has set out to identify certain traits of French policy which have traditionally been considered as indicative of the French exception. The articulation of a French 'distinctiveness' was aided, as we have seen, by the circumstances of the cold war. In more recent times, the nature of French exceptionalism has changed, and it is justifiable to talk of a gradual normalisation in the policy of the so-called 'exceptional partner' as external pressures for convergence grow. These external pressures can take various forms, ranging from changes in the international system itself after 1989, to economic imperatives and globalisation. This does not mean, however, that the accompanying rhetoric has changed as quickly and here, perhaps, we find that the nature of French exceptionalism today is to be located more in rhetoric than in substance. One reason for this may be found in the fact that the rhetoric that accompanies French activities is targeted towards a number of varied audiences. The domestic audience, for one, still arguably expects a particular framing of policy direction and choices. For others, in the U.S. and U.K. governments for example, the French role in the Iraq question may be perceived as yet another example of a French 'moment'. For others still, these 'moments' are what remains of a continuing exceptionalism.

PART III

Exceptionalism in French Culture, the Media and Sport

Chapter 10

PRESIDENTIAL DEBATES IN FRANCE: AN EXAMPLE OF AMERICANISATION?

Sheila Perry

The election of the president by universal suffrage was introduced in France by referendum in 1962; France held its first such election in 1965 and its first televised presidential debate in 1974. Televised debates became a regular feature of the second round of the presidential election until 2002, when the unprecedented success of the extreme right-wing candidate Jean-Marie Le Pen in getting through to the second round of voting led Jacques Chirac to refuse to take part. This chapter will examine the origins, format and interpretation of these debates, and compare these with similar debates held elsewhere, to establish to what extent and in what ways this is a distinctive feature of the French political scene. The chapter will then go on to determine whether the specificity of French debates justifies seeing them as an example of French exceptionalism.

The case for exceptionalism in this field is not promising, since France is clearly not unique in staging regular, televised debates as part of the campaign for important national elections. This is a practice France has shared not only with the U.S., the pioneer in the field, but with Australia and New Zealand, Canada, Israel and several of the new Latin American democracies, such as Mexico and Brazil. South Africa held its first such debate between Mandela and De Klerk in the first post-apartheid election in 1994, as a symbol of the arrival of democratic politics (Coleman 2000: 7). Nor, as this list shows, are these events confined to presidential regimes, notwithstanding the fact that in the U.K. they have frequently been rejected on the grounds that they are too personalised and unsuitable for a parliamentary democracy. Within Europe, for example, Sweden showed party leaders debating on television as early as the late 1950s, and West Germany held debates between the main party leaders in the Bundestag between 1972 and 1987, resumed in August 2002 with a head-to-head between Gerhard Schröder and Edmund Stoiber.

Furthermore, within France, politicians, media professionals and commentators have almost invariably invoked the precedent of the 1960 debates between Nixon and Kennedy as the inspiration for the French phenomenon, rather than make any claims to originality. This attribution of paternity to the U.S. is an element that France shares with most of the countries cited, which likewise see their own debates as an imitation of the American model – as early as 1976 U.S. debates were reportedly broadcast in ninety-one countries (Chaffee 1978: 345). However, reference to a single model can be misleading, because France has not imported the *format* of the debate, but rather the *idea* of the debate, and the symbol of democracy that it represents. That candidates should be required to defend their ideas simultaneously, and on an equal footing in a live broadcast, before the voting public, combines all the elements of true democracy – equality, fairness, transparency, accountability, comparability of candidates, etc. – it is unsurprising that such debates have been introduced in the newer democracies around the world. However, within the broad parameters of a live debate, any kind of format can be arranged, and in fact the French debates differ quite significantly from the American ones, as we shall show in the next section. A final section will compare French debates with those held in other countries of the world.

France and the U.S.

The French model for the format is, first of all, the *radios périphériques*. Television was seen to be lagging behind radio in the realm of politics and needed to introduce political debates to establish some legitimacy (Perry 1995: 115–16). Taking advantage of the new freedom accorded television by de Gaulle's decision to allow presidential candidates equal airtime for the 1965 election, television began debates between politicians in 1966 and regularised them from 1970–1973 with *A Armes Egales*, followed by *Les Trois Vérités* in 1973/4. During the 1974 presidential election campaign, there were radio debates between various candidates in the first round (Berne 1981: 85–86). It was these precedents that determined the format of the televised debate.

The most striking difference between the French and American debates is that the French debates are just that – debates, with direct interaction between the two participants in a head-to-head confrontation, whereas American debates are really joint press conferences, in which a panel of journalists puts questions to each of the politicians in turn. As the set designs show, the dynamics of the interaction are totally different: in France the two candidates sit opposite each other in direct confrontation, in the U.S. they face the journalists. In the French version, the function of the journalists is considerably reduced – indeed, in the first debate in 1974, they were merely timekeepers, ensuring an equal distribution of airtime. While they have been given marginally more freedom since, they are still only *animateurs*, facilitators, whose job it is to see that the main protagonists, the politicians, occupy centre stage in equal proportions. Their role is humble and minor, and deliberately so. In the U.S. on the other hand, the journalists lead the debate, devising questions to challenge the candidates; they are seated in front of the audience, a position which 'symbolises the competition between the political universe and the media universe for control of the public sphere' (Kaid et al. 1991: 280). In France, in contrast, the journalists take a back seat and are effaced; this has been quite literal in the debates since 1981, as cameras situated at the back of the stage framed the politicians at an angle that completely by-passed the journalists, seen only as new themes were introduced. American politicians address the journalists; French politicians address each other. As a result, American versions have been called 'counterfeit debates' (Bitzer and Rueter 1980), 'nondebates' (Salant 1979), and described as having a 'defective debate format' (Bitzer and Rueter 1980); Katz and Feldman (1968: 219) concluded their study of reactions to the debates with a recommendation that they should not be called debates at all.

In France, there can be no surprise or challenging questions from the journalists, as the themes of the debate are negotiated in advance by the politicians' campaign managers. The politicians come with their pre-prepared notes on each of the topics under discussion, and can develop their arguments at leisure – barring interruption and refutation by their opponents, of course – since they have twenty/thirty minutes on each theme, giving them up to ten/fifteen minutes each for their answers, and no time limit on any individual answer other than the overall time allotted to the theme, and French debates frequently surpass the scheduled time. This amounts to four or five themes per programme and contrasts sharply with the twelve or fourteen rounds of questioning on discrete themes which occur in American debates. American presidential hopefuls have to respond in a severely limited time span (this has varied, but is at most three minutes for an answer to an initial question, two minutes for a rebuttal, with similar times for a single follow-up question); they are not allowed to bring prepared notes, but can take notes during their opponent's answers in preparation for their counter-argument. American candidates are therefore engaged in an awkward two-way debate, in which they have to respond to questions put by the journalists, while at the same time taking account of the arguments presented by their political opponent. Bitzer and Rueter (1980: 194, 220) have argued that this is an almost impossible task in the allotted time. The same authors also criticised the format of the debates for the freedom it gives to journalists, who instead of merely asking questions, develop arguments of their own in lengthy preambles to the question. They estimated that in the 1976 debates, for example, the journalists occupied thirty-two minutes out of a total of ninety. The politicians cannot interrupt each other, or interject, but have to await their turn for rebuttal or refutation (Downs 1991: 191), by which time they frequently have another question to answer. The U.S. system has been criticised for its concentration on short-term, 'newsworthy now' subjects to the detriment of longer-term, wider issues, because of the domination by journalists with their own agenda (Bitzer and Rueter 1980: 223). With its more generous allocation of time, the French system presents an opportunity for rational argument. Kaid et al. (1991: 279) have asserted that there is a difference not only in the length of interventions, but in their substance: in France, they claim, politicians can adopt a more complicated logic, deal with subjects in more depth and provide more detailed supporting evidence than in the U.S.

French debates are therefore inspired by the American example of media democracy but introduced within French political culture and with its specificity. The difference in format reflects the different status of journalists in the U.S. and France, and greater deference towards politicians in the latter. Downs (1991: 192) refers to the hostility of the questions from the panelists and their refutation of politicians' responses in the American debates. The French journalist Véronique Brocard (1994: 57), on the other hand, asserts that in France it is considered bad manners to badger politicians with questions. The French system may allow more time for rational argument, but also for demagogy. French television channels are little more than 'public address systems' for the politicians, to use Salant's phrase (1979: 184); Salant, president of CBS, was not referring to French television, but arguing in favour of the role played by journalists within U.S. debates on the grounds that the media should *not* simply be a vehicle for politicians to address the public. In his opinion, the fact that politicians have a say in the choice of journalists or the camera shots allowed infringes basic journalistic principles, and he argues for greater journalistic freedom. In contrast, French journalists report the negotiations over the choice of journalists to participate in the debate with little or no comment (only Albert Du Roy has declared that he would refuse participation in a debate on the grounds that he is more than just a timekeeper). Political incursions into the production of the debates are seen as evidence of media neutrality: if both candidates are satisfied with the choice of journalists, the latter cannot be accused of complicity with one and antagonism towards the other.

It may appear from this lack of journalistic opposition that French politicians get a relatively easy ride in comparison with their American counterparts, but this is not so. They have to defend themselves in the face of counter-argument from the other candidate, and no one has more vested interest in destroying his adversary's credibility than the other politician. It is difficult to imagine any journalist delivering a more politically devastating blow than that dealt by Mitterrand in his 1988 debate with Chirac, in which he accused his prime minister of liberating Wahid Gordji, in spite of overwhelming evidence of his involvement in terrorist activities. Chirac's attempt to portray Mitterrand's tactics as an unworthy transgression of protocol (he had divulged a private conversation between president and prime minister) was a weak response, and when he challenged him to look him in the eye and contest his (Chirac's) version of events; Mitterrand did. Chirac rather lamely conceded the point on the grounds that he '[didn't] play poker' (Hayward 1989). French viewers sat and watched as the veneer of good relations which both men had displayed during their two years of *cohabitation* was publicly destroyed. This was supremely dramatic television. Indeed, in spite of the length of interventions in French debates, and the opportunities to develop sound, rational arguments, the moments that have gone down in French media history are the soundbites with which one of the candidates has demolished the other and come out the winner.

This brings us on to another major difference between French and American debates, and which has reinforced this tendency to draw a correlation between the perceived winner of the debate and the winner of the election in France. This is the timing of debates, their regularity. In France, debates were held in the second round of every presidential election without fail between 1974 and 1995, and so became ritualised; on the other hand, this means they have been held only every seven years, at a rate of one per election, totalling only four, which makes each one more momentous. In the U.S., after the first debates in 1960, there were none in 1964, 1968 or 1972 (Chaffee 1978: 343), the next one being held in 1976 and continuing regularly since then. However, there have been more of them: in addition to a shorter presidential term of office of four years (making seven elections since 1976), there are more debates per election, (between two and four presidential, plus vice-presidential debates). Each individual debate is therefore less important, and the format has been less ritualised in the U.S. There has also been a greater variety of political participants in the U.S., whereas in France, François Mitterrand took part in three of the four debates, twice with Giscard, and Chirac figured in two; Chirac's third was expected in 2002, and, had the first round results been as anticipated, he would have been pitted against Lionel Jospin for a second time. In particular, this ritualisation-cum-dramatisation of the debate in France has been reinforced by the fact that the first two debates were mirror-images of each other, both in terms of the perceived winner of the debate in each case and the outcome of the election. Debate number three then confirmed this view, with Mitterrand going on to win a second term of office after defeating Chirac in the debate described above. The Chirac-Jospin debate of 1995 had no clear winner, but was merely the exception that proved the rule: both protagonists were at great pains not to *lose* the debate, a tactic illustrative of the belief in its impact. Not only has the genre of the presidential debate been introduced in France via national political culture, it has also developed independently of external influence, each debate being determined by previous ones. This is only to be expected, given that earlier programmes are systematically viewed by politicians and their campaign teams in planning strategy, but the need for such an approach has been reinforced by the specificity of the French context, in which the debate is the culminating point of the election campaign, and where the correlation between the winner of the debate and the winner of the election has been firmly established.

Much could be said regarding this supposed correlation. Studies have shown (Cayrol 1988, for example) that the perceived winner is usually the person who was dominating the polls in the first place, which implies that, at best, the debate reinforces but does not change the fortunes of the contenders.[1] Belief in debates as decisive *was* imported from the U.S., as a result of the translation into French of Theodore White's book *The Making of a President*, which argued that television was the deciding influence in the 1960 election result. Katz and Feldman (1968: 205–13), studying the 1960 debates and White's arguments, show that there is little evidence of the effect of debates on voting decisions, but that if people are *asked*, they say, yes, it did influence them; the authors conclude that at most debates give viewers greater confidence in their voting choice. As Champagne (1989) has demonstrated, the belief in the influence of such debates can itself magnify the success for a candidate declared the winner. In a culture where the correlation between winner of the debate and winner of the election has repeatedly been made, it is hardly surprising that reviewers of the 1995 debate questioned whether it had been worth watching: in *Le Monde* (1995), for example, Agathe Logeart not only criticised it for its poor entertainment value, but also pitied the undecided voters whom she thought would be none the wiser. A debate without a winner apparently serves no useful purpose.

This brings us on to another point of difference. In France, attention of all commentators has been on the manipulative power of such debates. Politicians, more than anyone, subscribe to the myth of all-powerful media: nowhere is fear of media influence more evident than in the refusal to allow counter shots (views of the opponent while one candidate is speaking)[2] or audience reaction. Journalists have a vested interest in emphasising the impact of debates so as to achieve the viewing figures they need (see Ockrent 1988). Within academic circles, analysis and debate – already much scarcer than in the U.S.[3] – has focused on a critique of the dangers of manipulation by the media, and a deconstruction of media strategies. Controversy among researchers has focused on the respective validity of 'internal' or 'external' studies – analysing programmes as independent artefacts that produce meaning, or setting them in their sociological context (Champagne 1989) – but both sides concentrate on media production, what is on offer, as a means of assessing likely public responses (Legavre 1991).[4] In the U.S., on the other hand, the debate about the debates has been much less output-centred, and more viewer/voter-centred, and examined the usefulness of debates as a source of information (see for example Chaffee 1978; Miller and Mackuen 1979; Carlin 2000; Hall and Adasiewicz 2000). In fact, researchers in the U.S., led by Diana B. Carlin and aided by the Commission on Presidential Debates, have set up a viewer education programme called DebateWatch – including, *inter alia*, advice on *not* choosing a winner of the debate. This pragmatic approach recognises the usefulness of debates while also attempting to counter their more negative effects, and contrasts with the intellectual antagonism displayed in France, which has had little impact on the dramatisation of the debates by the press.

We can conclude from this comparison that in spite of its ready acceptance of American influence in this domain, France did not import the American model, but merely the notion of presidential debate; that this has been implemented and has functioned in ways that reveal marked differences between American and French political cultures, and that critical response, the debate about the debates, has been markedly different in the two countries. But does this French specificity equal French exceptionalism? For that, a wider comparison is necessary.

France and the world

In the previous section we observed that French debates differ from American ones in a number of respects, such that the French model can be characterised as follows: a head-to-head confrontation, in invariable, 'pure' debate format, with a tradition of a single programme per election between the two second-round contenders, and a strong correlation between the winner of the debate and the winner of the election. In this section we aim to show that while there may be many similarities in individual aspects of this model, none of the countries studied has the same *combination* of elements as does France.

Many countries, including parliamentary regimes, contrive to have head-to-head debates in spite of a multiparty system. One way to do this is to exclude minor party leaders: Australia (Ward and Walsh 2000) and, on occasions, New Zealand (H. Clark 2000) have used this method, and in this they are following in the footsteps of the U.S.[5] Another approach is to organise a series of debates: for example, in Canada, the three contenders in 1979 took part in two-way debates in three separate programmes, while in 1988 each programme consisted of a series of rotating debates between two of the three candidates (Amber 2000). France has resolved the problem of the fair treatment of all candidates by only holding these debates prior to the second round of voting, when only two candidates remain. Moreover, the confrontations held elsewhere differ from French debates in a number of aspects. Many have remained more faithful to the American model, with a strong element of journalist interview or press conference rather than a 'pure' confrontation between the respective politicians. This is true, for example, of Israel (Blum-Kulka and Liebes 2000) and Canada, while Australia has sometimes adopted a half-and-half debate and interview format, or else they have no set format or regular pattern (Australia and Canada). Yet more countries, including presidential regimes, broadcast debates with more than two participants: Mexico (Adler 1993, Domínguez and Poiré 1999), Brazil (Straubhaar et al. 1993), New Zealand, Canada, and Germany (Baker et al., 1981; Schoenbach 1987; Semetko and Schoenbach 1995). Prior to unification, West Germany held debates with the leaders of the four main parliamentary parties – on occasions this was a bipolar debate between government and opposition representatives, and included would-be chancellors (Baker and Norpoth 1981); as such they came closest to the French presidential model within Europe, but within a parliamentary regime. When in 2002 the Schröder-Stoiber debate adopted a fully presidential model, it reflected the American tradition, with the politicians standing at lecterns facing the journalists putting the questions. To date, moreover, German debates have not followed a set format, some consisting of journalist interviews with little interaction between candidates, others almost entirely a direct confrontation between politicians. Most of the countries cited have several debates per election and, where a two-round voting system exists, debates take place in both rounds, unlike in France. France does indeed appear unique in having translated its regime and voting system directly into a single, one-off confrontation as a culmination of the election campaign.

In France presidential debates have persistently run without viewer or audience participation (political programmes broadcast on French television in the first round have had elements of audience participation, but these programmes have taken the form of individual interviews and not debates). This lack of participation was also true of the U.S., but this changed in 1992 when undecided voters selected by Gallup asked the questions (Carlin 2000: 159). There has been audience participation in political debates in New Zealand and Canada, while Australia and New Zealand flirted briefly with the 'worm', an on-screen, instantaneous and dynamic measure of positive or negative response to the debaters – used in France only once, in 1985 in *Face à la Trois*, and never in a presidential election debate. Claude Estier (1995: 320) claims that he discovered a plot to use a 'worm' for the 1995 presidential election debate, but managed to stop it. The practice was abandoned in Australia on the grounds that it concentrated too much on the horse-race element, and has since been used only for the after-debate analysis, and not shown on screen (correspondence with Ian Ward). 'Worms' have been used in this way in Israel, and in the U.S. (Katz and Feldman 1968: 175). All countries use immediate pre- and post-debate polls to determine a winner – in 1984, Australia even used hired judges to adjudicate the debate (Ward and Walsh 2000: 54) – but the correlation made in France between the winner of the debate and the winner of the election has been less sure elsewhere for a number of reasons: because the number of debates meant that there was not necessarily one overall winner, or because there has been no consensus over who won, or because the winner of the debate did not always turn out to be the winner of the election. In this, also, France has proved distinctive.

One feature shared by debates in all countries is that it is ultimately the politicians who are in control, irrespective of the existence of independent bodies designed to see fair play. These bodies have no powers, and merely act as arbiters between the negotiating participants – politicians and media – but they determine little beyond the rule, accepted by all, that airtime should be equal. In France, the regulatory body, the Conseil Supérieur de l'Audiovisuel (CSA) is not officially responsible for the debate, and operates only by invitation; the debate is run under the same rules of equality as the official campaign broadcasts, but this is by custom and practice, not from any written law – unlike the rest of the campaign (CSA 1995: 46, 47). Everything else, from the colour of the carpet to the agenda, is determined by the media professionals and the politicians, and the politicians have the last say. French politicians even have their own chosen directors who determine which camera shots will be used when their candidate is speaking. Media professionals agree to this as the price they have to pay in order to be sure of broadcasting the event. For, ultimately, nowhere in the world is there a legal obligation for politicians to participate, and they can, and do, refuse.

The reason there were no debates in Germany between 1987 and 2002 was that Kohl persistently refused to participate (Semetko and Schoenbach 2000). The absence of a presidential-style debate in countries such as the U.K. is really because of this political expediency factor – there has never, so far, been an occasion on which two party leaders have both simultaneously seen it as being in their interest to participate, and so agreement has never been reached (Mitchell 2000). This is also the reason there has never been a first-round debate in France: besides all other considerations, a debate implies equality between participants, and few candidates will confer such legitimacy on adversaries. Similarly, Berlusconi refused a debate in the 2000 Italian election, as he claimed his opponent Francesco Rutelli was 'not worthy' (*New York Times*, 11 May 2001), while the one refusal in the second round in France – Chirac's in 2002 – was justified on the grounds of Le Pen's unworthiness, and possible because Chirac, certain to win the election without a debate, but by no means certain to win the debate, had nothing to gain, and much to lose, politically speaking, by agreeing to participate. Politicians may succumb to pressure to take part, but that pressure is political and not legal. However, in France it has been strong and persistent, and it may be that the ritualisation and dramatisation of the event in France has made the pressure particularly difficult to resist. Against such a tradition, only the exceptional circumstances of an extreme right-wing candidate winning through to the second round prevented a return engagement between Chirac and Jospin in 2002. Interestingly enough, this unexpected turn of events has created the only other circumstances that might provide sufficient counterpoint to the tradition: a second round in 2007 in which there may be no incumbent president – this was the factor which made the first debate possible in 1974 (Cotteret et al. 1976: 29) – and no previous participant, since both Chirac *and* Jospin are likely to be out of the frame.[6] Assuming this to be the case, neither of the second-round candidates in 2007 will have been in a previous presidential debate, and so both might feel freer than their precursors to avoid this hurdle – unless, of course, it is to their political advantage. If there *is* a debate in 2007, there may be attempts to vary the format: in spite of there being 20 percent of voters who were still undecided on the eve of the 1995 debate, viewing figures dropped to 16.7 million (from 25–30 million for previous debates),[7] and the debate was seen as a non-event, so television channels may wish to add new elements to rekindle viewer interest. Whether the politicians concerned will agree to this remains to be seen, but the 2002 hiatus, and the potential for new candidates, make this more possible than has hitherto been the case.

Conclusion

In conclusion, France is quite distinctive in the way in which between 1974 and 1995 debates became institutionalised in the political system, *and shares less similarity to the U.S. in this regard than many other countries.* Indeed, rather than an example of the Americanisation of French politics, a term usually used to designate something alien, even threatening to French culture (and resulting from American hegemony),[8] it is the suitability of the presidential debate to home-grown French political institutions that has led to its establishment as an integral feature. In France, the presidential election is 'the focal point of the regime' (Elgie 1999: 67) and its introduction led to 'powerful bipolarisation effects' in the political system (Bréchon 2002: 13). More specifically – since France's multiparty system makes an absolute majority unlikely for a first-round candidate – it is the existence of a second round of voting which institutionalises the bipolarisation process and confers on the winner of the election a legitimacy unsurpassed elsewhere in the electoral process. The televised debate, which takes place between the two surviving candidates in the second round, has been organised to epitomise this bipolarisation. It is a dramatic embodiment of political conflict, but in keeping with traditional French journalistic style, the confrontation takes place between two politicians, and not between the media and the political class.

However, while France has adapted American-style debates to suit its own needs, to talk of exceptionalism in this context would imply that all other countries share a common pattern and this is clearly far from the case: not only is there no commonality between countries, there is very little between debates broadcast within a given country. Presidential debates reflect the specificity of French political culture, but in this regard they are similar to debates elsewhere, since all nations have adapted the American model to suit their own specific needs. France is distinctive in this domain, but so is Australia, Mexico, Germany, etc., each in its own way and for reasons relating its own national traditions. However, other countries have generally adopted varying strategies according to changing circumstances, whereas France has stood out in the persistence of the same model. In that sense, France is unique among the countries studied here.

The notion of exceptionalism has therefore been a useful tool in enabling us to establish in what precise ways France differs from many other countries, even in an area in which the French themselves have made no particular claims to originality. However, the events of 2002 have shown the danger inherent in seeing what may be a conjunctural difference as something more permanent and fundamental to 'the French way of doing things'. Prior to 2002, the debate became an integral part of French political institutions; it mapped so well onto them that the presidential election and the debate appeared inseparable, and the debate unavoidable. Although it took exceptional and unforeseen circumstances to bring about change, the election of 2002 showed that even in France this symbiosis was conditional on other criteria being met, and that the one factor that all countries share in this domain, the power of the politicians to choose in their own interest, can, in certain circumstances, override national traditions. This illustrates that the long view is fundamental to a definition of exceptionalism, and the extent to which France will retain its distinctiveness depends on whether the absence of a debate in the 2002 presidential election will prove to have been a hiatus, or the end of an era.

Notes

1. Schrott (1990) argues the opposite in the case of Germany.
2. This restriction was introduced in 1981 on Mitterrand's insistence.
3. Katz and Feldman (1968: 173) located thirty-one independent studies of public response to the Kennedy-Nixon debates.
4. Cayrol (1988) is an exception, but his analysis was published in the U.S. See also studies on Germany: Noelle-Neumann (1978); Norpoth and Baker (1980).
5. In the U.S., debates became possible only with the involvement of the League of Women Voters, which, as an independent body, was exempt from the provisions of Section 315.

This stipulates that networks cannot undertake debates unless all candidates are involved (a practical impossibility due to the huge numbers of candidates). Since 1988 debates have been overseen by the Commission on Presidential Debates.

6. Both could be eligible to stand again if they so desired, but Jospin resigned from politics immediately after his first-round defeat, and any attempt at a come-back would need Socialist Party endorsement; Chirac might be tempting fate to go for a third mandate, given his previous failures, his poor performance for an out-going president in the first round in 2002, and potential accusations that he is seeking to stay in office to avoid corruption charges in the courts.

7. These figures are even more striking when one bears in mind that in 1974 30 million was the size of the electorate, compared with 40 million in 1995.

8. See Kuhn in chapter 12.

Chapter 11

The Myth of Exceptionalism? French Television in a West European Context

Raymond Kuhn

In the early summer of 2001 the French terrestrial television channel M6 broadcast a programme that attracted large audience ratings, especially among young viewers. *Loft Story* was the French version of *Big Brother*, the reality show which had originated in the Netherlands, and the format for which had then been imported into the U.K. to become one of the most talked about programmes of 2000. M6 had taken a proven format, tweaked it for its domestic market and then sat back to watch the rise in audience figures, which was helped no doubt by the attendant blaze of controversial media publicity (*Le Monde*, 4 May 2001). France, one of the self-appointed defenders of high cultural values in Western European broadcasting, had apparently capitulated to join the ranks of those who showed no respect for programme standards. At least, this was one way in which newspaper stories about the screening of the programme were framed, influenced in part by the views of television executives such as Patrick Le Lay, head of TF1, who had a vested interest in venting their spleen on the output of a competitor channel (Le Lay 2001).

It is tempting to use the *Loft Story* controversy to illustrate the contemporary alignment of French television with that of its Western European neighbours and, further, to bemoan the loss of national exceptionalism which such a development seems to exemplify. Where are the audiovisual snows of yesteryear? Yet before one rushes to pass such a judgement, it is sensible to pause and ask two related questions. First, was French television ever especially exceptional? Second, is it unexceptional now? This chapter seeks to address these two questions. More particularly, the chapter examines and assesses the validity of the concept of exceptionalism as applied to French television past and present, using a Western European context for cross-national comparative purposes. The chapter's central argument is that while French television has exhibited and continues to manifest certain elements of difference and even distinctiveness, in several key respects it fits quite neatly into the dominant Western European paradigm of the relevant time period. In short, to a significant extent the development of television in France from its origins to the present day can be satisfactorily regarded as a national variant of wider Western European trends, rather than a special case apart.

The chapter is organised in two main sections. The first raises some conceptual and methodological issues concerning both the idea of exceptionalism and the limits of the analysis undertaken in this chapter. The second contains the core empirical material and is divided into three successive chronological periods that together cover the evolution of television in both Western Europe and France from 1945 to the present day. These three time periods are distinguished by certain features related to the organisation and functioning of the medium: the first is marked by the dominance of public service values and institutions (from 1945 to the late 1970s); the second is characterised by the creation of a competitive market (from the late 1970s to the mid-1990s); the third has been profoundly affected by the dual impact of digital convergence and transnationalisation (from the mid-1990s to the present day).

Conceptual and methodological issues

It is essential at the outset to define and operationalise the concept of exceptionalism which lies at the heart of our analysis. In particular, it is important to try to distinguish between the related and overlapping ideas of difference, distinctiveness, specificity and exceptionalism. For instance, to uphold France's claim to exceptional status it is necessary but not sufficient to establish that, by whatever criteria selected, the French case is different to or distinct from that of other individual countries in the relevant peer group. In addition, one must be able to separate the French experience on the one hand from that of the rest of the group collectively on the other: the other countries have to share certain features in common to the (self-)exclusion of France, thus setting the latter apart from the rest of the group as a whole.[1] Furthermore, any reflection on the possible end of French exceptionalism inevitably involves some sort of historical perspective.

This chapter, therefore, uses a two-dimensional matrix. The first dimension is cross-national. Along this dimension comparisons can be drawn between selected features of French television at any given moment and those of the other members of the relevant comparator group – in this case, the television systems of other Western European countries. To have methodological validity such a cross-national approach should be as inclusive and broad-ranging as possible. It certainly cannot be confined to a simple bilateral comparison. A Franco-British study, for instance, may demonstrate important differences between systems in the two countries, but by definition it can tell us nothing about the exceptionalism of either (Scriven and Lecomte 1999). The second dimension is temporal. Along this dimension elements of change and continuity within any Western European televison system, including that of France, can be examined over a specified period of time.

In the context of this chapter, it is important to emphasise that neither dimension has sufficient explanatory value on its own. A cross-national dimension without a temporal focus can indicate only the extent to which French television is, or is not, exceptional at a particular moment. Such an approach has nothing to say about the dynamic nature of the claim to exceptionalism – how this may have changed over time. Conversely, a temporal dimension without a cross-national framework can point to elements of change and continuity within the French television system, but can tell us nothing about its relative exceptionalist qualities, if any.

The importance of these conceptual and methodological concerns can be illustrated by considering the following four hypotheses. While it is quite possible that all of these hypotheses are valid, none of them on its own sheds any light on the question of French exceptionalism within a Western European context.

1. *Contemporary French television is significantly different from what it was forty or even twenty years ago.* This is manifestly true. However, such a statement tells us nothing about the exceptionalist status of French television past or present.
2. *French television is less nationally specific now than at some period in the past.* This may well be the case in certain respects, though equally this view should not be overstated. However, inasmuch as such an assessment might well apply with equal force to other national television systems in Western Europe, such an assertion cannot of itself support any claims to French exceptionalism.
3. *In the past national televisions systems across Western Europe were different from each other in several important respects.* This may be true, although it probably underestimates historic elements of cross-national commonality. In any event, however, to the extent that these systems were all different from each other, France was not an exception.
4. *National television systems across Western Europe now share many features in common.* Again, this hypothesis may well be valid, though it probably underestimates contemporary elements of cross-national difference. However, inasmuch as this is a general trend affecting these national television systems, once again France has no particular claim to exceptional status.

As well as these conceptual considerations, it is important to recognise the methodological limits of the analysis undertaken here. First, the chapter takes a macro level approach that concentrates on certain broad features of French and Western European television over a period of more than half a century. Such an approach means that micro level examples of possible French exceptionalism may inevitably be passed over: for instance, the representation of minority identities in programming (Scriven and Roberts 2003). Our contention is that even if any such examples of exceptionalist French practice can be shown to have existed in the past or to be present now, these do not significantly undermine the macro level validity of the central argument of this chapter. Second, we recognise that academic research on the subject of television embraces many different aspects of the medium, including *inter alia* structure, production, form, content, genres, distribution, reception and effects. It is quite possible that French television in a Western European context may have been and/or may be more or less exceptional depending on the aspect considered. Third, it is clear that there exists a wide range of disciplinary approaches to the study of television within academe. Television is a technology of communication, an economic good, a means of information, a medium of entertainment and a major production industry. As such, it continues to be studied by electronic engineers, economists, political scientists, cultural theorists and organisational sociologists among others. All of these bring their own discipline-based perspective to their research projects. If one puts these three caveats together, it is evident that it is foolhardy to affirm that over such a long time period no aspect of French television past or present can be considered as exceptional in a Western European context. The argument of this chapter is more modest in its claim that with regard to certain key macro level features the case for French exceptionalism is difficult to substantiate.

What then are these features? The cross-national comparative framework used in the second part of this chapter is loosely based on a general set of variables outlined by Denis McQuail in the most recent edition of his book on mass communication theory (2000: 210–211). McQuail proposes five variables of media system difference:

- scale and centralisation
- degree of politicisation
- diversity profile
- sources of finance
- degree of public regulation and control

Two points need to be made about these variables in the context of this chapter. First, while McQuail is concerned with differences across media systems as a whole, in this chapter we are concerned with only one medium

– that of television. Second, the variables are used here not so much in the form of a prescriptive checklist but more as a prompt for heuristic inquiry. The confines of this chapter do not allow us to test all the variables in a rigorously systematic cross-national comparison over our three time periods. Their usage, however, is sufficient to enable us to make a reasonable test of the French exceptionalist hypothesis at a high level of generality.

Three ages of television

This section is organised in terms of three ages of television in both Western Europe in general and France in particular. Each era is characterised by the prevalence of particular structural and operational features. In practice, of course, the boundaries between these different time periods are fluid rather than rigid. This applies both within the context of any one national television system and, *a fortiori*, across different Western European systems brought together for the purpose of cross-national comparison. In particular, due allowance always needs to be made for national particularities. Moreover, rather in the manner of geological strata, institutions and practices from a previous age sometimes survive the transition into the succeeding time period. For instance, the BBC can be found playing an important, but rather different, role in all three ages of television in Britain. Nonetheless, while national and cross-national changes across the different variables have not been precisely synchronous, there are good reasons for analysing and explaining developments in French and Western European television in terms of the three ages analysed below.

The first age: the dominance of public service values and institutions

The first age of television refers to the period dating from the advent of television as a mass medium after the end of the Second World War up to roughly the end of the 1970s. Across Western Europe this first age was characterised by the domination of the medium by large public service broadcasting institutions such as the BBC in Britain, the ARD in West Germany and the RAI in Italy (Brants and De Bens 2000). In the French context the symbol of this first age of television was the state broadcasting service, the RTF (1949–64) and its successor the ORTF (1964–74).

During this period the medium was usually organised as a state monopoly, especially in its formative years. Responsibility for production, programming and transmission rested with a single integrated public broadcaster, which enjoyed considerable in-house production facilities for programme genres such as light entertainment and fiction. The organisation of the medium was geographically highly centralised, with most facilities based in or around the national capital. Political control over news content by government or leading political parties was a feature of several countries, as was a certain deference on the part of television journalists to political elites.

This first age was marked by spectrum scarcity, with the result that the supply of television was severely limited. Not only was the number of channels highly restricted, but each national system grew slowly and incrementally with roughly one additional channel coming on stream every decade or so. By the late 1970s, several Western European countries had a maximum of only three nationwide television networks in operation. These channels tended to be generalist in their scheduling policy, combining news, sport, drama, documentaries, quiz programmes and variety shows in their schedules. Television began as a medium for evening viewing and only gradually extended its schedules to the afternoon. The overall amount of television broadcast annually was tiny by contemporary standards. In most countries television was predominantly or solely funded through the licence-fee, which was effectively a flat-rate tax set by the government, the proceeds of which went to the public service broadcaster.

Political authorities in the form of the government or leading political parties played a major role in the organisation and regulation of the medium. Commercial interests were largely excluded from running channels or their influence mitigated through the application of detailed content regulation. Such regulation had public service values at its core (Blumler 1992). In this context television was widely regarded as a means for the dissemination of national cultural artefacts, as a medium that brought the nation together in an act of viewing solidarity and as a pedagogic device through which knowledge could be imparted and audiences educated and informed. Programme content was predominantly, though not exclusively, national – not only produced in the country but also tailored to meet the tastes of the domestic audience. This audience was of necessity targeted by programme schedulers as a largely undifferentiated mass.

The development of French television during this first age fits this Western European paradigm in many, indeed most, respects. French television remained a state monopoly throughout this period. The (O)RTF was a public broadcasting organisation that by the early 1970s managed three television networks and a large production division. Although a regional channel was established in 1972/3, much of its output, with the exception of regional news programmes, was dictated from the channel's headquarters in Paris. Tight political control over news content was exercised through the Ministry of Information, which during the de Gaulle presidency (1958–69) was a powerful symbol of the government's control of television (Bourdon 1990; Chalaby 2002). The output of French television increased very gradually during this first age, whether measured by the number of channels or the length of programme schedules. While advertising was introduced into the system in 1968, tight upper limits on the amount it could contribute to television revenues ensured that it did not drive scheduling policy. The licence fee remained the main source of finance.

Especially following the creation of the Fifth Republic in 1958, which coincided with the take-off of television as a truly mass medium in France, the government was the single most important actor influencing the medium's evolution. Television was regarded by ministers such as Malraux as a vehicle for disseminating French high culture to a mass audience. Gaullist sympathisers occupied the top managerial and editorial positions in a bid to ensure not just television's political allegiance, but also its administrative efficiency. Commercial interests were kept at a distance, and plans to launch a commercial channel met with stauch political opposition not just from Gaullists, but also from Socialists and Communists. The centre-right Giscardians were more sympathetic to the establishment of a commercial channel, but President Giscard d'Estaing lacked the necessary parliamentary majority during his septennate (1974–81) (Kuhn 1995). Government-inspired regulation underpinned programming policy.

During this first age of television France was certainly exceptional by some criteria. For example, during the 1960s its adoption of the Secam rather than Pal transmission standard for reasons of Gaullist-inspired national prestige made France unique among major Western European broadcasters of the time. Yet in other respects, French television not only conformed to the essential features of the dominant public service paradigm but did so more clearly than the broadcasting systems of some other countries. In the U.K., for example, the BBC lost its monopoly in television programming in 1954/5 with the introduction of the advertising-funded ITV, even if both broadcasters remained subject to public service regulation (Negrine 1994). In West Germany responsibility for the organisation of television was decentralised to the level of the regional states by the federal government's Basic Law (Humphreys 1994). Because of its own peculiar geopolitical status, Luxembourg never had a public service broadcaster, while the Netherlands chose to adopt a pluralistic television system in which different currents in Dutch society (such as Catholic, Protestant, Liberal and Socialist) each had responsibility for the management of its own television channel (Brants 1985). In short, French television during this first age was in many ways part of the mainstream in Western European broadcasting, while in contrast some other national systems often appeared more distinctive and even exceptional.

The second age: the creation of a competitive market

The second age of television covers the period from the end of the 1970s up to the middle of the 1990s. Across Western Europe this second age was characterised by a significant expansion in the supply of terrestrial television, the arrival of commercial competition in the form of privately owned channels and the spread of new programme delivery systems such as cable and satellite. State monopolies were abolished and public broadcasters exposed to competitive markets. In the French context the symbol of this second age of television was the privatised national channel, TF1.

During this period spectrum scarcity arguments began to lose their force. The supply of television programming was considerably increased, as a result of, first, an expansion in the number of channels distributed free-to-air and via cable/satellite systems and, second, a lengthening of schedules to include previous no-go areas such as breakfast and all-night programming. On the demand side, however, many sections of the audience continued to receive a limited number of terrestrial channels and only marginally increased their weekly consumption of television content. Commercial interests entered the market, owning and running television channels for the first time. Large-scale public service broadcasting organisations lost their previously guaranteed audience share. In responding to the new market conditions, established public broadcasters reformed their management practices, for example through internal marketisation, and hived off some of their functions, for instance by outsourcing some of their programme production to external independent companies. In several countries regional television channels became more important, reflecting a growing sociopolitical awareness of the importance of regional identity (Garitaonandia 1993).

Political control had to adapt to the changed environment, becoming more nuanced in at least two ways. First, with regard to the general functioning of the medium, the abolition of public monopolies meant that the state moved from an ownership to a regulatory role, defining a new relationship with the medium of television in the changed market conditions. Content regulation was reviewed and in general lightened in what some commentators described as a process of deregulation (Dahlgren 2000). Some state functions previously exercised directly by government ministries were now delegated to (quasi-)independent regulatory authorities. However, the state continued to play a powerful role with regard to the public television sector via control of key appointments, finance and regulation. Second, in terms of news management political elites tended to move away from heavy-handed direct mechanisms of control such as ministerial ukase towards more indirect means of pressure, for example via the appointment of sympathetic editorial staff. There was a marked decline in deference on the part of television towards the political class generally, as demonstrated through challenging interviews of politicians, investigative journalism and political satire programmes.

This period witnessed the gradual emergence of niche channels, catering for specific sections of the audience either in terms of sociological characteristics (such as age, gender and ethnic identity) or programming interests (including films, sport and news). For example, music channels aimed at young viewers made an appearance, with MTV entering the European market in 1987 (Papathanassopoulos 2002: 214–26). The audience was no longer regarded as an undifferentiated mass. With some notable exceptions, such as major sporting events, this period saw the beginning of the end of television as a national unifier in terms of the nation gathering together simultaneously to watch the same event. Commercial advertising became widely accepted as an integral means of funding television, while licence fee revenue for public service broadcasters plateaued, after a temporary boost provided by the switch-over to colour sets.

In this new television landscape public service values came under attack from a combined technological, ideological and economic offensive. The idea that television was above all a medium for entertainment became more rooted, while the notion of television as a public good was challenged in media policy debates. Entertainment values not only pushed 'serious' genres such as current affairs programming to the edge of programme schedules, but also infiltrated non-entertainment genres such as news programmes. A degree of convergence between public and private values in television output was evident, frequently, though not exclusively, on the latter's terms. There was a tendency for cultural output in the sense of 'high culture' to become ghettoised both in non-prime time slots on generalist channels and in specialist niche channels. A lot of television content remained domestically produced. However, boundaries between national television systems were becoming more permeable as national television channels opened up to foreign ownership holdings and imported product.

The development of French television during this second age largely fits this Western European paradigm. The state monopoly was abolished in 1982. Eight years previously, the ORTF had been dismantled and three separate television companies – TF1, Antenne 2 and FR3 – established (Bachmann 1997). The abolition of the ORTF at the start of the Giscard d'Estaing presidency resulted in the disintegration of the previously unifed public broadcaster, with transmission, programming and production services reallocated to separate, functionally independent companies. In the French case the period from 1974 to 1982 can thus be seen as a transitional stage from the first to the second age of television. Greater competition was introduced between television channels for audiences and revenue, while advertising became a more important source of finance for the two main national television networks. Yet at the same time during the

Giscard d'Estaing septennate the state refused fully to embrace marketisation and allow a television channel to be run by the private sector.

This situation changed after the 1982 Socialist reform. First, the pay-tv service, Canal+, was set up in 1984, winning subscribers with its mix of films and sports coverage. Then in 1985/6 two free-to-air commercial channels, La Cinq and TV6 (later renamed M6), were set up in the dying days of the Socialist government (Chamard and Kieffer 1992). Finally, and most spectacularly, in 1986/7 the incoming conservative government led by Jacques Chirac introduced its own reform which resulted in the privatisation of the most important public channel, TF1 (*Le Monde dossiers et documents* 1988). In addition, during the 1980s and 1990s cable television became increasingly available, especially in urban areas. The take-up rate for cable was low by the standards of Germany, the Netherlands and Scandinavia, higher than in Italy and Spain, and by the end of the twentieth century roughly on a par with the U.K. at around 10 percent of all households.

The regulatory environment of French television also altered significantly during this second age. Regulatory authorities were set up by government and given responsibility for top appointments in public television and for the allocation of commercial franchises (Franceschini 1995). This marked a shift away from the direct links between government and television which had been such a prominent feature of the first age. However, years of political interference in the medium did not disappear overnight. First, the regulatory authorities were frequently regarded, especially by the political opposition, as being largely subservient to the executive or a mere cipher. Thus, the Haute Autorité de la Communication Audiovisuelle set up by the Socialists in 1982 was replaced by the Commission Nationale de la Communication et des Libertés when the right came to power in 1986 (Chauvau 1997). The CNCL was in turn abolished by the incoming Socialist government and a new authority, the Conseil Supérieur de l'Audiovisuel, set up in 1989. Second, appointments to the regulatory authorities were frequently guided by party political considerations.

While television output remained heavily regulated, especially for the remaining public channels, the need to attract audiences and advertising revenue was a major driver for television companies. In the case of La Cinq the tension between regulatory compliance and commercial imperatives was not satisfactorily resolved, and the channel went out of service in 1992 (Perry 1997). After the privatisation of TF1 the balance between private and public sectors tilted dramatically in favour of the former. For much of the 1990s the public television channels, now grouped together under the banner of France-Télévision, appeared to stagger from crisis to crisis. With its emphasis on entertainment programming TF1 dominated free-to-air television in terms of audience ratings, while its owner scorned the idea that the channel should be a vehicle for cultural output. As a result, public service values informed only the public sector tranche of what had become a highly competitive television system. The creation of a Franco-German cultural channel, Arte, may have represented an against-the-tide victory for public service values during this period, but its audience figures remained disappointingly low.

The major shareholdings in private television held by industrial companies such as Bouygues (TF1) and Suez (M6) distinguished the French case from its Western European counterparts (Vulser 2002). In addition, the creation of the pay-tv channel Canal+ and the privatisation of the public television company TF1 appeared to mark France out as exceptional during this second age. However, Canal+ was distinctive from other pay services mainly because it used a terrestrial rather than cable or satellite platform, while the change in the status of TF1 went with – rather than against – the grain of the marketisation of television in Western Europe.

In any case it could be argued that in some respects other countries were just as or even more exceptional than France. Italy, for example, was not only the first major national system to break with the public service tradition, but throughout the 1980s also had a totally deregulated private sector dominated by Silvio Berlusconi's networks (Sassoon 1985). Thanks to a highly successful cable policy Germany moved from restricted public service provision to a multi-channel system in a relatively short space of time. Conversely, other Western European countries avoided the radical systemic changes which affected France, Italy, Germany and others. In Britain, for example, the main terrestrial innovation of this period was the creation of Channel 4 in the early 1980s (Goodwin 1998). Particularly in its early years Channel 4 represented an extension of public service television, not a competitive threat to it. Channel 5 belatedly came on air as the second age was already coming to an end, while in audience terms the challenge from satellite services to the established terrestrial broadcasters in Britain increased only gradually during the 1990s.

The third age: the era of digital convergence and transnationalisation

The third age of television began in the late 1990s and continues to the present day. Across Western Europe this third age is characterised by the transition from analogue to digital technology, the globalisation of communication and information flows, and the market power of vertically integrated, multimedia companies operating on a transnational basis and sometimes forming interlocking alliances with internet providers in an attempt to control both media content and distribution. In the French context the symbol of this third age of television is the Canal+ group and its parent communications conglomerate Vivendi Universal.

Two developments in particular have changed the configuration of the television landscape in the third age. The first is technological convergence. Digitisation has massively increased the number of television channels available to audiences, giving a new impetus to the distribution of multi-channel television to Western European households. By increasing the number and range of specialist channels aimed at particular niche markets, the spread of digital television further segments broadcasting supply and fragments national audiences (Murdock 2000). More importantly, by radically altering the ways in which information is reproduced, stored and transmitted, digital technology removes the barriers between the previously discrete communication sectors of broadcasting, telecommunications and information technology and allows the same product to be delivered through a range of different conduits (van Cuilenburg and Slaa 1993).

Technological convergence has had consequences for economic markets and regulatory policies. In facilitating the movement of economic actors across previously distinct communication and media sectors, convergence has encouraged global corporate mergers and strategic alliances, none more impressive than that between the U.S. media conglomerate Time-Warner and the internet provider AOL at the start of 2000. Convergence has also helped change the regulatory landscape by undermining sector specific regulations, bringing on to the policy agenda at national and supranational levels the possibility of a more integrated regulatory framework running across the communications media as a whole. In short, technological convergence has led to both economic and, to a lesser degree, regulatory convergence (Robillard 1999).

The second principal characteristic of the third age is its increasingly transnational character – the declining importance of national boundaries in the structures, functioning and regulation of television in Western Europe. The transnationalisation of television is frequently discussed in the context of globalisation, whereby economic and communication systems have become more interdependent on a worldwide scale. It is certainly true that the major international players in contemporary television, such as Rupert Murdoch's News Corporation, increasingly operate as global players. Meanwhile, satellite technology has undermined the capacity of any nation-state to control television content flows, several television channels are available in similar multi-channel packages in different countries, the same programmes are imported, often from the United States, to fill ever expanding schedules and successful formats across a range of genres (*Big Brother, Who Wants to be a Millionaire, The Weakest Link*) easily travel across national frontiers. Yet some commentators have emphasised the capacity of audiences to respond differently to the same transnational media product because of well-implanted local/national cultural norms and practices (Tomlinson 1999). As a result, for commercial reasons, transnational media firms frequently take account of the tastes and preferences of local audiences in adapting their product for consumption in particular national and subnational markets – hence the twin-track concept of 'glocalisation': the fusion of global and local.

In the third age of television it is evident that developments in France cannot be isolated from wider European and global trends. At the turn of the century, about 25 percent of households had access to digital television, and France was the leading country in Western Europe in the field of digital satellite services (Sergeant 2000: 242). In terms of consumer demand, the transition from analogue to digital in France was well in line with general Western European trends. The introduction of a digital terrestrial platform – scheduled for 2004/5 – will further push French television firmly into the third age.

One response by French elites to the transnationalisation of television has been to protect and promote national players in domestic and international markets respectively. In external markets French authorities have long been keen to ensure that a national company has the status and power to be a major player at the European and global levels. The Gaullist model of the state 'picking winners' by giving its backing to a preselected national champion is no longer considered appropriate. Nonetheless, so as to encourage the formation of strong French-owned media companies, the state ensures that France remains a relatively protected market. In particular, regulations limit ownership shares held by foreigners from outside of the European Union to a maximum 20 percent of the capital of French language free-to-air television channels (Regourd 2001: 200–1). This contrasts sharply with the provisions of the 2003 Communications Act in Britain, which opens up the possibility of a American media giant taking over a major commercial terrestrial franchise such as ITV.

The Vivendi communications and utilities conglomerate has in recent years been the principal flagbearer of French hopes in international media markets. Its purchase of the North American group Seagram in 2000 confirmed its status as a global media conglomerate, symbolised in the change of name to Vivendi Universal. At the height of its market power, when it was being written up as a potential European rival to AOL-Time Warner, Vivendi Universal had shares in the following media-related sectors: telecommunications (Cegetel, SRF), the music industry (Universal Music), cinema (Universal Studios), publishing (VUP), the internet (Vizzavi) and television (Canal+ group). The serious financial problems encountered by Vivendi Universal in 2002, however, made it necessary for the group to relinquish many of its assets and seriously revise its corporate strategy (Johnson and Orange 2003). Ironically, the value of AOL-Time Warner also plummeted from 350 billion dollars in January 2000 to around 50 billion by the summer of 2002, in a stark reminder of the uncertain benefits of economic convergence as media and internet shares took a pounding on international stock markets. The Canal+ group, owned by Vivendi Universal, has long had vertically integrated interests along the value chain of production, programming and distribution, as well as owning a stake in Paris-Saint-Germain football club and being involved in a number of television holdings outside France, including Italy and Spain (Buob and Mérigeau 2001). The financial problems of Vivendi Universal caused a crisis at the Canal+ group in 2002, involving the emotional dismissal of the chairman, Pierre Lescure, and the subsequent sale of the company's shares in the Italian pay-tv channel Telepiù. Yet even traversing a period of corporate crisis, Canal+ did not represent a French exception. With the collapse of the Kirch media empire in Germany and the liquidation of ITVDigital in the U.K., the Canal+ group was only one of various television ventures across Western Europe to run into financial difficulties at this time.

With regard to media content, French authorities have tried to mitigate what they regard as some of the more undesirable consequences of more open television markets by supporting French productions at both national and supranational levels. For instance, content regulation has long been used to protect domestic television programme production, especially in key areas such as drama and fiction. Moreover, the French authorities have actively used the supranational arena of European institutional decision-making to support quotas for European productions on television channels across the European Union as a whole (Collins 1994; Levy 1999).

This regulatory activity is partly driven by *economic* considerations as the French government seeks to maintain employment in the country's media production industries. However, among Western European states the French authorities have long been in the vanguard of those making a strong *cultural* case for protectionist measures in the broadcasting and audiovisual fields. This has been particularly evident in the various moves to defend the French cinema industry as a 'cultural exception' in the face of what French elites have presented as the global dominance of Hollywood (Harris 2000). In the light of the close links between the cinema and television industries in France – for example, through the film production wing of Canal+ and the aid to the cinema industry provided by the main channels – television content is also implicated in this debate. Back in the 1980s, Jack Lang, the Minister of Culture under President Mitterrand, warned of the dangers of 'Coca Cola satellites' undermining the integrity of the national culture, while the perceived threat of the 'Americanisation' of French culture has been a constant theme in political rhetoric since the de Gaulle presidency (Regourd 2002).

It is perhaps here in the defence of its cultural heritage that France might be expected to be most exceptional in the Western European context. Certainly French television does at times act as a medium for the discussion and expression of a certain French 'high culture' in public sector channel programmes such as *Bouillon de culture* and *Campus*, as well as on the

Arte cultural channel. Yet this is by no means the whole story. For example, if one considers the important programme genre of television fiction, France does not stand out as a statistical exception when compared with other major national television systems in Western Europe (such as Italy and Spain) with regard to the percentage of American imports in its schedules (Brants and De Bens 2000: 20). At the same time, while French audiences may show a marked preference for domestically produced programmes, this does not differentiate them from audiences in other Western European countries. In the case of major Western European nation-states such as France, Germany and Britain, language and dominant cultural norms are powerful barriers to the cross-border flow of television programming and the formation of transnational or supranational audiences (Biltereyst 1992).

Conclusion

This chapter has argued that a broad historical overview of French television within a Western European context does not substantiate any comprehensive macro level claim to exceptionalist status. Rather in many key aspects France can be more satisfactorily analysed and assessed as part of the mainstream, occasionally distinctive but rarely unique. Even in the area where one might have expected a strong claim to French exceptionalism – programming reflecting national cultural values – the evidence is more mixed than might have been anticipated. Of course, even to ask questions about the nature of French exceptionalism demonstrates to some extent the success of cultural and political elites in influencing external perceptions of French television. This may well tap into a desire on the part of some to see in the French experience something different and, therefore, 'exceptional'.

To argue that in the Western European context of the past fifty or more years French television rarely merits an exceptionalist label should not be taken to mean that there is no value in examining the French experience in its own right. Nor do we seek to deny the frequent distinctiveness of the French case from that of other individual countries in Western Europe, which continues to make cross-national comparison a valid and enriching exercise. Elements of national specificity within a common Western European paradigm are more than sufficient to make French television worth studying in depth, without us becoming too hung up on the applicability of the label of 'exceptionalism'.

Note

1. A weaker interpretation of the concept of exceptionalism might allow it to be applied to more than one member of a group under the same heading, for example to claim that two countries in Western Europe were exceptional in the same respect. This would require the group of countries to be sufficiently large, the similarities between the two countries to be very strong and the differences between the two members on the one hand and the rest of the group on the other to be particularly significant. If the criteria are not specified, then it may be possible to argue that all members of the group are in some way exceptional. While this may be true, it is not especially helpful. It is important to know, therefore, on what basis and by what criteria any claim to exceptionalism is being advocated.

Chapter 12

CULTURAL EXCEPTION(S) IN FRENCH CINEMA

*Brigitte Rollet**

There are few areas in which the idea of a possible French exception has asserted itself to such an extent as in the field of culture, and it is actually hardly surprising that the term 'cultural exception' has come to be associated with France, or a certain idea of France. The issue came to the forefront during the 1993 round of GATT (General Agreement on Tariffs and Trade) negotiations, when France insisted on removing cultural products from the negotiations, on the grounds that 'culture is not just another commodity'. In so doing, the French representatives may have compounded France's bad reputation in international negotiations, but in a way they were only following a tradition that has strong roots in French society, where culture plays a very special role in many fields that are not strictly speaking cultural, such as politics and the economy.

When the word 'exception' is mentioned, it conjures up the idea of rules, norms or standards. In the cultural field, rules often only apply to the society, nation or group that produces them, so that logically an exception is only such in the eyes of those who do not share the same rules. However, given the great cultural diversity of the French nation, this in no way means that all the things that appear to be exceptions outside France, in the case of cinema for example, may not also be exceptions for certain groups inside France itself.

As soon as we start to examine the specificities of the seventh art in France in comparison to other national cinemas, there is the overriding feeling that the French film industry is no more than a series of exceptions. Whatever angle it is seen from, and particularly if compared with other national cinemas, French cinema has an immense variety of parameters and characteristics that help to make it *exceptional*, as if, far from proving the rule, exceptions had become the rule. This chapter, rather than giving a list of examples and describing each exception in turn, will look at this 'exceptionality' from different perspectives, to broaden our

---

* Translated by Alison Bissery.

view of the subject. By taking a step back and starting from a far-off time when cinema had yet to be invented, we are able to contemplate French cinema as an exception compared with other national cinemas, in Europe and above all the United States, but an exception that reflects other typically French traditions. The second part of the chapter will explore the limits of this 'exceptionality' in a French context. This will enable us to look at culture in general, and cinema in particular, in a wider perspective, with a view to demonstrating how cinema continues in the line of certain French traditions, but also how other French specificities can get in the way of such exceptionalities.

Without dissociating cinema from the society that produces and consumes it, we find a large number of interdependencies and also many exceptions. French cinema did not create these exceptionalities, they simply took on other forms in the cinema. Generally speaking, the film producers merely extended what the previous centuries had instituted, and/or what the French Revolution – on many counts the foundation stone of the French nation, which I take as a starting point – had helped establish. By drawing up a 'list' of the French specificities in the cinematic field and more widely in the field of culture, other exceptional trends appear and take shape implicitly, confirming my initial premise that the cinema has adopted and integrated, without really challenging them, certain founding principles of the French nation.

Obviously, the angles from which we choose to address the subject (wide and narrow, to use the film industry's vocabulary) will allow us to ask a certain number of questions and put forward certain hypotheses, not all of which will find clear-cut answers here. Nonetheless, they will open a more general debate on the importance of maintaining cultural diversity in a world environment that seems inexorably drawn towards a uniformisation of cultural forms and practices (i.e, conforming to the U.S 'model', imposed as the general norm and reference).

French cinema and the outside world

What rules can be established in the cultural field? Is it a question of France as opposed to Europe? On a wider scale, are the rules governing European (and French) cinema necessarily different from those applied in Hollywood? Going beyond the various programmes launched since the beginning of the 1990s to promote cinematographic production in EU member states (such as Eurimages and Media), the very notion of European cinema involves specificity – whether real or desired – and a different conception of culture in general, and the cinema in particular, in Europe and the U.S. Although attempts made to define it are not always successful, specialists do use the term 'European cinema', believing that it has characteristics that distinguish it radically from Hollywood-style cinema. Thus, with its perhaps more marked tendency for *auteur* cinema, and for 'the temptation towards introspection' (Nysenholc 1995: 88), also perceived as 'pursuing the romantic illusion of individual creativeness to such an extent that the film-maker himself is explicitly placed at the centre of the film' (38), is European cinema more than the sum of Europe's different national cinemas (Dyer and Vincendeau 1992: 5)? Others, such as the film director Jean-Luc Godard, offer different definitions and views of cultural Europe:

> Because there is the rule and then the exception. There is culture, which is the rule, and there is the exception, which is art. Everybody talks about the rule – computers, T-shirts, television – nobody talks about the exception; you don't talk about that sort of thing. You write about it – Flaubert, Dostoevsky, you compose it – Gershwin, Mozart, you paint it – Cézanne, Vermeer, you record it – Antonioni, Vigo. Or you live it, and it becomes an *art de vivre* – Srebrenica, Mostar, Sarajevo. It will be the rule for cultural Europe to organise the death of the *art de vivre* that still flowers at our feet. (1991).

In her book on French cinema, Susan Hayward set out to define the paradigms for the notion of 'national' when applied to the cinema. Based on Guy Gauthier's work on mapping national cinemas, she drew up what she calls three antagons, the first being 'the centre Hollywood/US and the indigenous cinema which is peripheral in relation to the epicentre *par excellence* that Hollywood/US represents'. She justifies the presence and position of Hollywood/U.S. cinema by adding that 'America/Hollywood is the epicentre because it is the leading exporter of films and because all other cinemas define their difference in relation to this dominant cinematic culture against which they cannot compete either on the economic or on the production level' (1993: 13). The figures for Europe are quite eloquent on this point as, according to Laurent Creton: '70 percent of cinema and audio-visual programmes broadcast in Europe are American ... 80 percent of revenues from cinema and television productions made in Europe are made by American companies'. He goes on to add, giving us the first French exception, that 'only France enjoys a relatively better position with a rate of 57 percent' (1995: 200).

Nation and cinema: from one exception to another?

In his book *Cinema and Nation*, Jean-Michel Frodon the film critic for the newspaper *Le Monde*, begins a chapter on the 'French paradox' by declaring: 'Enough futile controversy: France invented the cinema. Because it was its role or, if you prefer, because it needed it to accomplish what it considered to be its role, i.e., to enlighten the peoples of the world and lead them on the paths of freedom and equality, no less. If France had thought that it had accomplished its task in the nineteenth century, it would not have needed to invent cinema'. He continues with this wonderful phrase: 'If *les Lumières* (the Enlightenment) had triumphed, *les Lumière* (the brothers, Louis and Auguste) would not have been French, they might even have been unnecessary' (Frodon 1998: 82).

This statement exemplifies the relationship between the invention of cinema and the Revolution, between the invention of cinema and the invention of the nation.[1] Although they are in principle of a very different nature, it seems to me that this association of two major events, on a national and international level, is fundamental in more than one respect. Not only does it take the French Revolution out of the purely political framework, but it also puts cinema into a system that is not purely cultural. Whether declaring that 'the nation is an image', or quoting Pierre Nora: '… the nation is nothing but a representation' (1998: 18), Frodon agrees with Benedict Anderson's definitions of the nation as 'an imaginary and imagined community', both adjectives being taken literally here. Further, by linking politics and culture, he illustrates a major French characteristic, which I am not aware exists elsewhere, a characteristic that dates back even further than the French Revolution, that is the almost 'incestuous' relationship between the state and culture in France (Fumaroli 1992; Patriat 1998; Djian 1996).

Since Louis XIV and Versailles, the political powers have established themselves as patrons of the French arts.[2] Even more importantly, their role in the creation, protection and distribution of the arts in question has never really decreased, whether it be for the ' legitimate ' arts (from which the cinema was excluded not so very long ago) or the other, more popular arts. In the following century, the philosophers of the Enlightenment, by their attempts to democratise the arts and culture and encourage enlightened despotism, made a significant contribution towards linking the political and social development of the nation and the development and acquisition of 'culture'.

If we carefully examine the laws, decrees and various institutional reforms affecting French cinema since the end of the Second World War, the tradition of state support designed to spread the influence of culture – in this case, cinematographic art – continues in a number of different forms. Examples include the creation of the Institut des Hautes Etudes Cinématographiques (IDHEC) in 1944[3] and, above all, the Centre National de la Cinématographie (CNC), a public body created in 1946. The latter is responsible 'for examining draft bills or regulations, for controlling financing and revenues, for encouraging and financing national production, the broadcasting of documentaries and the non-commercial sector, for organising vocational and technical training and, lastly, for co-ordinating benefit schemes for the cinema' (Ministère de la Culture et de la

Communciation1992: 53). In 1945, the film industry support fund introduced a 7 percent tax on takings in cinemas. Whatever the period in question, these support policies (in favour of training, creation and distribution) represent different forms of protectionism and have contributed to the establishment of the wide range of systems that enable French cinema to survive today. Thus, France developed a protectionist system in the cultural field.

From the 1980s onwards, following the major changes introduced by the Socialist governments in the world of culture, institutional and political support for French cinema made a very important contribution to maintaining its presence in the international arena, where other national cinemas collapsed, including some, such as Italian cinema, which initially had relatively similar operating structures. There is also the obvious comparison with Great Britain during the same period: although it was 'one of the first countries in Europe to adopt measures to protect its film industry (in 1909 and 1927), today it has stopped granting subsidies and tax incentives' (Jackel 1995: 293). Once the National Film Finance Corporation had been disbanded by Margaret Thatcher in 1985, the only bodies offering help in the production of feature films were British Screen, a private company set up in 1986, and the British Film Institute.[4] In terms of percentages, national cinema only accounted for 3.6 percent of the total in Great Britain in the 1990s (against 85.8 percent for films imported from the U.S.) with only forty-eight feature films produced. Although the UK is the only country to have such an acute imbalance, US cinema also dominates national production in other European countries. For example, data from the CNC show that Germany and Spain are in a similar situation, with ratios of national/U.S. cinema of 9.5/82.8 percent and 9.3/77.1 percent respectively.

The French state's *exceptional* intervention in culture in general and the cinema in particular can still be found today at all the different levels of creation, from financing to production and distribution, although the system of distribution is likely to be affected by recent changes at Vivendi Universal and Canal Plus following the departure of Jean-Marie Messier. Among the numerous examples of the state's involvement are the various taxes payable by the French television channels to finance film-making. First, with the creation of the Institut pour le Financement du Cinéma et des Industries Culturelles (IFIC) in 1983, then the Sociétés de Financement des Industries Cinématographiques et Audiovisuelles (SOFICA) in 1985, the television channels were required to make direct contributions. Then a tax introduced in 1986 obliged the television companies to invest a growing percentage of their profits in the production and creation of films: from 3 percent in 1986, to 4 percent in 1987 and 5.5 percent since 1992. The direct result is that today practically all French films are produced thanks to television, which at least partially recovers the initial investment through future broadcasts and so-called spin-off products. In addition, the television companies' terms of reference now include very strict rules concerning the broadcasting of films on television. The first restriction concerns the minimum period of time between a film's first showing in cinemas and it being broadcast on television (for a long time this was one year, but has now been reduced to six months for certain channels), and also its distribution on video cassette or DVD. The total number of films that the French channels can show is stipulated in their terms of reference, which also specify the days and times films can be shown on television, as an incentive for the French population to go to the cinema. Although all the TV channels are not subject to the same restrictions for showing films, none of them are authorised to programme films on Wednesday evenings, the day films are released in the cinemas in France, and on Friday evenings and Saturdays (Looseley, 1995). CNC statistics for 1999 clearly demonstrate the importance of the latter: 56 percent of seats were sold between Friday and Sunday, with 22 percent of sales on Saturday.

In addition, the various types of subsidy introduced by the CNC to encourage the production of films in French are eloquent illustrations of the 'institutionalisation' of culture. On this last point the sometimes fierce defence of the French language and the development of Francophonie can be seen as continuing a tradition initiated in the seventeenth century with the creation of the Académie Française. Within the wider field of audiovisual production, it was not enough for France to simply encourage or (even) impose the defence of its culture.[5] It also attempted in 1993/1994, albeit without great success, to encourage its European partners to do the same. Since 1992, there has been a quota for 'European language works' on French television, fixed at 40 percent and also subject to restrictions concerning the days and hours of broadcast.[6] Still these different types of support do not eliminate the problems faced by film-makers, a point underlined by Truffaut's joke about Abel Gance and his Napoléon : 'To let Abel Gance get on with his work, seeking a Louis XIV-like sponsor' (Frodon: 88).

On another level, a factor that greatly contributes to the survival of French cinema is the continual renewal of film-makers in France. Since the first film production subsidies were introduced, such as the truly unique system of advances against takings introduced in 1959 and which provided a great stimulus to the development of the Nouvelle Vague, the number of first films and new film-makers has grown accordingly. For example, sixty-two first films were produced in France in 2000 (out of a total of 180 French films, including co-productions). To put this into perspective, the number of first films in France is higher than the total production of most countries in Western Europe: for example, CNC data for 1992 show that sixty-three German films, fifty-two Spanish films and sixty-three British films were produced in that year, compared to 127 in Italy and 155 in France.

Another strategy has been used to ensure the survival of French cinema in the increasingly Americanised national and European markets. Since the mid-1980s, with the gradual increase in the number of tickets sold for films from the United States, French films now only attract roughly a third of total audiences.[7] The means employed to preserve and retain French audiences at any price can also be seen as exceptions. For instance, in the 1980s, there was an increase in epic, blockbuster films with huge budgets which, in line with the wishes expressed by the then Minister of Culture, Jack Lang, combined popular and cultural themes. The immense success of adaptations of classics of French literature such as Pagnol briefly changed the situation: *Jean de Florette* and *Manon des Sources* directed by Claude Berri in 1986 accounted for nearly 14 million ticket sales alone. Other blockbusters of the 1980s included epic films (Alain Corneau's *Fort Saganne*, 1982), adventure films (Luc Besson's *Le Grand Bleu*, 1988) and even a medieval *polar* (Jean-Jacques Annaud's *Le Nom de la Rose*, 1986), all of which drew audiences of several million spectators. It was not the first time that a certain type of French cinema tried to beat Hollywood at its own game, although adaptations of literary works are part of a cinematic tradition in France, the same tradition, in fact, that the young wolves of the New Wave rose up against.

What is new today is the choice of a film genre that is rare, to say the least, in the history of French cinema. Taking as a starting point Lewis Strauss, for whom 'narrative [is] a culture's way of making sense of itself' (1993: 9), Susan Hayward identified national typologies not only in these Straussian narratives, but also in the narrative *genres*, underlining that: 'there are filmic modalities which are specific to a particular nation' (1993: 10). Comedies, *polars* and psychological dramas were for a long time the dominant genres for films produced in France and were a great success with the public. Apart from the epic films, adventure films and westerns – which, according to Susan Hayward, do not belong to French filmic culture – we can add science fiction and/or films with special effects. Here there is clearly a change since the beginning of the new century, another trend seems to be emerging, with the arrival of high-budget films crammed full of special effects, a very un-French and typically Hollywood-style. Up until now, only Luc Besson and Marco Caro used new technologies in their films, which is hardly surprising given their experience in producing films in America. The most surprising – and 'exceptional' – thing about the special effects used in the films released in France since 2000 is that they are used in films that return to national sources, reinterpreting the national myths (literary or otherwise) and legends, such as the Beast of Gévaudan in *Le Pacte des Loups* (Christophe Ganz 2001), or the Phantom of the Louvre in *Belphégor, le Fantôme du Louvre* (J-P Salomé 2001), with Sophie Marceau taking the part played by Juliette Gréco in the cult television series.[8] In autumn 2001, *Vidocq*, revised and updated by

Pitof, was the first French feature film to be produced solely with digital technology, based entirely on special effects. Claude Zidi with *Astérix et Obélix contre César* in 1998 and Luc Besson with yet another adaptation of the Joan of Arc legend/history in 1999, had opened the way to the production of films which relied on a large number of special effects. Given the importance of the 'myths' of Astérix and Joan of Arc in French culture, in the very wide sense of the term, this is less anecdotal than it may seem. With over nine million tickets sold for the former and nearly three million for the latter, these films that were at the same time very and yet so little French, helped rebalance the figures. With his *Jeanne d'Arc*, Luc Besson probably attracted an audience that was more interested in the productions of the author of the *Cinquième Element* than in the life of the Maid of Orleans. *Le Pacte des Loups*, another film with a spectacular budget of 200 million francs, was seen by over five million people in France, which meant that the film topped the box office for French films in 2001, but above all, that it beat the Hollywood-style blockbusters with which it was in competition. These French films with special effects were among the box office hits (i.e, films with seven-digit ticket sales), with Vidocq recording over one million sales in the first two weeks. It is worth noting, in passing, that the same team of technicians worked on all these films with Caro, Jeunet, Besson and Zidi.

It is doubtless too soon to draw precise conclusions about this trend which, if it is confirmed, could perhaps open the way to a new form of filmic intertextuality in which the form is imported and adapted to 'dress up', so to speak, a national content. Even if intertextual references to Hollywood are not infrequent (Forbes 1993), those made in the French super-productions mentioned above doubtless had far clearer commercial targets.

From one exception to another: cinema and universalism

However, one exception can sometimes conflict with another, for another major, *exceptional* principle inherited from the French Revolution is *universalism*. This is a key point, since it probably explains why exceptionality tends to develop in a relatively unprogressive way. The significance of universalism should not be underestimated, given its influence in all areas of French society and above all in the field of culture. It is by virtue of this so-called universalism whereby all French citizens are equal, whatever their origin (social or ethnic), their age, their sexual orientation or their religion, that the recognition, or even just the conception, of minorities in France has proved to be extremely problematic. There is an extremely strong tradition of this in the cultural field that influences the financing, the content and even the reception of films, although some recent legislation has somewhat altered this situation. For example, two laws voted by the National Assembly in 1999, the first on gender parity in politics and the second giving legal recognition to same-sex couples (PACS), both in their own way contradict this universalist trend by indirectly recognising the specificity and needs of certain groups.

In cinema, immense problems arise where women, *'beur'*[9] or 'gay' film-directors are concerned, due mainly to the lack of recognition, and therefore legitimacy, offered to these groups. The first reason for this is that the CNC's data do not recognise a distinction between these groups. Hence, following in this respect another French tradition, the CNC provides no information regarding the gender or ethnic origin of film-makers. Culture is not the only area concerned by this. A similar controversy flared up in 1999 when it was suggested that people's ethnic origin should be included in the statistics prepared by the National Institute of Demographic Studies (INED). Although they do not necessarily demand it, this non-recognition of a major element of the film-maker's identity is quite problematic, given the importance of these same data when it comes to the film's financing (by the CNC or the production companies) and the acceptance or refusal of projects. For instance, there are a large number of *beur* film-makers whose films have not received any advances against takings or other support, although this has not actually prevented them from making their films: I am thinking here in particular of Malik Chibane and Zhora Ghorab-Volta, neither of whom comes from the 'establishment' nor has been through cinema school. It would no doubt be interesting to work on the CNC's archives to study the evolution of projects, between the first versions submitted to the commission and the final version accepted for financing. The account given by the actor-turned-film-producer Abdel Kechiche about his first film *La Faute à Voltaire* (2001) is quite telling on this point. Kechiche stressed the amount of time he took to set up the project and make the film (four years), and above all the different versions submitted to the CNC before he obtained the advance against takings. The film's subject (a Moroccan illegal immigrant's stay in Paris) could have suggested that it was a denunciatory, political, or at least 'socially-oriented' film, but in the end this was not the case, as the producer opted for a light, toned-down version of the story.

In this context, it is interesting to note a current trend among a large number of cinema critics who are inspired by France's republican tradition and have no fear of paradox, for instance when they say that a film made by a *beur* speaks too much about *beurs*, or when they congratulate a *beur* director for not filming *beur* characters or issues. While recognising that France has become a multicultural society, the same people implicitly refuse any demonstration of differences in the field of artistic creation. Since the 1980s and the end of the activism that had marked certain films in the previous decade, it is not good form to venture into the sociological realm, except under the banner of *auteur* cinema, which allowed the Dardenne brothers to get very good reviews for films such as *La Promesse* or *Rosetta*. All the same, it is as if women, *beurs* or gays are indirectly discouraged from making films dealing with issues that are particular to them. Whereas the development of specific legislation (anti-sexist, anti-racist, anti-antisemite and perhaps soon anti-homophobic laws) clearly exposes the existence of the groups which, in principle, they target, these same groups are repudiated in practice. The arguments put forward by the anti-PACS and anti-parity movements clearly stated that separatist, minority groups were a threat to the tradition of the one and indivisible republic (Hayward 1983). This is similar to the phenomenon witnessed during the debates on promoting minority languages in Europe, which raised the spectre of France as a country prone to division, with its Republic nearing breaking point and explosion.

The aim here is not to advocate a ghettoisation of culture, but at least to enable differences to be expressed. It is ironical to see that, whenever one of these 'minority' film-makers ventures onto ground where he or she is not expected to tread, the reactions are, to say the least, surprising. For instance, the recent reappropriation by certain women creators of areas of cultural creation that were formerly exclusively male domains, such as violence and pornography (or explicit sexuality), affects what the majority of people already take for granted, i.e., the idea that there can be a women's cinema or literature. The fact that the scenes filmed or written by women[10] were seen as taboo, although they would not have been perceived in this way if male film-makers had done the same, highlights the flagrant contradictions of a universalism that is in fact synonymous with masculine, white, heterosexual and Catholic.

Concluding questions

At a time when the question of the right to difference or otherness is posed, in a context of unbridled globalisation in which the adjective 'citizen' is constantly used in speeches as a synonym for 'showing solidarity ', (the French even talk of '*films citoyens*', literally citizens' films, for socially aware films where solidarity plays a central role), what exactly is the current status of these revolutionary principles within the film industry? In other words, have the Lumière brothers succeeded where les *Lumières* (the Enlightenment) failed? Is it possible today to prevent cultural creation from becoming simply the tool of a majority of privileged people who already have access to cinema schools (given that the Republican ideal of 'school for all' does not in practice eliminate, far from it, the inequalities arising from social origin)?

There is also a very good case for wondering whether contemporary cinema, and in a broader context the audiovisual world in France, is not in the process of becoming another means of introducing and strengthening the idea of monoculture. French schools were for a long time seen as a mould and filter whereby young pupils from Brittany or Corsica or elsewhere became fully-fledged citizens of the French Republic. Thus, Bretons or Corsicans were required to forget their language and culture, which constituted the cornerstone of their regional identity. Similarly, are we not witnessing a tendency to iron out anything that makes the identity of a group? Is this 'gay', 'feminine' or '*beur*' cinema the exception, the margin or the periphery of a universalist, universalising cinema? In this context, what alternatives are there to guarantee that film-making that falls outside this consensus can express itself?

In the film diary for her latest film *Chaos* (2001), filmed in digital video (DV), the producer Coline Serreau talks of her enthusiasm for digital technology. She declares that we are moving towards: 'a revolution in the art of filming … DV will completely transform world film production in the coming years. The younger generations will discover and invent a new language, within everyone's means; they will be able to make the films they want to, without having to worry about whether such-and-such a decision-maker, caught up in humdrum concerns over audience ratings, is thinking about their project, because we will be able to shoot highly professional feature films with a ridiculously low budget. There will be an explosion of films freed from constraints, leading to a radical change in content' (Serreau 2001). Although this will not solve the problem of how these films are distributed,[11] the (utopian?) idea that digital technology, which has previously been seen as an indirect factor in formal uniformisation (by special effects) in a costly form of cinema, can also provide the ways and means of both democratising the cinema on the one hand, and of offering freedom in the choice of subjects on the other, is nothing short of revolutionary.

Notes

1. Later in the text he develops the idea by stating: 'Great Britain arrived before the cinema …, it didn't need it … England, the first modern nation, made itself before the cinema, in the splendid reserve of its insularity, which had no concern to "project" itself materially further afield in any other way than by its ships and its merchants' (Frodon 1998: 144).
2. The chronology of the French Ministry of Culture's internet site starts with the Capetian Monarchy, from which 'the beginnings of a French cultural policy' can be dated. See: www.culture.gouv.fr./culture/historique/index.htm. Retrieved 9 September 2003.
3. IDHEC became FEMIS (Ecole nationale supérieure des métiers de l'image et du son – The National Institute for the Image and Sound Trades) in 1986.

4. The National Lottery can now be added to these bodies, as it has been used to help finance British films since the end of the 1990s.
5. The law dated 9 September 1986 proposed by the National Communication and Freedom Commission (Commission Nationale de la Communication et des Libertés: CNCL) includes the promotion of Francophonie in audiovisual production (article 45).
6. To avoid certain channels programming European films at off-peak viewing times, the proposed slots are from 14.00 to 23.00 on Wednesdays and from 18.00 to 23.00 on the other days of the week.
7. Statistics from the French weekly, *Le Film Français*, on the evolution of market shares for French and U.S. films are as follows: 1990: 37.6/55.9; 1991: 30.6/58.2; 1992: 34.9/58.3; 1993: 35.1/57.1; 1994: 28.3/60.9; 1995: 35.2/53.9; 1996: 37.5/54.3; 1997: 34.5/53.8; 1998: 26.6/36.2; 1999: 29.7/53.9; 2000: 27/68 percent.
8. Arthur Bernède's novel was adapted by Henri Desfontaines in 1927, then filmed for television in 1965 by Claude Barma and Jacques Armand.
9. Although the term *'beur'* (second-generation North African living in France) may be outdated, I use it in overall, neutral terms to designate ethnic minorities from North Africa, as the other ethnic minority groups are very rare and seldom found in the French film industry.
10. I am particularly thinking of the films by Catherine Breillat (including *Romance*, 1999) and Virginie Despentes (*Baise-moi*, 2000). In literature, recent 'controversial' books include Catherine Millet's work, *La vie sexuelle de Catherine M* (2000).
11. The Franco-German television channel Arte, through the head of its fiction department Pierre Chevalier to whom we already owe successes such as the series *Tous les garçons et les filles de leur âge*, has recently launched a new series called *Petits Formats* for films shot exclusively in DV. The first productions, by Olivier Py and Brigitte Rouan, were on relatively controversial subjects for France, such as male homosexuality in the former case and prostitution in the latter case.

Chapter 13

SPORT AND POLITICS: ANOTHER FRENCH EXCEPTION

*Patrick Mignon**

The two sporting exceptions

In France, sport is characterised by strong intervention by both the state and local authorities. It is one of the manifestations of the famous French exception, which is embedded in a historic continuity that begins in the years following the war of 1870 and continues through the Popular Front, the Vichy regime and the Republics since 1947. What began as material and financial support has come to define sport as the state's field of competence. The reasons for this intervention are no different from those of other countries which, depending on the period, may be concern for the physical and moral regeneration of the population or a quest for national prestige. To this is added, in France's case, a long history of political centralisation in which the state guarantees the general interest and as such becomes society's teacher.

At the same time, the place of sport in France is also exceptional. It is often stated that the sporting culture in France is weak. Not that the French are not sporty; on the contrary, the number of clubs and participants is similar to that of other European countries, as is the practising of sport outside the context of competition. However, the difference is:

> that in France sport is not the object of a strong infatuation, that French supporters are rather less numerous and less passionate than elsewhere, that they are distant and cold towards their national teams and that the latter do not have the same taste for victory that characterises other great sporting nations. It is these sorts of ideas, for example, that have led foreign commentators to remark that the 1998 Football World Cup should never have happened in a country like France that is so lacking in sporting enthusiasm. (Mignon and Truchot 2002)

---

* Translated by Emma Lelliott and Tony Chafer.

These two exceptions are a result of a particular way of moulding both individuals and their relationships to the state. Its sociopolitical manifestation is the weakness of civil society vis-à-vis the state, which means, for the purposes of our argument here, the weakness of sporting associations vis-à-vis sport's governing bodies and of sport vis-à-vis politics.

Sport and politics: the anthropological approach

Sport and the English model

In his book on sport in France during the Belle Epoque, Richard Holt (1981) cites the example of an English traveller who marvelled at the fact that 'the French excel at different sports'. Against the already well established popularity of football, for example in Great Britain, the French tend to mix new English sports, practised by the upper classes, with gymnastics or traditional French sports practised by the working-class, especially in rural areas. Although France invented the word, it did not invent sport. The model for competitive sport came from Great Britain and spread progressively from the 1870s onwards, thanks as much to the development of international trade, tourism, the progress of industrialisation and urbanisation as to the First World War, colonisation and the anglophilia of part of the French political and social elites. It was introduced to France through the secondary schools of Paris, Lyon and Bordeaux, the ports (in 1872, the first football club was founded at Le Havre) and the seaside resorts of the Normandy coast (tennis), but also came in from the industrial areas of the north and east. The Paris schools organised timed races, and football and rugby matches became more commonplace, while a wider public became interested in cycle races. There was a slow acclimatisation to sport, despite the reticence of patriots who preferred shooting and gymnastics clubs that were more suited to forging patriotic sentiment and for preparing men's bodies for revenge against Germany. The need to set an example was felt particularly in gymnastics. Popularised in France by Colonel Amoros from 1820 onwards, it was seen as an activity that was both educational and morally uplifting, that aimed to strengthen the body while at the same time engendering national sentiment. The gymnastics associations, the fencing and shooting clubs and cycling associations, which sprang up in France towards the end of the Second Empire, were therefore seen as cells of physical and moral rearmament for the French nation, which had to take revenge after the defeat of 1870. In 1873 in France, the Union of French Gymnastics Societies (USGF) was therefore created to bring together the different gymnastics and shooting clubs.

This movement was controlled by teachers, members of the armed forces and doctors, depending on the circumstances, each vying for influence and seeking to define the meaning of the activity. But whether they were seeking to strengthen the sense of civic pride, to 'give Marianne muscles', to combat physical and moral degeneration or to provide physical training for future soldiers, physical activity was not an end in itself: it was undertaken in the service of a greater cause: the fatherland. It was these patriotic gym associations that benefited, from the 1870s onwards, from state and local council funding. As a result, in 1914 there were more gymnastics, archery and cycling societies than football clubs in the Pas-de-Calais region.

The notion of competition as a value in itself independent of any educational project or mobilisation of national sentiment was not readily accepted. English sport was not always welcome, firstly because of its English origins (this was before the *entente cordiale*) which made it an easy target for virulent nationalists who wanted to defend national sports, such as kickboxing, or regional sports such as *barette* and the Basque *pelota*. It was also criticised for its overly frivolous, individualist and disinterested nature, with no other purpose than the pleasure of physical confrontation. Furthermore, by the time they were introduced in France, sports of British origin, such as football, were already professionalised, which shocked all who attributed moral virtues to physical exercise.

Several associations were created from the middle of the 1870s onwards to practice these new types of sport. In 1889, they came together to form the Union of French Societies for Athletic Sports (USFSA), which was the first large grouping of sports clubs in France independent of the state. This move towards organising sport gathered momentum in 1903, with the setting up of the Gymnastic and Sporting Federation of France (FGSPF), a Catholic-run group that brought together gymnasts and fans of English sport. But it was not until 1918 that sport truly became established in France, in the sense that it attracted enthusiasts from outside the elite circles that had introduced it. This is why it is generally thought that football only really became established in rural areas in the 1920s (Dumons et al. 1987; Hubscher et al. 2000; Vigarello 2000). The process of establishing sporting federations was not completed until the 1930s.

Social or political history of sport?

Reasons can be found for this weakness of sport in the structure of French society. The process of urbanisation for example: the rapid implantation of sport assumes the existence of large towns, where values and routines can be transmitted. France was a rural country of small towns, so that there was not a true market for sport in France, as there was in large towns such as London, Milan or Barcelona, that was capable of sustaining, for example, professional football clubs. Nor were there rivalries between towns or regions for national leadership or to become the national centre for a particular sport: Paris and the Jacobin tradition crushed any rivals' claims, unlike in Italy and Spain. There were also no local bourgeoisies seeking to compete with each other, only the mayors of large towns such as Lyon and Toulouse, who were looking to build a political career at national level and who used sport as a way of showing that they were dynamic and entrepreneurial. It is also worth noting that it was a long time before professionalism, which was introduced into football in 1932, became a means of social promotion for the working class. Unlike in England, where players generally came from the working class, or in Italy, where they were often young people of peasant stock who had come to Milan or Turin to work, the French professional footballer, who was in fact more often than not a semi-professional, generally came from the middle class and was a student, for whom football was an amusing and lucrative diversion. It was only in the 1950s that football became a working-class profession, and even then it was not uncommon, right up until the 1960s, for players to prefer to remain amateurs, adding to their salary the benefits of possible promotion within the company of the local club's sponsor and the bonuses that he paid (Wahl and Lanfranchi 1995). French-style industrialisation, which remained 'gentle' despite its painful consequences for some, is one explanation for the fact that the working class attached less importance to professionalism, since it was, after all, not the only way of escaping from working class roots. The salaries offered by clubs were not large enough for a skilled worker to abandon his work or for a semi-rural worker to leave his job on the farm. For most people, school and the hope of becoming a civil servant, or taking on the family farm, or going to work at the steelworks like their father, or gaining a qualification, represented the realistic dreams of social promotion. The move to true professionalism, from the 1950s onwards, which saw a massive influx and domination of workers among professional players, took place largely thanks to immigrants (Beaud and Noiriel 1990). Only immigrants, Poles and Italians at first, then the Spanish and North Africans, thought that football was really the best way to escape from working down in the mines. A good example of this is Kopa, for whom professional football took the place of a job as an electrician, which anti-Polish prejudice had made difficult.

Sporting passion and political passion

We must also perhaps consider that other passions were in competition with the taste for sport. A number of hypotheses can be put forward concerning the link between sport and politics and sport and the state in France. These hypotheses, from the work of Huizinga and Elias (Huizinga 1977; Elias and Dunning 1998), link French political centralisation to the predominance of physical activity related to military-type activity for the defence of the country. The importance attached to horse-riding, fencing and shooting is a product of this military culture that developed under the monopoly of the centralised state and that we find throughout the nineteenth century in gymnastics societies. Elias emphasises the parallel development, in Great Britain's case, of democratic political competition and sporting competition, whereas in France the absolute monarchy was replaced by centralised Jacobinism. In the former case, sport developed in a society where an autonomous civil society created its institutions, while in France the state sought to retain control over civil society.

The reference to Parisian centralism is reflected in the republican character of the state, which is fundamental to the definition of a French identity that is superior to local and social identities. Since the Revolution, the state has fought against any notion of local specificities. In the republican and secular school system it created an instrument to forge a national identity that went against traditional affiliations and a means of defining membership of the national community as a form of detachment, even if its role in promoting social mobility is more modest than current nostalgia is prepared to acknowledge. More generally, by introducing the notion of citizenship, it has made access to the latter one of the major issues at stake in social and political struggles. The passions of the French, such as they were expressed during the nineteenth and twentieth centuries, were political passions that militated against involvement in particularistic cultural practices. For many years, all sport enthusiasts and their potential supporters were also passionately engaged in the fight for citizenship, the defence of the nation and the recognition of their rights by the state. Thus football, which quickly became the most popular sport, was as much a symbol of integration into a national community as it was of belonging to a particular social class or region. French peasants learnt French and football in the trenches during the First World War, in the same way that Polish and North African immigrants playing for French teams were proof of republican universalism. If one accepts the hypothesis (Ehrenberg 1991) that the impact of sport is as important as the passion for equality, both in the legal and the real sense, in terms of providing the opportunity for social mobility, one can understand how, in a country where this is achieved through social struggle and through the political struggle for access to citizenship rather than through a struggle for the right to live according to one's own rules, one can accord second place to the passions whose roots lie in the private sphere and which may even represent an obstacle to achieving this ideal. This is why there was widespread reticence towards sport in France before 1914, which always had to be subordinated to higher ideals: the motherland, the Revolution, and those institutions that are the real 'producers' of citizens (Wahl 1989).

Therefore, from the moment it was introduced in France, sport found itself highly ideologically loaded. It played a key role in the struggles between church and state and had an effect on competition between sports: in the south, secular primary school teachers created rugby clubs, while the Catholic FGSPF was working to create football and basketball clubs. This had an effect on the organisation of common competitions and therefore on the possibilities for the faster development of sport. In 1906, the USFSA banned its clubs from playing against those of the FGSPF; as a result it was 1917 before the first French Football Cup could be organised, 1919 before the French Football Federation was created, and 1932 before the national league came into being. Another example is the attempts to create a working class sport before the First World War, in the hope of escaping from the paternalism of employers and of developing a socialist sport ethic. Working-class sport then suffered from rivalries between socialist and communist sports federations, resulting in separate competitions and audiences, before they came together again in 1934.

The question arises: how significant were the political strategies of the different parties in the relative weakness of an autonomous working-class culture, of which sport was a part? For example, the idea was prevalent among the working-class parties that the advancement of the working class depended on access to culture, that this was one of the aspects of its emancipation and of its admission to true citizenship. This in turn was seen as the condition for gaining access to universal culture, and was thus seen as more important than promoting a purely working-class culture. In France, all the workers' organisations were constructed around the idea of opposition to an autonomous working class or popular culture: the socialist and communist organisations were fighting for access to the universal, in the same way as they were fighting to gain political power. For them, emancipation was achieved through refusing conventional leisure activities that carried the risk of alienation. One could love sport in a private capacity, but this love was not a value. In France until the 1960s, culture remained culture in the widest sense, something that was always linked to the idea of a united social and national body. Popular culture, of which sport was a part, played a secondary role in the definition of communities.

The Republic and Olympic ideal

France nevertheless occupies a unique position in the history of sport. It has long appeared to be less sporty than other nations and more intermittent in the performance of its champions. Yet, it was responsible for launching two of the greatest international competitions: Pierre de Coubertin organised the first Games of the modern era at Athens in 1896, while Jules Rimet, president of the International Federation of Football Associations (FIFA), organised the first Football World Cup in 1930. If British sport spread thanks to its economic significance and the desire of local elites to promote it, the French, with Coubertin and the Olympic Games, made it into a project of global proportions which propelled the state and the Republic from the status of national to that of universal teacher. This is because the promotion of sport within the context of the Olympic ideal is linked to issues around the fate of democratic societies. From a diversion for the well-heeled and a spectacle for the people, sport became, under de Coubertin, a contribution to education and a possible recourse for those confronted with the decline of religion and the ideological battles of the day. It was able to play this role thanks to the benefits of physical exercise taken in the fresh air and the moral virtues of an undertaking framed by rules that everyone must respect, the unavoidable result of which was the establishment of the values of equality and justice. Where society was imperfect, sport proposed, within the Olympic doctrine, a counter-model that was a synthesis of the virtues that were in decline. These virtues manifested themselves in gymnastics, in the projects of English missionaries and indeed throughout the long history of games: fair play, exercise, physical commitment, selflessness, respect for one's opponent, setting oneself new goals, justice, chivalry, generosity and a concern for education. It was this synthesis that was able to reconcile gymnasts, sportsmen and the Republic with sport.

State intervention: national grandeur and the education of society

Physical recovery, national grandeur and the role of local councils (1919–1939)

During the period from 1919 to 1936, the administration of sport and physical education passed gradually from the Minister for War to the Minister for Health and Education. After the First World War, it was vital to ensure the physical and moral renaissance of the nation. The state therefore arranged for the training of the first teachers specialised in physical education and actively promoted gymnastics. It also intervened by obliging communes of more than 10,000 inhabitants to build facilities that contributed to the well-being of their population. This marked the beginning of the active involvement of local councils in the building of sports facilities. But the state also had to promote national grandeur.

When the government created the National Committee for Physical Education, Sport and Military Training in 1919, it was attached to the Ministry for War. In the same way, when an appeal was made to the government after the disappointing results of French athletes in the Olympic

Games at Antwerp, they entrusted the preparation of the athletes for the Games in Paris in 1924 to the Ministry for War, under the slogan 'be better prepared to win'. The important thing was to be able to compare oneself to others and to demonstrate, through sport, one's power and efficiency, whether against totalitarian countries or one's former adversaries of 1918. But this was achieved not by being the best in competitions, but by preventing French athletes from taking part in certain competitions. Moreover, within the context of international comparison, left-wing parties pressed for more sports facilities, with the aim of demonstrating a politics of sport that was different from that of totalitarian countries, while right-wing parties compared Italian and German policies of regeneration with French degeneration. This also explains the permanent tension between sport and physical activity linked to military preparations (Arnaud and Wahl 1994).

Local town councils already played an important role. The1920s saw the emergence of municipal policies to promote sporting activities and develop urbanisation through the creation of sports facilities. Edouard Herriot, Mayor of Lyon, began building the Gerland Stadium in 1913 in anticipation of the 1920 Olympic Games. Others, elsewhere, built swimming pools and velodromes. Town councils began giving subsidies to sporting associations, setting the precedent for clubs to ask for government help. This was what happened in professional football, which began in 1932 and which advised clubs to look to their local councillors for financial support.

In 1936, under the Popular Front and Léo Lagrange, an Under-Secretariat of State for Sport and Leisure was created, under the jurisdiction of the Ministry for Education. It combined a programme of building sports facilities with the law on paid holidays and a reduction in working hours, to promote the development of physical activity. It was also during this period that, with the introduction of the Sport and Physical Activity Diploma, the foundations were laid for a body to emerge whose primary responsibility would be to develop sport for the masses. Right-wing parties criticised these measures as signs of a creeping authoritarianism, but for the left in power, the sporting movement had to find its own sources of funding and not look to the state for help: the government therefore refused to finance the great football stadium that its leaders wanted for the 1938 World Cup.

Under the Vichy regime, sport was given a key role in the renewal of physical and moral order as part of the National Revolution. The great tennis player, J. Borotra, became Commissioner General for Sport in 1940, promoted the Olympic ideal of sport and strengthened the administration of sport. He was replaced in 1942 by Colonel Pascot, who adopted a more authoritarian policy, suppressing youth movements and appointing most

of the directors of the different sporting federations at a time when public
subsidies for the sporting federations were becoming commonplace.

The creation of the sporting welfare state

From 1945 onwards, the French sporting model was put in place, founded
on the joint management of sport by the state and the sporting movement.
A 1945 decree gave the sporting federations the task, subject to state
approval, of providing sport as a public service in France. Sporting associations regained their autonomy after the authoritarianism of Vichy but,
unlike in Germany, there was no split between the state and the sporting
associations. Sport was a part of the project of national reconstruction,
which meant building sports facilities and guaranteeing its place within
the school curriculum. This is why the creation of a General Committee for
Physical Education and Sport and the founding of an Under-Secretariat for
Youth and Sport in 1946 came under the jurisdiction of the Ministry of
Education. But there was no real policy, due to lack of money (sport was
not a priority) and the lack of an effective administration, until the Fifth
Republic, when Maurice Herzog, the well-known mountaineer, created
first a Commissariat, then in 1963 a Secretariat, and finally in 1966, a Min-
istry for Youth and Sport.

From then on, sport policy became linked to state reform. The state was
expected to intervene in specific problem areas where sport could play a
role, such as that of youth policy (the Black Shirts, the fallout from the
Algerian war and the physical and moral education of a growing number
of secondary school children) or in promoting the international prestige of
France. This was because the cold war gave sport once again an important
role in the politics of grandeur. The struggle for supremacy between the
U.S. and the USSR concealed other struggles, such as that of Third World
countries and small nations that also wanted to play a part in the international sporting scene. Thus sport became a central preoccupation after the
failure of French athletes at the Rome Olympics in 1960. This failure, at a
time when General de Gaulle was seeking to define a national policy of
independence symbolised by the creation of an atomic strike force, led to
the introduction of a sports policy that aimed to develop a sporting elite.

Sport was therefore a crucial part of the Fifth Plan. New sports facilities,
(swimming pools especially) aimed to create a virtuous pyramid whereby
the development of sport for the masses and educational sport would lead
to the emergence of a sporting elite. The welfare state also became sports-
oriented: subsidies were given to federations through a new contract
between the state and the sporting movement. In 1975 Pierre Mazeaud,
who had become minister three years earlier, put forward a law carrying
his name, which organised definitively the French model of sport. It was

based on the idea that the state should not just distribute subsidies and then leave well alone: it had to intervene in order to control the uses to which the aid was put. The left, which was in power from 1981, continued in the same vein: the Avice law of 1984 maintained the practice of intervention in different areas such as the organisation of competition-level sport, but also attributed to it a new social mission by defining Physical and Sporting Activities (Activités Physiques et Sportives: APS) as a public service. This was subsequently confirmed by the so-called Buffet law of 2000.

The1960s also saw the expansion of municipal policies (via subsidies to sports clubs, but also through local council control of facilities and organisation events, by 'helping' clubs become 'professional' and reorganising them). To this day, the state gives barely one percent of its budget, whereas local councils give between ten and fifteen percent of theirs (Callède 2000). It is a trend that has grown since 1982, in the years following decentralisation. In 2000, out of the twenty-five billion euros spent in France on sport nearly three billion was spent by the state and nearly eight billion by local councils (Ministère des Sports 2002). This was because, with the recession that began in the middle of the 1970s, sport was given new missions. The idea of sport as part of an individual's education was extended to include the idea of sport as a tool for integration, with emphasis being put on its role in the fight against delinquency, in the integration of foreigners and in the search for solutions to the problem of economic integration. But the mission assigned to sport is much larger. The state, in conjunction with local authorities, sees sport as an instrument for development. It is a way for a mayor to make his town or region known and to attract inhabitants through the provision of sporting activities, alongside cultural activities and other urban facilities (from school transport to hospitals). It is also a way of attracting investors, thanks to the image transmitted by sporting activity. It is the same for the state, which got involved in the sporting movement by supporting the French applications to organise the 1998 World Cup and the 2008 Olympic Games. Several things are at stake here. There is no doubt that sport is today the only area in which massive intervention in the urban fabric is accepted. The 1998 World Cup was a tool for urban development, by making possible the reclamation of an urban space and an industrial wasteland to attract new inhabitants and businesses, by creating jobs during the development phase and by turning the town of Saint-Denis into a tourist attraction. It was also a communication tool, to sell French technology for the construction of large buildings and transport infrastructure, such as the railways, to get people to the event. Finally, it was a political tool that aimed to attract world attention to the country for the duration of the event, to demonstrate the ability of the country, the state and the society to put on a large-scale event, and highlight the efficiency of its public services and the true spirit of the country (Callède 2000; Arnaud and Augustin 2000; Arnaud 2001).

The French sporting system

The present French model for the organisation of sport only really became established in 1960, on the basis of the distribution of tasks set out in 1945: the state gave the sporting federations a monopoly on organising competitions, conferring awards, selecting national teams and developing sport. The state reserved the right to intervene in the federations while recognising the independence of the sporting movement. From the Mazeaud law of 1975 to the Buffet law of 2000, ideas were put forward to legitimise state intervention: the place of sport in education, with APS being the joint responsibility of the Ministry for Sport (or its equivalent) and the sporting movement, while Physical and Sports Education came under the purview of the Ministry of Education; national representation in competition level sport; and the protection of sporting citizens' health and safety.

The state exercised increasing administrative and financial control of sporting associations and devised a set of regulations designed to ensure the safety of users, through agreement with the sporting associations, and the upkeep of sports facilities, to provide a system of compulsory insurance and medical checks, to prevent drug use and regulate the sporting professions and in particular the qualifications needed to become a coach. The sporting federations were required to sign a contract with the state stipulating the conditions for their participation in the movement for the democratisation of sport and the development of competition level sport, as the precondition for receiving subsidies.

APS thus became a genuine public service, with the task of ensuring the democratisation of its activities and its promotion in all sectors (civil society, schools, the armed forces and at work). The mission of social integration, which was the basis of its public service status, covered not only the safety of spectators in stadiums but also wider access to televised sport, which is why, for example, the state intervened so that great sporting events such as the Tour de France, the Rolland-Garros tennis championship and French team matches are shown on free-to-air television channels. The idea of sport as a public service also includes the struggle for the defence and promotion of the French model of integration between professional sport and sport for the masses, especially by maintaining the centralised allocation of television rights (currently a very thorny issue in the world of professional football) and by defining the status of the different professional groupings. Thus, the professional leagues remain part of the federations and the clubs can be commercial businesses, but they must remain subject to the 1901 law on associations, which is the basis for club status and bans them, at the present time, from distributing dividends and being quoted on the Stock Exchange. It was also this principle of public service and solidarity that led to the creation, in 1991, of the National Committee for Control and Management (DNCG), which is responsible for

auditing the accounts of professional football clubs and avoiding bank-
ruptcies. This model was then extended to all professional team sports.
These principles also meant that companies providing sporting leisure
facilities, such as fitness centres, were not officially recognised. Finally,
these ideas supported the notion of a 'sporting exception', which enabled
sport to be exempt from normal market rules in the name of the preservation of social values that were expressed through sport, such as identity,
equality and integration.

As for the policy on competition-level sport, this was justified as being
the ultimate outcome of top-level sport and in the name of national representation. This was reflected in the setting up of a specific organisation at
the beginning of the 1970s, which opened up new paths to sporting
achievement, such as the Football Centre at Clairefontaine or the new
National Rugby Centre. It also led to the training of specialist managers
(about 1500 people), who were then placed at the federations' disposal by
the state according to a hierarchy that went from the national technical
director down to department-level sports advisers, and established new
sources of funding that were linked to signed agreements with the federations for the delivery of certain agreed objectives. Furthermore, a new title
of high-level athlete was introduced, the attainment of which entitles the
selected sportsman or woman the right to aid (financial and social), just as
there exist high-level coaches, paid for by the state (a large proportion of
whom are civil servants). The public finance package was completed by the
National Fund for Sport Development (FNDS), created by the state in 1979,
which manages money arising from a percentage of the tax on betting.
Moreover, local councils intervene, especially by helping athletes from their
region, although the state tends to concentrate on funding competition-
level sport, while local councils mainly finance sport for the masses. For all
these reasons, we can consider that the Olympic medals as well as the
recent successes in football are the result of public intervention in sport.
This is true even of professional sports like football, by making possible,
from the 1960s onwards, the training of coaches and players and the financing of national sports facilities. Public intervention thus contributed to the
new organisation of sport and the new culture of success that we find in
judo, rowing, kayaking, basketball, volleyball, handball, fencing and tennis
(Barreau 2001). It also, along with the economic and social transformations
in France from the 1960s onwards, contributed to the move towards a
diversification of lifestyles and leisure activities, which resulted in a steady
increase in sporting activity (Mendras 1988). In 2000, 83 percent of the population aged between fifteen and seventy-five said they took part in some
kind of physical activity, compared to twenty-five percent in 1967 (Mignon
and Truchot 2002). This increase in physical exercise and the growth in
sporting practices of all kinds has led people to speak of a 'sportivisation'
of French society, as a way of describing both greater attention being paid

to health and the body, and a new definition of social relationships in terms of individualistic values, both ascetic and hedonistic, of competition and of team-working in business (Ehrenberg 1991).

The end of the French exception?

'France plays sport and France wins'. That was indeed the case in the 1996 Olympic Games and the 1998 Football World Cup. This is at least one of the exceptions that seemed to be in the process of disappearing after the 2002 World Cup. But what about the second exception, state intervention? This exception may disappear because it is no longer exceptional: for example, a country such as Australia presents many similarities with France in terms of the organisation of competition-level sport and public intervention, while Great Britain has moved away from the strictly *laissez-faire* approach it adopted for a number of years. It may also disappear because we have now perhaps reached the system's limits. We now have a very small administration for a large range of activities where, unlike in the 1960s, the main participants are private actors. As a result, a number of problems have arisen, such as the cost to the public purse of this intervention; its effectiveness, which has made France, for example, very successful in a small number of sports such as judo, fencing, horseriding, off-road cycling and synchronised swimming, but not so good at gymnastics and athletics; the fact that the advantages of the French training system and the resulting solidarity between professional and amateur football clubs comes at the cost of the financial and sporting fragility of professional clubs; and the permanent imbalance between elite sport and sport for the masses. Finally, sports clubs are seeing their memberships peak as an increasing number of individuals perform some form of sport (Baudillon 2000).

We must also keep in perspective the state's power, insofar as its financial means are limited. Since 1979, it has had to call on the resources of the FNDS and rely on the increased role of local councils (even if sport was not originally an area for which they were responsible). The result is the paradox of an interventionist system that lacks financial means in an area where the missions assigned to it have multiplied and its organisation has become increasingly complex. There is also the constant recourse to the state because of the weakness of the associations, as one can see with the drug issue, where the federations have been unable to deal with this rising phenomenon, and the problem of hooliganism. There have also been economic issues, as for example when the state set up the DNCG or when it intervened to arbitrate between the Rugby Federation and its professional league. In both cases, it was the state that took the initiative by passing a law or by putting pressure on the federations and clubs to take their share of responsibility in the matter and by reminding them of the importance of devising long- term strategies. It seems as if, if the state withdrew, no-one would be in a position to guarantee the long-term development of professional sport and its competitions. One could respond to this by suggesting that it is constant state intervention that has led to the irresponsibility of the sports associations. But is this situation unique to France? This is not certain.

In analysing the links between sport and politics, it is important to note the difference between the present context and the context in which sport was established in France: its origins were heavily marked by ideological considerations, whereas the 'end of political passions' no doubt explains its importance today. When there are no longer any visions for the future, when revolutionary hopes have disappeared along with great religious commitments, only the present counts, the emotions experienced and the result attained. This is what is at stake when sport is watched or played. Sport is never a trivial event: it is always the playing out of an exploit and of what remains of the ideals of equality and justice, of attachment to, and identification with, the nation or one's home town. From this point of view, if the French system has now reached its limits, perhaps it at least has the merit, through the theme of the sporting exception, of placing great new sportsmen and women in front of an inescapable question: how can excellence in sport be reconciled with the need for equality between those who practise it, which is what enables them to attain excellence?

Chapter 14

FRENCH INTELLECTUALS: THE LEGENDARY EXCEPTION

Michael Kelly

> Many foreign observers have quipped that intellectuals are a French speciality, attributable to our exceptional monarchic and Jacobin tradition. This is untrue, of course. As Raymond Aron demonstrated in his *Opium of the intellectuals,* every society eventually secretes a body of people specialising in defining norms and producing values. But it is certainly true that the peculiar effervescence of this corporation, and its place in national political debates, are one of the most striking features of France, from the eighteenth century to the present day. (Julliard and Winock 1996: 13)[1]

This nuanced denial of the French 'intellectual exception' is a graceful way of accepting a compliment. It is true that foreign commentators have often remarked on the extraordinary place of intellectuals in France. Theodore Zeldin, for example, describes them as 'a small group that have cast a magic spell on the way the French are perceived by themselves and by foreigners' (Zeldin 1983: 398). The result is a glorious legend that France has always been the privileged homeland of the intellectual. It is echoed in many of the scholarly studies that have been undertaken in recent years. And it figures as a supporting feature of the wider French 'cultural exception'. This chapter will attempt to clarify the basis on which the legend has arisen, and assess how well it stands up to close scrutiny. In particular, it will suggest that the legend arose from the period immediately following the Second World War, when French intellectuals played a highly distinctive role in French society. This remarkable period lasted for almost thirty years, but its 'halo effect' has surrounded intellectual activity in France up to the present day, and has also inflected the way that earlier periods have been understood. While most scholarly accounts date them from the Dreyfus case, the legend has it that intellectuals have always been an exceptional French feature, from the eighteenth century, or perhaps even the

Middle Ages. The legend may be gaining greater lustre from recent prog-
nostications of the 'end of the intellectual'.

Intellectual exception or cultural diversity?

Most countries regard themselves as exceptional, and some countries
achieve international recognition for their exceptional characteristics. Of
late, it has become an orthodoxy of global business that the role of
national governments is to seek competitive advantage by identifying
and promoting their country's areas of distinctive excellence (Porter
1990). This is an important part of the context in which France has
debated *l'exception française*, and as Susan Collard notes, the notion of a
French exception has come to be associated with many disparate and
unlikely fields. She aptly points out that the notion 'only began to take on
a reality (at least in discursive terms) from the point in time which was
identified as being the moment of its demise'.[2] And one might add that its
discursive afterlives have been particularly vigorous. Four or five years
after the seminal announcement of its threatened demise (Furet, Julliard,
and Rosanvallon 1988), the Uruguay Round of GATT negotiations
erupted into a dispute over the French cultural exception, where France
led European opposition to U.S. proposals for deregulating the audiovisual industries. Subsequently, the notion of the exception was extended to
cover the entire cultural domain, for example by Jacques Rigaud (Rigaud
1996), head of the RTL broadcasting company, former senior civil servant
in the Ministry of Culture, and author of several books on cultural policy
(Rigaud 1975, 1990). When this exception was itself declared dead in late
2001 by Jean-Marie Messier, head of the Vivendi-Universal corporation
and a key figure in implementing French cultural exceptionalism, a storm
of protest ensued in France, revitalising the supposed corpse (Regourd
2002). By that time, it had become apparent that the notion of *l'exception*,
cultural or otherwise, had become an established feature of French
national identity and, as Nick Hewlett suggests, come to stand in constant
opposition to the processes of 'normalisation' by which France sees itself
threatened.[3] Consequently, the question of whether there is an 'intellectual exception' remains a delicate one in France, as reflected in Julliard
and Winock's nuanced treatment of it.

The richness of France's cultural and intellectual life from the Middle
Ages to the present day is unquestionable, as is its importance in the
broader life of the country. But as Julliard and Winock point out, every
country has its cultural figures, with important roles in articulating norms
and values for their society. And while there is a long popular tradition of
comparing one country's cultural figures with those of another, the case
for exceptionalism could not be founded on vaunting the respective mer-

its of Racine against Shakespeare, or Jean-Paul Sartre against Bertrand Russell. There has until recently been relatively little academic interest in comparing one country's cultural figures with those of another, and Susan Collard is right to point to the prevalence of unproven assertions over rigorous comparisons in this. But the task of drawing rigorous comparisons between intellectuals of different countries is by no means straightforward. Relatively few works have attempted it, and with few exceptions, such as Frank Field's study of French and British writers of the First World War (Field 1991), those that do attempt it are edited volumes based on colloquia (Granjon, Racine, and Trebitsch 1997; Kemp-Welch and Jennings 1997; Hill 2000; Racine 2003). Valuable though these are, they offer only limited elements of synthesis of the kind that address issues of differentiation and exception. The reasons for this relative lack are not difficult to find.[4] Among other practical difficulties, any scholar undertaking a comparative study of this kind would need a formidable range of knowledge, skills and resources spanning two or more cultures. The objects of comparison do not often present enough historical symmetry to compare like with like. And the scholar's work is suffused with his or her own particular identities, audiences and communities of reference. Though these may be counterbalanced by the advances of information technology, and by increased opportunities to travel and develop international contacts, the comparative approach is a difficult one to pursue in intellectual history.

It is striking that French discourse on *l'exception* has not been hampered by the lack of serious comparative study. On the contrary, it has perhaps been assisted by it. Exceptionalism is an inherently ambiguous notion, located within the interplay between identity and difference. An exception can only exist if there is some rule or norm with which it is identified, but from which it diverges in some significant respect. This was clear in the GATT negotiations, where it was agreed to exclude the audiovisual industries from the rules of international trade applying to all other industries. But it is less clear that the culture of a particular country can be seen as diverging from a general rule to which all other countries conform. It is significant that international trade negotiations have moved to focus on cultural *diversity*, rather than exceptionalism, as the means of recognising the differences between countries (Regourd 2002). In this perspective, it may be argued that exceptionalism is nothing other than the way diversity is experienced within a particular country, in this case France. If this is so, then the presentation of an exception is not dependent on any particular comparison, but requires only that the possibility of comparison should be acknowledged. Roland Barthes might have stigmatised this as the strategy of the *alibi* (Barthes 1957): references to possible comparisons give permission for the particular case to be presented as exceptional. A 'light touch' acknowledgement also masks the danger that too close an analysis of comparisons would emphasise the relativity of each particular case within a context of pervasive diversity, and would consequently undermine the sense of exceptionalism.

The legend of French intellectuals

In these circumstances, it is therefore less useful to ask whether French intellectuals have been historically exceptional in comparison to other countries, and more useful to ask what French and foreign commentators consider distinctive about French intellectuals. The answer to this is largely to be found in the legend that has now grown up around them. The term 'legend' is used advisedly. It is a term present in both English and French since the Middle Ages, whose first meaning is the story of the life of a saint (*Oxford English Dictionary Online* 2003). It is exemplified in the medieval collection of saints' lives written by Jacobus de Voragine, Archbishop of Genoa, in the thirteenth century, now usually called *The Golden Legend* (*Legenda Aurea*), the name popularly given to it in the Middle Ages. Later it was extended to a wider range of stories, handed down by tradition from early times and popularly regarded as historical. The idea of the intellectual as a kind of saint is not far removed from the French notion that they are 'clerics' (*clercs*), albeit of a secular type, and that their lives are exemplary, at least in the commitments they espouse (Benda 1927).[5] Moreover, like the lives of saints, a legend is presumed to have some grounding in historical fact, and there can be no doubt that the French intellectuals have such a grounding, even if its 'halo effect' exceeds its historical basis.

Historical information is plentiful, and the history of intellectuals in France is a well-established area of study in France itself, as demonstrated by Julliard and Winock's Dictionary of French Intellectuals, which extends to 1,260 pages, and covers all the main figures and movements, as well as the places and events in which intellectuals have been prominent during the twentieth century. With some 240 contributors, the scale of the work itself demonstrates the importance of intellectuals in French historiography. There is an impressive body of work by a substantial group of high-profile historians, who together make up a cohesive scholarly community concerned with the area.[6] Though less extensive, there is also a significant body of work by non-French scholars, especially in the English-speaking world.[7] With such authoritative analyses available, the historical basis for understanding French intellectuals is unquestionable. The legendary dimension arises from ways in which the importance and distinctiveness of French intellectuals has been taken to extend beyond what can be historically supported.

Who are the intellectuals?

To some extent the historical and legendary aspects can be distinguished by clarifying definitions. French historians have come to broad agreement on their object of study: a recognisable intellectual community that has developed over a century in France, and has shown a notable degree of self-awareness at key moments in its history. For Michel Winock the task is to provide 'the description of political confrontations that have opposed writers, philosophers, artists and scientists' (Winock 1999b: 7). He and Jacques Julliard confine their Dictionary to those who have shown a polit-ical commitment (*engagement*) (Julliard and Winock 1996). For Pascal Ory and Jean-François Sirinelli, 'the intellectual will therefore be a man of the cultural sphere, a creator or mediator, put in the position of a man of poli-tics, a producer or consumer of ideology' (Ory and Sirinelli 2002: 10). In the same vein, for Michel Leymarie, the intellectual is 'a man – much more often than a woman – master of the spoken word and familiar with the written, whose job is to think, and who, from outside the political world, speaks on behalf of values in public debate, formulates its terms and its implications, and has – or claims to have – the vocation of the universal' (Leymarie 2001: 3). The markedly masculine profile conveyed is part of the specificity of the French construction of the intellectual, despite the recent attention that has been paid to 'les intellectuelles' (Racine 2003). The defi-nition clearly echoes Sartre's characterisation of the intellectual as a tech-nician of practical knowledge who meddles in what does not concern him, namely politics (Sartre 1972). Ory and Sirinelli propose, however, a signif-icant shift of emphasis away from Sartre's solitary figure toward the intel-lectuals as a social group, 'an intellectual community' (*société intellectuelle*), with its own methods and networks, and a degree of self-awareness as a group (2002: 10). The collectivity took its origins in the debates around the Dreyfus case in France at the end of the nineteenth century, in the particu-lar context of a highly centralised national state with a radical revolution-ary and democratic political tradition, at a time when mass education and literacy were spreading to the whole population. Although the intellectual therefore constitutes a specific formation in the context of French history, Ory and Sirinelli point out that the concept has gained wider currency and has been applied anachronistically to other periods of history, includ-ing the Middle Ages (Le Goff 1975).

The pre-history of French intellectuals

This wider currency forms the outer fringes of the golden legend of French intellectuals. Jacques Le Goff's use of the concept to describe medieval Schoolmen is deliberately provocative, and successfully enables the period to be viewed in a fresh perspective, generating sparkling insights and suggestive analogies. But the social and political contexts that made intellectuals a distinctive feature of twentieth-century life were almost wholly lacking in the Middle Ages. Moreover, the role of clerics in medieval France, far from being unique, was common to most of Western Christendom. Their co-option into a French 'exception' could only be conceived from the particular standpoint of late twentieth-century France. Much the same can be said of the eighteenth-century writers who are frequently quoted as intellectuals *avant la lettre*. While it is true that national identities were assuming a higher profile, the Republic of Letters was an assertively cosmopolitan affair. It is difficult to disentangle the specifically French contribution to the Enlightenment, without doing violence to the relations between writers from different countries and to the role played by many neighbouring countries in supporting and developing the French *philosophes*. While Voltaire's crusades on behalf of victims of religious intolerance have often been compared with the Dreyfus case, they remain early precursors, rather than examples of a tradition. The nineteenth century produced a pantheon of French writers and artists deeply engaged in the political struggles of the century, through monarchies, empires and republics. Several held high political office, several endured prison or exile, in the name of their beliefs (Winock 2001). Some experienced both. They are among the most distinguished names in French culture and include, for example, Balzac, Chateaubriand, Constant, Daumier, Delacroix, Flaubert, Géricault, Hugo, Lamartine, Maupassant, Michelet, Quinet, Renan, Sand, Stendhal, and Zola. But looking at the life and works of these figures and other contemporaries, it is difficult to assign the label 'intellectual' to them, without diminishing their stature, either in terms of their writings or in terms of their public role. If commentators can happily accommodate eighteenth-century predecessors, their curious reluctance to claim nineteenth-century writers as intellectuals raises interesting questions.[8]

Emergence of the intellectuals during the Dreyfus Case

For the most part, historians are content to make broad gestures of inclusion towards the more distant past. This academic curtsey may nourish the impression of an apostolic succession of intellectuals and therefore burnish the halo effect of the golden legend, but it does not press a strong historical claim. By general consent, the story begins in earnest with the Dreyfus case. To some extent, the consensus is led by the emergence of the noun 'intellectual' into common currency at this point. Though the word can be found sporadically in earlier writings by Saint-Simon, Balzac or Renan (Julliard and Winock 1996: 14), it was popularised in the vehement polemics that began in January 1898 around the trials and imprisonment of Captain Dreyfus on charges of spying and was identified with the group of dissident writers, artists and academics who campaigned for truth and justice against the institutions of the state, the judicial system, the army and the church (Cahm 1996). Since this public baptism coincided with the turn of the century, it has generally been agreed that the twentieth century was the 'century of the intellectuals' (Winock 1999b), and several recent historical studies of the French intellectuals have taken this to define their scope (Ory and Sirinelli 2002; Julliard and Winock 1996; Leymarie 2001). In a sense, this approach is uncontentious, since it begins with the naming of the phenomenon. The emergence of the name in France still leaves open the question of how the newly baptised French intellectuals differed from their counterparts in other countries. More significant, it leaves open the question of how the phenomenon differed from what existed before, and how far it constituted a sustained change.

French commentators have tended to assume that French usage led to the adoption of the idea of the intellectual by other countries. The French example did in due course become an influential model, but in fact, the term 'intellectual' was used with broadly the same meaning in other languages during the nineteenth century. In English, there are attested uses of the term by Byron and Ruskin in the early part of the century (1813 and 1847 respectively), and it was in common usage in the press by the end of the century (*Oxford English Dictionary Online* 2003). Undoubtedly similar patterns could be traced in other languages, with a range of differences and similarities between French intellectuals and their British, German or indeed Turkish counterparts at this period.[9] The difficulties of pursuing a comparative analysis have already been noted, but it may support the French perception of a distinctive or exceptional status if it were established that the experience of the Dreyfus case had transformed the body of people who henceforth might be considered intellectuals in France.

The turbulence of the Dreyfus case was soon superseded in public opinion by more pressing issues, increasingly those of peace and war. In Charles Péguy's terms (Péguy 1910; Cahm 1972), the *mystique* deteriorated into politics as protagonist intellectuals on both sides of the argument gravitated to more traditionally political commitments on the nationalist right and the socialist left until these long-running polarisations were dampened by the 'sacred union' of national unanimity in the face of foreign aggression in the First World War (Hanna 1996). The participants in rhetorical battles of the Dreyfus case may not have created a sustainable sense of community among intellectuals, but their action did mark the arrival of a certain number of innovations with longer term significance. Two are particularly noteworthy. One of the most significant was the emergence of manifestoes and petitions as a form of action (Sirinelli 1990). Emphasising the growing role of the media and the importance of public opinion, they also created, on paper at least, the sense of intellectuals as a significant body of people, willing to use their cultural capital in support of a social or political cause. A second legacy of Dreyfus was the meeting of writers and artists with scholars and scientists. Science and education were national priorities for France in the Third Republic. In particular, the laws brought forward by Jules Ferry during the 1880s introduced free compulsory state schooling and began a social revolution. Among other things, they created a large secular workforce of educators, from which many of the new intellectuals arose. The French university system doubled in size in the fifteen years 1891–1906, stabilising at that point (Prost 1968). The role of teachers and academics in the Dreyfus case was significant, even if their presence in petitions and newspaper articles was less prominent than writers and journalists. As the century progressed, their presence among the recognised intellectuals grew sharply.

Return of the intellectuals in the 1930s

Though the Dreyfus case focused attention on the rise of the media and of public education, these were by no means uniquely French developments. On the contrary, they were common to most industrial countries at the period, and produced similar cultural changes. The social and political conflicts of the 1920s and 1930s, fuelled by economic crisis, provided a further spur for educators and scientists to join with writers and artists in campaigning on the issues of the day. The magnetic force of the new communist and fascist movements added to the polarisation of opinion, and gave increased intensity and vehemence to the debates in France and in other countries. For a long time, however, French participants did not engage battle under the banner of intellectuals. Two of the most noted polemics of the interwar era, Julien Benda's *La Trahison des clercs* (Benda 1927) and Paul Nizan's *Les Chiens de garde* (Nizan 1932), dealt trenchantly with the maladies affecting what would now be called the intellectuals of the period. Strikingly, neither used the term 'intellectual', but addressed their strictures to the 'clercs' or the 'philosophers' whom, from their different stances, they accused of betraying the human race.

The re-emergence of 'intellectuals' as an acknowledged category dates from the mid-1930s, when organisations of the political left and right intensified their campaigning around issues of war and peace (Sirinelli 1990: 132–214). The best-known examples are on the left, with the Vigilance Committee of Anti-fascist Intellectuals (Comité de vigilance des intellectuels antifascistes), founded in 1934, and the Union of French Intellectuals for Justice, Liberty and Peace (Union des intellectuels français pour la justice, la liberté et la paix), founded in 1938. But on the right too, declarations were issued, identifying their signatories specifically as intellectuals. Henri Massis, for example, organised a Manifesto of Intellectuals for Peace in Europe and the Defence of the West (*Manifeste des intellectuels pour la paix en Europe et la défense de l'Occident*) in October 1935 supporting the Italian intervention in Ethiopia, and similar other declarations followed on the civil war in Spain. The resurgence of self-identified intellectuals was brought to an abrupt end by the outbreak of war.

Up to this point, it is difficult to see any basis for an exceptional status for French intellectuals, either in comparison with events in other countries, or in comparison with the role played by writers, artists and academics in earlier periods of French history. Certainly, writers like Romain Rolland and Henri Barbusse were influential in the early stages of the movement that led to the Popular Front government. But the extent of most intellectuals' public profile was distinctly modest, and largely focused within a narrow Parisian milieu. Their debates were mainly conducted across the pages of small reviews, with petitions or manifestoes sometimes achieving publication in the daily press, and disputes occasionally spilling over into confrontations on the streets of the Latin Quarter. From the perspective of French intellectuals, probably the most lasting significance of the interwar period is that it provided opportunities for the younger generation of writers, artists and academics to gain experience of political involvement. Born after the Dreyfus case, and too young to have fought in the Great War, this new generation were the novices and junior partners in many of the interwar disputes. Some, like Emmanuel Mounier or Andrée Viollis, threw themselves into action, while others, like Jean-Paul Sartre and Simone de Beauvoir, watched from the sidelines. Either way, they obtained an apprenticeship that bore fruit in the exceptional circumstances of the Liberation.

The Golden Age of the intellectuals

Immediately after the Second World War, France faced complex post-conflict circumstances in the wake of what would now be called 'regime change'. The provisional government recognised that cultural and intellectual reconstruction was at least as important and possibly no less difficult than economic and political reconstruction. In the postwar penury, one thing that was in plentiful supply was a cultural heritage of language, images, and ideas, and a highly educated body of writers, artists, scholars and scientists, who had learned political and social commitment, whether in the 1930s or during the occupation. These 'intellectuals' were mobilised for internal purposes, to assist the country in reinventing itself, in reshaping the hearts and minds of the people, and in rebuilding the 'imagined community' of the nation. They were also mobilised for external representation, as cultural ambassadors, promoting French culture around the world as a key part of restoring France's prestige and its international position. The task fell particularly to the generation who had been intellectual apprentices before the war, and particularly with those who had a left-wing affiliation. In 1945, Sartre suggests, no author could publish without having some link with the Resistance, or at least a cousin in the *maquis*. As a result, in the field of literature for example, many senior figures in the literary establishment were discredited by their wartime activities, while others had died or been forgotten. The result of what called 'this sudden massacre of the Grand Old Men' (*Cette brusque hécatombe des doyens*)', (Sartre 1948b: 46) was an urgent need to fill the void left behind. An important factor, in his view, was that France had been humiliated internationally as a result of the war, and that its literature was one of the few things for which it was still admired, especially by the Western Allies. The widespread international interest in French literature prompted France to take it more seriously than in the past. Sartre observed wryly that many French people would prefer their country to be best known for military leaders like Turenne or Bonaparte, but for the time being they were willing to settle for poets like Rimbaud or Valéry. As a result, young writers were being prematurely boosted into great men, who could be dispatched to London, Stockholm or Washington. Sartre was as well placed as anyone to attest to the pressures on French writers to play a representative role in the nation in 1945. He spent several months visiting the U.S. as a willing spokesman and literary ambassador on behalf of France. And at home he was prominent in the National Writers' Committee (Comité national des écrivains: CNE), which was issuing blacklists and ensuring that writers had the kind of wartime credentials he described.

At this period, it was still rare for writers such as Sartre to refer to themselves as intellectuals, but in the months following the Liberation, writers gradually internalised the status and began to 'come out' as intellectuals. This is particularly visible in three groups of writers who are now generally regarded as archetypal intellectuals. The first group are the existentialists and the wider constituency surrounding the review *Les Temps modernes*. As well as Sartre, Simone de Beauvoir and Maurice Merleau-Ponty, it includes such writers as Albert Camus, Raymond Aron and Boris Vian, among many others. The second group are the Left Catholics and their sympathisers around reviews like *Esprit* and *Témoignage chrétien* and the éditions du Seuil publishers. As well as the directors of these, Emmanuel Mounier, André Mandouze and Paul Flamand, it includes writers such as Jean Lacroix, Claude-Edmonde Magny, Jean-Marie Domenach, Denis de Rougemont, and Paul Ricoeur. The third group are the Christian Democrats, whose spiritual leader, Jacques Maritain, was more often in New York and Rome than in Paris, but which included philosophers like Pierre Teilhard de Chardin and Gaston Fessard as well as writers and journalists like François Mauriac, Stanislas Fumet and Louis

Terrenoire. The texts written by the members of these groupings made remarkably few references to intellectuals, and when they did so, it is in the same spirit as Sartre, who wrote pityingly that 'Anglo-Saxon intellectuals, who form a race apart, cut off from the rest of the nation, are always dazzled when they find in France men of letters and artists closely involved in the life and affairs of their country' (Sartre 1948b: 42). It is striking that Anglo-Saxon 'intellectuals' are contrasted with French 'men of letters and artists', all the more remarkable since the American and British writers of the period would have been even less likely than the French to describe themselves as intellectuals. Two main factors contributed to the emergence of intellectuals as a self-conscious group: the importance of the Resistance role and the policies of the French Communist Party (PCF).

The Resistance and the Communist Party

The role of intellectuals during the occupation was one of the most prominent themes of the Liberation. Those writers, artists and journalists who had supported Vichy or the Germans had done so recently and visibly in the public arena. Conversely, those who had supported the Resistance now found their clandestine writings republished for a mass readership, which regarded them as custodians of the nation's honour. The trial and execution of the writer Robert Brasillach for intelligence with the enemy made the question of the intellectual's responsibility into one of the most hotly debated issues of the year. The galaxy of luminaries from the worlds of culture and science who petitioned General de Gaulle to exercise clemency, made it clear that they fully accepted the responsibility of intellectuals, and the text of their request identified them as 'the undersigned intellectuals' (Sirinelli 1990). Writers who had joined the Resistance, for their part, looked back nostalgically at what they now saw as their finest hour. The unique nature of the Resistance experience was a frequent theme for writers, who as Merleau-Ponty suggested, tended to want its spirit to be maintained in the postwar arrangements:

> The experience of resistance was for them a unique experience, and they wanted to retain its spirit in the new French politics, because it at last escaped the notorious dilemma of being and doing, which every intellectual feels when confronted by action. (Merleau-Ponty 1996: 183–84)

The identity of 'Resistance intellectual' was in 1945 a positive and valorising one, which largely overcame the pejorative associations that had previously clung to the term intellectual. There were counter-examples, in people like Brasillach, Drieu la Rochelle and the dozens of writers and artists named in lists of collaborators by the CNE (Assouline 1985). However, for the most part, these were considered as exceptions. Sartre, speaking primarily to an American readership, declared that 'almost all the intellectuals fought against the occupying power' (Sartre 1949: 45). This was a point taken up energetically by the PCF, which played an influential role in highlighting the role of intellectuals in the Resistance, especially those of its own members who had been executed or died in deportation, most prominently Georges Politzer, Jacques Salomon and Jacques Decour (Daniel Decourdemanche), later joined by Danielle Casanova. Initially, the task of mobilising intellectuals was given to the experienced teacher, turned politician, Georges Cogniot, and the young philosopher Roger Garaudy. In keynote interventions at the Tenth Congress of the party in 1945, they saluted 'all the heroes of our intelligentsia who died for their Country' (Cogniot and Garaudy 1945: 17). They celebrated the great French artistic, literary and scientific traditions. And they called on intellectuals in all branches of culture and education to put their weight behind the work of national reconstruction, led by the party. The party recognised not only the symbolic value of prominent figures, but also the importance of intellectuals as a rapidly growing social and electoral group (Caute 1964; Verdès-Leroux 1983). It set an agenda in which intellectuals were invited to become more aware of their specificity and at the same time to extend their political partisanship into their intellectual activity. Largely as a result of this, and from the onset of the Cold War, the intellectual became a prominent part of the French political landscape, and a figure that seemed always to have been there (Kelly 1997).

Intellectuals as national treasures

The dissident stance of so many intellectuals during the following decades did not prevent them from being national treasures, however inconvenient they may at times have been for a particular government. General de Gaulle was more aware of this than most, and twenty years or so later, when his advisers approached him about one of Sartre's current skirmishes with the law, he is reported to have commented that 'you don't arrest Voltaire' (Atack 1999: 74). The comparison with the celebrated Enlightenment philosopher is often made of Sartre, and betokens not simply his high cultural prestige, but also his importance as a national figure. Recent studies of French intellectuals have largely focused on their struggles for political power or cultural capital within the overall social field (Boschetti 1988; Jennings 1993; Debray 1979). They consider the often-difficult relations of intellectuals to this or that French institution, organisation, issue or policy. But underpinning all the battles and controversies is a prior commitment to the primacy of the French nation, as incarnated by the state. This now appears too self-evident to mention, following half a century in which the worst taunt that could be flung at an intellectual is that they are lacking in national commitment. But the specifically national commitment of the French intellectuals was constructed in the historical circumstances of the Liberation.

The end of the intellectual exception?

For the thirty glorious years (*trente glorieuses*) of postwar prosperity, the integration of French intellectuals with the nation gave them a privileged role in articulating national identity. This was not a tranquil role. On the contrary, contending groups of intellectuals pitched into bitter conflicts with one another in a succession of high-profile quarrels, attacks, counter attacks, campaigns and court cases. Issues of national and international politics, of philosophy and social theory, as well as personal histories and conflicts formed a heady mixture, which were endlessly fascinating to cultivated audiences in France and across the world. Or so it seemed for thirty years. But the lustre of this Golden Age of intellectuals eventually began to fade. From the mid-1970s, there was a noticeable increase in anti-intellectualism in France, reflected in prolonged bouts of self-questioning among the intellectuals themselves (Flower 1991). Some recent commentators now go so far as to suggest that the intellectual has either ceased to matter, or even ceased to exist, in contemporary France. The intellectual review *Esprit* recently devoted two special numbers to the 'Splendours and poverty of intellectual life'.[10] Several contributors examined the issue of whether the day of the intellectuals was over, and if they did not all consider that it was, at least they were sharply aware that the question was on the table. Shortly afterwards, Régis Debray launched a polemic through his book *I.F. suite et fin*, suggesting that the French Intellectual (*intellectuel français*, I.F.) has been transformed into the Last Intellectual (*intellectuel terminal*), reaching its final incarnation before disappearing entirely (Debray 2000). This work has aroused considerable controversy and is far from articulating a consensus, though it does resonate with the mood of doubt and self-questioning in intellectual circles. Michel Leymarie and Michel Winock both conclude their recent works of synthesis with a chapter entitled interrogatively, 'the end of the intellectuals?' Each offers a balanced answer recognising the probable end of the era of high-profile prophet-like individuals, and emphasising 'mutations' in the role of moral questioning and democratic debate. This suggests the analogy of Minerva's Owl, the symbol of wisdom, which in Hegel's account only flies out at dusk. Similarly, the scholarly history of intellectuals has emerged and flourished in France, just as the exceptionalism of French intellectuals begins to fade into the past.

There are many explanations of why this might have happened. The expansion of higher education from the 1960s probably played a role in rendering more commonplace the debates of the elite. The re-emergence of militant right-wing intellectuals in the mid-1970s was certainly a factor, led by the 'New Philosophers', who were committed to demolishing the fascination of the earlier generation of intellectuals. The deaths during the 1980s of leading figures like Sartre (1980), Barthes (1980), Foucault (1984), and Beauvoir (1986) played a part, as did the advent of the Mitterrand presidency (1981–1995), which demobilised many left-wing intellectuals. The growth of the mass media contributed its insatiable demand for celebrities, among whom intellectuals were just another group of talking heads. And the accelerating internationalisation of intellectual life provided both opportunities and threats, giving amplified prominence to a few French stars while opening the French market to a plethora of international figures.

The evident demoralisation and loss of prestige affecting current intellectuals has combined with the emergence of a vigorous historiography to add lustre to the reputation of earlier generations of intellectuals. Nostalgia for the Golden Age easily leads to optimistic denials that it has come to an end, and both contribute to the legend of the French intellectual as a permanent figure of the French exception. However, there is a significant consolation in the twilight of these gods: they have passed on their most important achievements to mere mortals. Their engagements have contributed to widening the base of political debate and asserting the rights of non-specialists to speak on the most important national and international issues. To a large extent, this has borne fruit in the widespread acceptance of a renovated notion of citizenship (Schnapper and Bachelier 2000). The duty of taking part in public life, whatever one's professional expertise, has now become recognised as a democratic responsibility for all citizens, an achievement that was dear to the heart of Eric Cahm, and to which he contributed so actively. It is this change that may ultimately have robbed the intellectuals of their special role in articulating political and social commitment. Eric would no doubt have considered this a price worth paying and would perhaps have seen it more positively as the great intellectuals' parting gift to their more numerous but also less exceptional successors.

Notes

1. All translations are my own, except where otherwise stated.
2. See Chapter 3 'The Elusive French Exception'.
3. See Chapter 1 'France and exceptionalism'.

4. For a fuller discussion of these issues, see Kelly 2003.
5. This notion is developed by Jean-Paul Sartre in his work on Jean Genet (Sartre 1952).
6. There is a useful bibliography of their key works in Leymarie 2001. See among others Racine 2003; Ory and Sirinelli 2002; Charle 1990; Winock 1999b.
7. See, among others Caute 1964; Drake 2002; Flood and Hewlett 2000; Hazareesingh 1991; Judt 1992; Mathy 1993; Nelson 1995; Reader 1987; Jennings 1993.
8. Space does not permit this topic to be pursued here, but several lines of inquiry could be suggested, including the increased importance of academics (as opposed to writers) in the intellectual life of the Third Republic; the contrast between the nineteenth and twentieth centuries, heightened by the perceived turning point of the Dreyfus case; and the widely observed scholarly division of labour between political and literary historians.
9. The *OED Online* entry quotes a newspaper reference in the *Daily News* (30 November 1898) to 'the so-called intellectuals of Constantinople, who were engaged in discussion while the Turks were taking possession of the city'.
10. 'Splendeurs et misères de la vie intellectuelle', *Esprit*, March & May 2000.

BIBLIOGRAPHY

Actuel Marx. 2000: 'Y a-t-il une pensée unique en philosophie politique?' Special issue, no 28. Paris: Presses universitaires de France.

Adam, G. 2000. *Les Relations sociales année zéro.* Paris: Bayard.

Adams, D. and C. van Minnen, eds. 1994. *Reflections on American Exceptionalism.* Keele: Ryburn.

Adda, J. and M.-C. Smouts. 1989. *La France face au Sud. Le Miroir brisé.* Paris: Karthala.

Adler, I. 1993. 'The Mexican Case: The Media in the 1988 Presidential Election'. In R. Skidmore (ed.), *Television, Politics and the Transition to Democracy in Latin America.* Baltimore: The John Hopkins University Press.

Aglietta, M. 1998. *Le Capitalisme de demain.* Paris: Fondation Saint-Simon.

Agulhon, M. 1987. *Essais d'ego histoire.* Paris: Gallimard.

Amber, A. 2000. 'Making the Debates Happen: A Television Producer's Perspective'. In S. Coleman (ed.), *Televised Election Debates. International Perspectives.* Basingstoke: Macmillan.

Amin, S. 1989. *Eurocentrism.* London: Zed Books.

Andersen, J. and Bjørlund, T. 2000. 'Radical Right-Wing Populism in Scandinavia: From Tax Revolt to Neo-Liberalism and Xenophobia'. In P. Hainsworth (ed.), *The Politics of the Extreme Right: From the Margins to the Mainstream.* London: Pinter.

Anderson, B. 1983. *Imagined Communities. Reflections on the Origin and Spread of Nationalism.* London: Verso.

Anderson, P. 1964. 'Origins of the Present Crisis', *New Left Review* 23: 26–53. Reprinted in P. Anderson, *English Questions.* London: Verso.

Andolfatto, D. 2000. 'Les principales organisations syndicales des salariés'. In *L'Etat de la France, 2000–2001.* Paris: La Découverte & Syros.

———— 2001. 'Le plus faible taux de syndicalisation des pays industrialisés'. In *L'Etat de la France, 2001–2002.* Paris: La Découverte & Syros.

Andolfatto, D. and D. Labbé. 2000. *Sociologie des syndicats.* Paris: La Découverte.

Anon. 1996. 'The Civil Service'. In *An Introduction to French Administration.* Paris: La Documentation Française.

Arnaud, P. 2001. ' Genèse des politiques sportives publiques : le cas français', *Revue française d'administration publique,* 97: 29–38.

Arnaud, P. and J.-P. Augustin. 2000. ' L'Etat et le sport : construction et transformation d'un service public'. In P. Arnaud (ed.), *Le Sport en France: une approche politique, économique et sociale.* Paris: La Documentation Française.

Arnaud, P. and A. Wahl. 1994. *Sports et relations internationales*. Centre d'études des civilisations européennes, Université de Metz.

Ashcroft, B., G. Griffiths and H. Tiffin, eds. 1995. *The Post-Colonial Reader*. London: Routledge.

Assouline, P. 1985. *L'Épuration des intellectuels: 1944–1945*. Brussels: Editions Complexe.

Atack, M. 1999. *May 68 in French Fiction and Film*. Oxford: Oxford University Press.

Azéma, J.-P., J.-P. Rioux and H. Rousso. 1985. 'Les guerres franco-françaises', *Vingtième siècle*, special issue, 5.

Bachmann, S. 1997. *L'Éclatement de l'ORTF*. Paris: L'Harmattan.

Baker, K.L. and H. Norpoth. 1981. 'Candidates on Television: The 1972 Electoral Debates in West Germany', *Public Opinion Quarterly* 45: 329–45.

Baker, K.L., H. Norpoth and K. Schoenbach. 1981. 'Die Fernsehdebatten der Spitzenpolitiker vor den Bundestagswahlen 1972 & 1976', *Publizistik* 26: 530–40.

Barreau, G. 2001. 'Le modèle français du sport', *Revue française d'administration publique*, 97: 15–28.

Barret-Kriegel, B. 1989. *La République incertaine*. Paris: Presses Universitaires de France.

Barthes, R. 1957. *Mythologies*. Paris: Seuil.

Baudillon, P. 2000. 'Sport: assouplir le modèle français'. In R. Fauroux and F. Spitz (eds), *Notre Etat: le livre vérité de la fonction publique*. Paris: Laffont.

Baverez, N. 2003. *La France qui tombe. Un constat clinique du déclin français*. Paris: Perrin.

Beaud, S. and G. Noiriel. 1990. ' L'immigration dans le football', *Vingtième Siècle*, special issue: 'Le football, sport du 20ème siècle', 26.

Bell, D. 2002. *French Politics Today*. Manchester: Manchester University Press.

Belloc, B. 1998 'La Fonction publique: un emploi sur quatre'. In F. Gallouédec-Genuys (ed.) *A propos de l'administration française*. Paris: La Documentation Française.

Benda, J. 1927. *La Trahison des clercs*. Paris: Grasset.

Berne, J. 1981. *La Campagne présidentielle de Valéry Giscard d'Estaing en 1974*. Paris: Presses Universitaires de France.

Berstein, S. 1991. 'Political Consensus in 20th Century France'. In S. Berstein and P. Morris (eds), *Political Consensus in France and Britain*, Studies in European Culture and Society: Paper 5, European Research Centre, Loughborough University of Technology.

Béroud, S., R. Mouriaux and M. Vakaloulis. 1998. *Le Mouvement social en France. Essai de sociologie politique*. Paris: La Dispute.

Besançon, A. 2000. 'Nous allons en Russie' *Commentaire*, 90: 321–28.

Betz, H.-G. 1994. *Radical Right Wing Populism in Western Europe*. Basingstoke: Macmillan.

Betz, H.-G. and S. Immerfall. 1998. *The New Politics of the Right: Neopopulist Parties and Movements in Established Democracy*. Basingstoke: Macmillan.

Bezès, P. 2001. 'Bureaucrats and politicians in the politics of administrative reforms in France (1988–1997). In B.G. Peters and J. Pierre (eds), *Politicians, Bureaucrats and Administrative Reforms*. London: Routledge/ECPR Studies in European Political Science.

Bihr, A. 1998. 'Alsace, exception à la règle', *Le Monde diplomatique*, May: 16–17.

Biltereyst, D. 1992. 'Language and culture as ultimate barriers?', *European Journal of Communication* 7: 517–40.

Birnbaum, P. 1977. *Les Sommets de l'Etat*. Paris: Seuil.

Bitzer, L. and T. Rueter. 1980. *Carter vs Ford. The Counterfeit Debates of 1976*. Madison, WI: University of Wisconsin Press.

Black, I. and H. Smith. 2003. 'Blair mends fences with Chirac on Iraq', *The Guardian*, 17 February.

Blackbourn, D. and G. Eley. 1984. *The Peculiarities of German History*. Oxford: Oxford University Press.

Blanchard, O.-J. and P.-A. Muet. 1993. 'Competitiveness Through Disinflation: An Assessment of French Macro-economic Strategy', *Economic Policy*, 16: 12–50.

Blum-Kulka, S. and T. Liebes. 2000. 'Peres versus Netanyahou: Television Wins the Debate, Israel 1996'. In S. Coleman (ed.), *Televised Election Debates. International Perspectives*. Basingstoke: Macmillan.

Blumler, J.G, ed. 1992. *Television and the Public Interest*. London: Sage.

Bonnal, N. 1997. *Le Coq hérétique. Autopsie de l'exception française*. Paris: Les Belles Lettres.

Bonté L.-M. and P. Duchadeuil. 1988. *Eloge de la volonté à l'usage d'une France incertaine*. Paris: Editions Universitaires.

Boschetti, A. 1988. *The Intellectual Enterprise: Sartre and Les Temps Modernes*. Evanston, Ill.: Northwestern University Press.

Bostnavaron, F. 2001a. 'Les conducteurs de train se sont isolés de la grève', *Le Monde*, 8–9 April.

———— 2001b. 'La CGT critique vivement les organisations qui continuent la grève à la SNCF', *Le Monde*, 12 April.

Bourdieu, P. 1998. *Contre-feux. Propos pour servir à la résistance contre l'invasion néo-libérale*. Paris: Liber-Raisons d'agir.

Bourdon, J. 1990. *Histoire de la télévision sous de Gaulle*. Paris: Anthropos/INA.

Bourseiller, C. 1999. 'Sous le révolution, la réforme?', *Le Débat*, special issue: La gauche, l'extrême gauche, les intellectuels, 103: 60–66.

Boyer, R. 1988. 'Wage/Labour Relations, Growth and Crisis: A Hidden Dialectic'. In R. Boyer (ed.), *The Search for Labour Market Flexibility: The European Economies in Transition*. Oxford: Clarendon Press.

———— 1997. 'How does a new production system emerge?'. In R. Boyer and J.-P. Durand, *After Fordism*. London: Macmillan.

Brants, K. 1985. 'Broadcasting and Politics in the Netherlands: from Pillar to Post' in R. Kuhn (ed.), *Broadcasting and Politics in Western Europe*. London: Frank Cass.

Brants, K. and E. De Bens. 2000. 'The Status of TV Broadcasting in Europe'. In J. Wieten, G. Murdock and P. Dahlgren (eds), *Television Across Europe*. London: Sage.

Bréchont, P. 2002. 'Pourquoi le Languedoc-Roussillon a-t-il offert tant de voix au FN?', *Midi Libre*, 2 June.

Bréchon, P., ed. 2002. *Les Elections présidentielles en France. Quarante ans d'histoire politique*. Paris: La Documentation Française.

Bridgford, J., ed. 1987. *France: Image and Identity*. Newcastle- upon-Tyne: Newcastle Polytechnic Products.

Brocard, V. 1994. *La Télévision. Enquête sur un univers impitoyable*. Paris: Lieu Commun.

Brochier, J.-C. and H. Delouche. 2000. *Les Nouveaux sans-culottes. Enquête sur l'extrême gauche*. Paris: Grasset.

Brooks, W. 2000. 'French Intellectuals and anti-globalism', *Contemporary French Civilization*, 24, 2: 192–219.

Brown, G. 1996. Speech to the Friedrich Ebert foundation, 7 May.

_____ 1998. Statement on the Pre-Budget report, 3 November.

Bruckner, P. 1990. *La Mélancolie démocratique*. Paris: Seuil.

Brunet, J.-P. 1980. *Saint-Denis, la ville rouge*. Paris: Hachette.

Bryant, J. 1996. 'Changing Circumstances, Changing Policies? The 1994 Defence White Paper and Beyond'. In T. Chafer and B. Jenkins (eds), *France: From the Cold War to the New World Order*. Basingstoke: Macmillan.

_____ 2000. 'France and NATO from 1966 to Kosovo: Coming Full Circle?' *European Security*, 9, 3: 21–37.

Buchan, D. 1994. 'France goes on the defence offensive', *Financial Times*, 24 January.

Buob, J. and P. Mérigeau. 2001. *L'aventure vraie de Canal+*. Paris: Fayard.

Burin des Roziers, L. 1998. *Du Cinéma au multimédia: une brève histoire de l'exception culturelle*. Paris: IFRI.

Burton, R. and F. Reno. 1995. *French and West Indian: Martinique, Guadeloupe and French Guiana Today*. Basingstoke: Macmillan.

Cahm, E. 1972. *Péguy et le nationalisme français: de l'affaire Dreyfus à la Grande guerre*. Paris: Cahiers de l'Amitié Charles Péguy / Minard.

_____ 1996. *The Dreyfus Affair in French Society and Politics*. London: Longman.

Callède, J.-P. 2000. *Les Politiques sportives en France. Eléments de sociologie historique*. Paris: Economica.

Cameron, D. 1996. 'Exchange Rate Politics in France 1981–83: The Regime Defining Choices of the Mitterrand Presidency'. In T. Daley (ed.), *The Mitterrand Era*. London: Macmillan.

Camus, J.-Y.1998. *Les Extrêmismes en Europe*. La Tour d'Aigues: Editions de l'Aube.

_____ 2001. 'La structure du 'camp national' en France: la périphérie militante et organisationnelle du Front National et du Mouvenement National Républicain'. In P. Perrineau (ed.), *Les Croisés de la société fermée: l'Europe des extrêmes droites*. La Tour d'Aigues: Editions de l'Aube.

Capdevielle, J. and R. Mouriaux. 1988. *Mai 68: l'entre-deux de la modernité. Histoire de trente ans*. Paris: FNSP.

Carlin, D. 2000. 'Watching the Debates: a Guide for Viewers'. In S. Coleman (ed.), *Televised Election Debates. International Perspectives*. Basingstoke: Macmillan.

Carr, F., ed. 1998. *Europe: The Cold Divide*. Basingstoke: Macmillan.

Carr, F. and K. Ifantis. 1996. *NATO in the New European Order*. Basingstoke: Macmillan.

Casals, X. 2001. 'Le néo-populisme en Espagne: les raisons d'une absence'. In P. Perrineau (ed.), *Les Croisés de la société fermée: l'Europe des extrêmes droites*. La Tour-d'Aigues: Editions de l'Aube.

Casanova, J.-C. 1995. 'Dissuasion Concertée'. *L'Express.* 28 September.

Cassese, S. 1987. 'Divided Powers: European Administration and National Administrations'. In *The European Administration.* Brussels: International Institute of Administrative Sciences.

Caute, D. 1964. *Communism and the French Intellectuals, 1914–60.* London: Deutsch.

Cayrol, R. 1988. 'The Electoral Campaign and the Decision-Making Process of French Voters'. In H.R. Penniman (ed.), *France at the Polls, 1981 and 1986. Three National Elections.*Washington DC: American Enterprise Institute for Public Policy Research.

Ceaux, P. 2002. 'Sarkozy donne le tempo à la droite et un coup de vieux à Le Pen', *Le Monde,* 10 December.

Cerny, P. 1980a. 'The new rules of the game'. In P. Cerny and M. Schain (eds), *French Politics and Public Policy.* London: St. Martin's Press.

———— 1980b. *The Politics of Grandeur: The Ideological Aspects of de Gaulle's Foreign Policy.* Cambridge: Cambridge University Press.

———— 1984. 'Gaullism, Nuclear Weapons and the State' in J. Howorth and P. Chilton (eds), *Defence and Dissent in Contemporary France.* London: St Martin's Press.

———— 1989. 'The "Little Big Bang" in Paris: Financial Deregulation in a Dirigiste System', *European Journal of Political Research,* 17: 169–92.

Césaire, A. 1957. *Letter to Maurice Thorez.* Paris: Présence Africaine.

Chafer, T. 2002. 'Franco-African Relations: No Longer So Exceptional?' *African Affairs* 101: 343–63.

Chaffee, S. 1978. 'Presidential Debates – are they helpful to voters?', *Communication Monographs,* 45: 330–46.

Chalaby, J.K. 2002. *The de Gaulle Presidency and the Media.* Basingstoke: Palgrave Macmillan.

Chamard, M.E. and P. Kieffer. 1992. *La Télé: dix ans d'histoires secrètes.* Paris: Flammarion.

Champagne, P. 1989 'Qui a gagné? Analyse interne et analyse externe des débats politiques à la television', *Mots* 20: 5–21.

Chanet, J.-F. 1996. *L'Ecole républicaine et les petites patries.* Paris: Aubier.

Chardon, J.-M. and D. Lensel, eds. 1998. *La Pensée unique. Le vrai procès.* Paris: Economica.

Charette, H. de. 1995. 'European Peace Role for NATO.' *The Guardian,* 6 December.

Charle, C. 1990. *Naissance des 'intellectuels', 1880–1900, Sens commun.* Paris: Editions de Minuit.

Chatterjee, P. 1986. *Nationalist Thought and the Colonial World: A Derivative Discourse.* Tokyo/ London: Zed Press for United Nations University.

Chauveau, A. 1997. *L'Audiovisuel en liberté?* Paris: Presses de Sciences Po.

Chesnais, F. 1997. *La Mondialisation du capital.* Paris: Syros.

Cieutat, B and N. Tenzer. 2000. *Fonctions publiques: Enjeux et stratégies pour le renouvellement.* Rapport du Commissariat Général du Plan. Paris: La Documentation Française, [http://www.ladocfrancaise.gouv.fr/rapports]. Consulté 24 August 2001.

Clark, D. 1998. 'The Modernization of the French Civil Service: Crisis, Continuity and Change', *Public Administration* 76,1: 97–115.

―――― 2000. 'The Changing Face of Audit and Evaluation in Government: A Franco-British Comparison'. Paper for the PSA Public Administration and French Politics specialist groups meeting on Current Issues in British and French Public Administrative Reform on 14 September 2000.

Clark, H. 2000. 'The Worm that Turned: New Zealand's 1996 General Election and the Televised 'Worm' Debates'. In S. Coleman (ed.), *Televised Election Debates. International Perspectives*. Basingstoke: Macmillan.

Clift, B. 2003a. *French Socialism in a Global Era*. London: Continuum.

―――― 2003b. 'The Changing Political Economy of France: *Dirigisme* under Duress'. In M. Ryner and A. Cafruny (eds), *A Ruined Fortress? Neoliberal Hegemony and Transformation Europe*. New York: Rowman & Littlefield.

Closets, F de. 1982. *Toujours plus*. Paris: Grasset.

Cogniot, G. and R. Garaudy. 1945. *Les Intellectuels et la Renaissance française*. Paris: Editions du PCF.

Cohen, E. 1995. 'France: National champions in search of a mission'. In J. Hayward (ed.), *Industrial Enterprise and European Integration: From National to International Champions in Europe*. Oxford: Oxford University Press.

―――― 1996. *La Tentation hexagonale. La souveraineté à l'épreuve de la mondialisation*. Paris: Fayard.

Cohen, R. 1997. 'France vs US: Warring Versions of Capitalism', *New York Times*, 20 October.

Cohen-Tanugi, L. 1989. *La Métamorphose de la démocratie*. Paris: Odile Jacob.

Cole, A. 1998. *French Politics and Society*. London: Prentice Hall.

―――― 1999. 'The *Service Public* Under Stress', *West European Politics* 22, 4: 166–84.

Cole, A. and P. John. 2000. 'Governing Education in England and France'. Paper for the PSA Public Administration and French Politics specialist groups meeting on Current Issues in British and French Public Administrative Reform on 14 September 2000.

Coleman, S. 2000. 'Meaningful Political Debate in the Age of the Soundbite'. In S. Coleman (ed.), *Televised Election Debates. International Perspectives*. Basingstoke: Macmillan.

Coleman, W. 1997. 'The French State, *Dirigisme*, and the Changing Global financial Environment'. In G. Underhill (ed.), *The New World Order in International Finance*. Basingstoke: Macmillan.

Collard, S. 2000: 'French Cultural Identity and the End of Exceptionalism'. In B. Axford, D.Berghahn and N.Hewlett (eds), *Unity and Diversity in the New Europe*. Bern: Peter Lang.

Colley, L. 1992. *Britons: Forging the Nation 1707–1837*. New Haven: Yale University Press.

―――― 1999. 'This Country Is Not So Special', *The New Statesman*, 1 May.

Collin, D. and J.Cotta. 2001. *L'Illusion plurielle. Pourquoi la gauche n'est plus la gauche*. Paris: Lattès.

Collins, R. 1994. *Broadcasting and Audio-Visual Policy in the European Single Market*. London: John Libbey.

Combault, P. 1999. 'La couverture conventionelle à la fin 1997', *Premières synthèses* 29,2. Paris: DARES.

Confiant, R. 1993. *Aimé Césaire. Une traversée paradoxale du siècle.* Paris: Stock.

Cotteret, J.-M., C. Emeri, J. Gerstlé and R. Moreau. 1976. *Giscard d'Estaing – Mitterrand, 54 774 mots pour convaincre.* Paris: Presses Universitaires de France.

Courtois, S. and M. Lazar. 1995. *Histoire du Parti communiste français.* Paris: Presses Universitaires de France.

Coutrot, T. and J.-Y. Boulin. 1994. 'Les accords de réduction du coût du travail et de partage de travail', *Premières synthèses*, 16 February. Paris: DARES.

Creton, L. 1995 'Analyses et options stratégiques pour le cinéma européen'. In F. Sojcher (ed.), *Cinéma européen et identités culturelles.* Brussels: Editions de l'Université de Bruxelles.

Crettiez, X. and I. Sommier. 2002. *La France rebelle. Tous les foyers, mouvements et acteurs de la contestation.* Paris: Michalon.

Crozier, M. 1971. *Le Phénomène bureaucratique.* Paris: Seuil.

——— 1991. *Etat modeste, état moderne.* Paris: Livre de Poche.

CSA. 1995. *Election du président de la République. Rapport sur la campagne électorale à la radio et à la télévision (20 septembre 1994 – 7 mai 1995).* Paris: CSA.

Cuilenburg, J. van and P. Slaa. 1993. 'From Media Policy towards a National Communications Policy: Broadening the Scope', *European Journal of Communication* 8: 149–76.

Cumming, G. 2001. *Aid to Africa: French and British Policies from the Cold War to the New Millennium.* Aldershot: Ashgate.

Dahlgren, P. 2000. 'Key Trends in European Television'. In J. Wieten, G. Murdock and P. Dahlgren (eds), *Television Across Europe.* London: Sage.

Debray, R. 1978. *Modeste contribution aux discours et cérémonies officielles du dixième anniversaire.* Paris: François Maspéro.

Debray, R. 1979. *Le pouvoir intellectuel en France.* Paris: Ramsay.

——— 1989. *Que vive la République.* Paris: Odile Jacob.

——— 2000. *I.F. suite et fin.* Paris: Gallimard.

Deniau, X. 1983. *La Francophonie.* Paris: Presses Universitaires de France.

Derville, J. and M. Croisat. 1979. 'La socialisation des communistes français', *Revue française de science politique* 29, 4–5: 760–90.

Dézé, A. 2001. ' Entre adaptation et démarcation: la question du rapport des formations d'extrême droite aux systèmes politiques des démocraties européennes'. In P. Perrineau (ed.), *Les Croisés de la société fermée: l'Europe des extrêmes droites.* La Tour d'Aigues: Editions de l'Aube.

Dilas-Rocherieux, Y. 1999/2000. 'Abandon et innovation', *Les cahiers d'histoire sociale* 13: 17–24.

Djian, J.-M. 1996. *La Politique culturelle.* Paris: Le Monde-Editions.

Domard, E. 2002. 'Elimination de l'équipe de France : une défaite politique', *Français d'abord!*, 367: June.

Domínguez, J.I. and A. Poiré, A.1999. *Towards Mexico's Democratization. Parties, Campaigns, Elections and Public Opinion.* London: Routledge.

Downs, V.C. 1991. 'The Debate about Debates: Production and Event Factors in the 1988 Broadcast Debates in France and the United States'. In L.L. Kaid, J. Gerstlé and K.R. Sanders (eds), *Mediated Politics in Two Cultures*. New York: Praeger.

Drake, D. 2002. *Intellectuals and Politics in Post-War France*. Basingstoke: Palgrave.

Dreyfus, F. 1999. *L'Invention de la bureaucratie*. Paris: La Découverte.

──── 2002. 'A la recherche du temps perdu: la science oublieuse de l'administration publique', *Politix* 15, 59: 171–94.

Duhamel, A. 1985. *Le Complexe d'Astérix*. Paris: Gallimard.

──── 1989. *Les Habits neufs de la politique*. Paris: Flammarion.

Duhamel, A., O. Duhamel and J. Jaffré. 1984. 'Consensus et dissensus français'. *Le Débat* 30: 4–26.

Dumons, B., G. Pollet and M. Berjat, 1987. *Naissance du sport moderne*. Lyon: La Manufacture.

Dunleavy, P. 1991. *Democracy, Bureaucracy and Public Choice*. Hemel Hempstead: Harvester Wheatsheaf.

Dunleavy, P. and C. Hood. 1994. 'From old public administration to new public management', *Public Money and Management* 14, 3: 9.

Dupont, G. 2003. 'Larzac 2003, carrefour de la contestation sociale', *Le Monde*, 8 August.

Duprat, F. 1972. *Les mouvements d'extrême-droite en France depuis 1944*. Paris: Editions Albatros.

Dupuy, F. and J.-C. Thoenig. 1985. *L'Administration en miettes*. Paris: Fayard.

Dupuy, F. 1999. 'Why Is It so Difficult to Reform Public Administration? Government of the Future: Getting from Here to There', *OECD Paper*, PUMA/SGF 99: 7.

Duval, G. 2000. 'Les nouveaux capitalistes français', *Alternatives économiques*, 182: 35–43.

Duverger, M. 1988. *La Nostalgie de l'impuissance*. Paris: Albin Michel.

Dyer, R. and G. Vincendeau. 1992. *Popular European Cinema*. London: Routledge.

Dyson, K. 1999a. 'The Franco-German Relationship and Economic and Monetary Union: Using Europe to Bind Leviathan', *West European Politics* 22, 1: 25–44.

──── 1999b. 'Benign or Malevolent Leviathan? Social Democratic Governments in a Neo-Liberal Area', *Political Quarterly* 70, 2: 195–209.

Eatwell, R. 2000. 'The Extreme Right and British Exceptionalism: the Primacy of Politics'. In P. Hainsworth (ed.), *The Politics of the Extreme-Right: From the Margins to the Mainstream*. London: Pinter.

Ebbinghaus, B. and J. Visser, eds. 2000. *The Societies of Europe: Trade Unions in Western Europe since 1945*. Basingstoke: Macmillan.

Economist, The. 2003a. 'France's Foreign Policy: Ever Awkward, Sometimes Risky', 1 February.

──── 2003b. 'When Squabbling Turns Too Dangerous', 15–21 February.

Eeckout, L. van. 2001. 'La panoplie des armes contre les licenciements', *Le Monde*, 12 April.

Ehrenberg, A. 1991. *Le Culte de la performance*. Paris: Calmann-Lévy.

Einaudi, M., J.-M. Domenach and A. Garosci, eds. 1951. *Communism in Western Europe*. Ithaca: Cornell University Press.

Elgie, R. 1991. 'La méthode Rocard existe-t-elle?' *Modern and Contemporary France*, 44: 11–19.

———— 2001. 'Departmental Secretaries in France'. In R.A.W. Rhodes and P. Weller (eds), *The Changing World of Top Officials*. London: Open University Press.

Elgie, R., ed. 1999. *Semi-presidentialism in Europe*. Oxford: Oxford University Press.

Elias, N. and E. Dunning. 1998. *Sport et civilisation. La violence maîtrisée*. Paris: Fayard.

Elliott, G. 1998. *The Merciless Laboratory of History*. Minneapolis: University of Minnesota Press.

Engels, F.[1885] 1968. 'Preface to the third German edition of Karl Marx, *The Eighteenth Brumaire of Louis Bonaparte*'. In K. Marx and F. Engels, *Selected Works in One Volume*. London: Lawrence and Wishart.

Espaces 89. 1985. *L'Identité française*. Paris: Editions Tiercé.

Esprit. 2000. 'Splendeurs et misères de la vie intellectuelle', dossier, March and May.

Estier, C. 1995. *De Mitterrand à Jospin. Trente ans de campagnes présidentielles*. Paris: Stock.

European Council. 1997. *Presidency Conclusion: Extraordinary European Council Meeting on Employment Luxembourg, 20 and 21 November 1997*. Brussels: European Council.

European Industrial Relations Review. 2001a. 'News France', 324 (January): 5–7.

———— 2001b. 'News France', 329 (June): 7–8.

———— 2001c. 'News France', 330 (July): 5–6.

Evans, J. and G. Ivaldi. 2002a. 'Les dynamiques électorales de l'extrême droite européenne', *Revue politique et parlementaire* 1019: 67–83

———— 2002b. 'Quand la crise du consensus profite à l'extrême-droite', *Le Figaro*, 18–19 May.

Fabre-Guillemant, R. 1998. *Les Réformes administratives en France et Grande Bretagne*. Paris: L'Harmattan.

Farchy, J. 1999. *La Fin de l'exception culturelle?* Paris: CNRS Editions.

Fauroux, R. 1986a. 'La Fondation Saint-Simon', *Le Débat*, 41: 131.

Fauroux, R. 1986b. Interview by Patrick Fridenson, 'L'industriel et le fonctionnaire', *Le Débat*, 40: 159–84.

Fenby, J. 1998. *France on the Brink. The Trouble with France*. London: Little Brown.

Ferenczi, T. 1989. *Défense du consensus*. Paris: Flammarion.

Ferner, A. and R. Hyman. 1998. 'Introduction. Towards European Industrial Relations?'. In A. Ferner and R.Hyman (eds), *Changing Industrial Relations in Europe*. Oxford: Blackwell.

Ferry, L. and A. Renaut. 1985. *La Pensée 68. Essai sur l'anti-humanisme contemporain*. Paris: Gallimard.

Field, F. 1991. *British and French Writers of the First World War*. Cambridge: Cambridge University Press.

Finkielkraut, A. 1987. *La Défaite de la pensée*. Paris: Gallimard.

———— 1991. 'L'abandon des principes révolutionnaires', *L'Histoire* 143: 63.

Finkielkraut, A., P. Ory, J. Revel and M. Winock. 1987. 'Changement intellectuel ou changement des intellectuels?', *Le Débat* 45: 40–58.

Fitoussi, J.-P. 1998. 'Table ronde: Comment appliquer les 35 heures?', *Revue politique et parlementaire* 993: 73–91.

Flood, C. and N. Hewlett, eds. 2000. *Currents in Contemporary French Intellectual Life.* London and New York: Macmillan and St. Martin's Press.

Flower, J. 1991. 'Wherefore the intellectuals?', *French Cultural Studies* 2, 3: 275–90.

Flynn, G., ed. 1995. *Remaking the Hexagon: the New France in the New Europe.* Oxford: Westview Press.

Forbes, J. 1993. *The Cinema in France. After the New Wave.* London: Macmillan/BFI.

Formesyn, R. 1984. 'Europeanisation and the Pursuit of National Interests'. In V. Wright (ed.) *Continuity and Change in France.* London: Allen and Unwin.

Forrester, V. 1996. *L'Horreur économique.* Paris: Fayard.

Fourcaut, A. 1986. *Bobigny, banlieue rouge.* Paris: Editions ouvrières.

Franceschini, L. 1995. *La régulation audiovisuelle en France.* Paris: Presses Universitaires de France.

Francophonie: [http://www.france.diplomatie.fr/francophonie]. Consulted 11 November 2003.

Frank, T. 1998. 'Vue des Etats-Unis. Cette impardonnable exception française', *Le Monde diplomatique*, April.

Freyssinet, J. 1993. 'France: toward flexibility'. In J. Hartog and J. Theeuws (eds), *Labour Market Contracts and Institutions: a Cross-national Comparison.* Amsterdam: North Holland.

Freyssinet, M. 1997. *Le Temps de travail en miettes: vingt ans de politique de l'emploi et de négociation collective.* Paris: Editions de l'Atelier.

Friend, J. 1991. *The Linchpin: French-German Relations 1950–1990.* New York: Praeger.

Frodon, J.-M. 1998. *La Projection nationale. Cinéma et nation.* Paris: Odile Jacob.

Fumaroli, M. 1992. *L Etat culturel: une religion moderne.* Paris: Éditions de Fallois.

Furet, F. 1978. *Penser la Révolution française.* Paris: Gallimard.

———— 1983. 'La Révolution dans l'imaginaire politique français', *Le Débat* 26: 173–81.

———— 1988.'La Révolution'. *Histoire de la France*, tome 4. Paris: Hachette.

———— 1995. *Le Passé d'une illusion.* Paris: Robert Laffont.

Furet, F., J. Julliard and P. Rosanvallon. 1988. *La République de centre. La fin de l'exception française.* Paris: Calmann-Lévy.

Furet, F. and M. Ozouf, eds. 1988. *Dictionnaire critique de la Révolution française.* Paris: Flammarion.

Gallagher, T. 2000. 'Exit from the Ghetto: the Italian Far Right in the 1990s'. In P. Hainsworth (ed.), *The Politics of the Extreme-Right: From the Margins to the Mainstream.* London: Pinter.

Gallouédec-Genuys, F., ed. 1998. *A propos de l'administration française.* Paris: La Documentation Française.

Gamble, A. and G. Kelly. 2000. 'The British Labour Party and Monetary Union', *West European Politics* 23, 1: 1–25.

Garitaonandia, C. 1993. 'Regional Television in Europe', *European Journal of Communication* 8: 277–94.

Gauchet, M. 1985. *Le Désenchantement du monde.* Paris: Gallimard.

_____ 1995: *La Révolution des pouvoirs. La souveraineté, le peuple et la représentation: 1789–1799*. Paris: Gallimard.

_____ 2002. *La Démocratie contre elle-même*. Paris: Gallimard.

Gaulle, C. de. 1954. *Mémoires de guerre, l'appel, 1940–1942*. Paris: Plon.

_____ 1970. 'Discours prononcé par le Général de Gaulle à Bayeux, le 16 juin 1946.' In C. de Gaulle, *Discours et messages*, vol. 2, 1946–58. Paris: Plon.

Gauzy, F. 1998. *L'Exception allemande*. Paris: A. Colin.

Girard, L. 2001. 'Phillips annonce la suppression de plus de 6.000 emplois', *Le Monde*, 18 April.

Giret, V. and B. Pellegrin. 2001. *Vingt ans de pouvoir: 1981–2001*. Paris: Seuil.

Glyn, A. ed. 2001. *Social democracy in neoliberal times: the left and economic policy since 1980*. Oxford : Oxford University Press.

Godard, J.-L. 1991. *JLG/JLG*, documentary by Joseph Strub.

Godin, E. 1996. ' Le néo-liberalisme à la française: une exception?' *Modern and Contemporary France*, NS4, 1: 61–70.

Goetschy, J. 1998. 'France: The Limits of Reform'. In A. Ferner and R. Hyman (eds), *Changing Industrial Relations in Europe*. Oxford: Blackwell.

Gonod, P. 1998. 'L'Administration publique dans la bande dessinée'. In F. Gallouédec-Genuys (ed.), *A propos de l'administration française*. Paris: La Documentation Française.

Goodwin, P. 1998. *Television under the Tories: Broadcasting Policy 1979–1997*. London: BFI.

Gordon, P. 1993. *A Certain Idea of France: French Security Policy and the Gaullist Legacy*. Princeton: Princeton University Press.

Gordon, P. and S. Meunier. 2001. 'Globalisation and French Cultural Identity', *French Politics, Culture and Society* 19, 1: 22–41.

Gramsci, A. 1971. *Selections from 'The Prison Notebooks' of A.Gramsci*. Edited by Q. Hoare and G. Smith. London: Lawrence and Wishart.

Granjon, M.-C., N. Racine and M. Trebitsch, eds. 1997. *Histoire comparée des intellectuels*. Paris: Institut d'histoire du temps présent.

Gregory, S. 2000. *French Defence Policy into the Twenty First Century*. Basingstoke: Macmillan Press.

Grémion, P. 1976. *Le Pouvoir périphérique: bureaucrates et notables dans le système politique*. Paris: Seuil.

Groux, G. 1998. *Vers un renouveau du conflit social*. Paris: Bayard.

Gubian, A. 1998. 'Les 35 heures et l'emploi: la loi Aubry de juin 1998', *Regards sur l'actualité* 245: 15–33.

Gutman, O. and E. Lefebvre. 1999. 'Le rééquilibrage de la fiscalité du travail et du capital', *Regards sur l'Actualité* 249: 3–16.

Guyomarch, A. 1999. ' "Public Service", "Public Management" and the "Modernization" of French Administration', *Public Administration* 77, 1: 71–193.

Guyomarch, A., H. Machin and E. Ritchie. 1998. *France in the European Union*. Basingstoke: Macmillan.

Guyomarch, A., H. Machin, P. Hall and J. Hayward. 2001. *Developments in French Politics*. Basingstoke: Palgrave.

Hague, R. and M. Harrop. 2001. *Comparative Government and Politics*. Basingstoke: Palgrave

Hainsworth, P. 2000 'Introduction: the Extreme Right'. In P. Hainsworth (ed.), *The Politics of the Extreme Right: From the Margins to the Mainstream*. London: Pinter.

Halimi, S. 1996. 'Less exceptional than meets the eye'. In A. Daley (ed.), *The Mitterrand Era. Policy Alternatives and Political Mobilization in France*. Basingstoke: Macmillan.

—— 1997. *Les Nouveaux chiens de garde*. Paris: Liber-Raisons d'agir.

—— 2000. *Quand la Gauche essayait. Les leçons de l'exercice du pouvoir 1924, 1936, 1944, 1981*. Paris: Arléa.

Hall, J.K. and C. Adasiewicz. 2000. 'What Can Voters Learn from Election Debates?'. In S. Coleman (ed.), *Televised Election Debates. International Perspectives*. Basingstoke: Macmillan.

Hall, P. 1986. *Governing the Economy*. Cambridge: Polity.

Hancké, B. 2001. 'Revisiting the French Model: Coordination and Restructuring in French Industry'. In D. Soskice and P. Hall (eds), *Varieties of Capitalism*. Oxford: Oxford University Press.

Hanna, M. 1996. *The Mobilization of Intellect: French Scholars and Writers during the Great War*. Cambridge, Mass.: Harvard University Press.

Harris, S. 2000. 'Cinema in a nation of filmgoers'. In W. Kidd and S. Reynolds (eds), *Contemporary French Cultural Studies*. London: Arnold.

Hastings, M. 1991. *Halluin la Rouge 1919–1939*. Lille: Presses Universitaires de Lille.

Hayward, J. 1983. *The One and Indivisible French Republic*. New York: Norton.

—— 1988. 'From trend-setter to fashion-follower in Europe: the demise of French distinctiveness'. In J. Howorth and G. Ross (eds), *Contemporary France: a review of inter-disciplinary studies*, vol. 2. London: Frances Pinter.

—— 1994. 'Ideological Change: The Exhaustion of the Revolutionary Impetus'. In P. Hall, J. Hayward, H. Machin (eds), *Developments in French Politics*. Basingstoke: Macmillan.

Hayward, S. 1989. 'Television and the Presidential Elections April–May 1988'. In J. Gaffney (ed.), *The French Presidential Elections of 1988*. Aldershot: Dartmouth.

—— 1993. *French National Cinema*. London: Routledge.

Hazareesingh, S. 1991. *Intellectuals and the French Communist Party: Disillusion and Decline*. Oxford: Clarendon Press.

—— 1994. *Political Traditions in Modern France*. Oxford: Oxford University Press.

Heilbroner, R. 1992. *The Worldly Philosophers*. New York: Touchstone.

Henley, J. 2003. 'Algerians Flock to Chirac the Hero', *The Guardian*, 3 March.

Hermet, G. 1997. 'Populisme et nationalisme',*Vingtième siècle*, 56: 34–47.

Hermet, G. 2001. *Les Populismes dans le monde*. Paris: Fayard.

Hewlett, N. 1998. *Modern French Politics. Analysing Conflict and Consensus since 1945*. Cambridge: Polity.

—— 2003: *Democracy in Modern France*. London: Continuum.

Hill, C. E., ed. 2000. *Intellectuals, Identities and Popular Movements: Ten Case Studies from France, Britain, Germany and the Balkans*. Manchester: Manchester University Press.

Hoffman, S., ed. 1963. *In Search of France*. Cambridge, Mass.: Harvard University Press.

Hollifield, J. and G. Ross. 1991. *Searching for the New France*. London: Routledge.

Holt, R. 1981. *Sport and Society in Modern France*. Basingstoke: Macmillan.

Hombach, B. 2000. *The Politics of the New Centre*. Cambridge: Polity.

Howarth, D. 2002. 'The French State in the Euro Zone'. In K. Dyson (ed.), *European States and the Euro-Zone*. Oxford: Oxford University Press.

Howarth, D.and G. Varouxakis. 2003. *Contemporary France: an Introduction to French Politics and Society*. London: Arnold.

Howell, C. 1992. *Regulating Labor: The State and Industrial Relations Reform in Postwar France*. Princeton: Princeton University Press.

Howorth, J. and P. Chilton. 1984. *Defence and Dissent in Contemporary France*. London: St Martin's Press.

Huber, E. and J. Stephens. 2001.'The Social Democratic Welfare State'. In A. Glyn, (ed.), *Social Democracy in Neoliberal Times*. Oxford: Oxford University Press.

Hubscher, R., J. Durry and B. Jeu. 2000. *L'Histoire en mouvement. Le sport dans la société française*. Paris: A. Colin.

Huizinga, J. 1977. *Homo Ludens. Essai sur la fonction sociale du jeu*. Paris: Gallimard.

Humanité, L'. 2002. 'Débat', 26 March.

Humphreys, P. 1994. *Media and Media Policy in Germany*. Oxford: Berg.

Hunter, M. 1998. 'L'extrême-droite à la conquête de l'Est', *Le Monde diplomatique*, December.

Ignazi, P. 1992. 'The Silent Counter-Revolution: Hypotheses on the Emergence of Extreme-Right Parties in Europe' *European Journal of Political Research* 22, 1/2: 3–34.

———— 1994. 'La force des racines: la culture politique du Mouvement Social Italien au seuil du gouvernement', *Revue française de science politique* 44, 6: 1014–34.

———— 1997. 'The Extreme Right in Europe: a Survey'. In P. Merkl and L. Weinberg (eds) *The Revival of Right-Wing Extremism in the 1990s*. London: Frank Cass.

———— 2001. 'Les partis d'extrême-droite: les fruits inachevés de la société postindustrielle'. In P. Perrineau (ed.), *Les Croisés de la société fermée: l'Europe des extrêmes droites*. La Tour d'Aigues: Editions de l'Aube.

Ignazi, P., ed. 2003. *Extreme-right parties in Western Europe*. Oxford: Oxford University Press.

Imbert, C. 1989. 'The End of French Exceptionalism', *Foreign Affairs* 68, 4: 48–60.

Jack, A. 1999: *The French Exception*. London: Profile Books.

Jackel, A. 1995. 'La France et l'Angleterre ont-elles une identité commune?'. In F. Sojcher (ed.), *Cinéma européen et identités culturelles*. Brussels: Editions de l'Université de Bruxelles.

Jacquier, J.-P. 1998. *Les Clés du social en France: manuel d'initiation sociale*. Paris: Liaisons.

Jaume, L. 1998. 'The Paradoxes of French Liberalism'. Paper to the Midlands Political Thought Seminar, University of Birmingham, 11 May.

Jennings, J., ed. 1993. *Intellectuals in Twentieth-Century France, Mandarins and Samurais*. London: Macmillan.

Jobert, A. 2000. *Les Espaces de la négociation collective, branches et territoires*. Paris: Octarès.

Jobert, B., ed. 1994. *Le Tournant néo-libéral en France*. Paris: L'Harmattan.

Johnson, J. and M. Orange. 2003. *Une Faillite française*. Paris: Albin Michel.

Jones, G. 2003. 'The Effects of the 1989–1997 French Administrative Reforms on the Ministerial Field Services' (unpublished Ph. D. thesis, Southampton Institute of Higher Education).

Jospin, L. 1999. *Modern Socialism* London, Fabian Society.

Judge, A. 1999. 'Voices and Policies'. In K. Salhi (ed.), *Francophone Voices*. Exeter: Elm Bank Publications.

Judt, T. 1992. *Past Imperfect: French Intellectuals, 1944–1956*. Berkeley: University of California Press.

Julliard, J. 1985. *La Faute à Rousseau: essai sur les conséquences historiques de l'idée de souveraineté populaire*. Paris: Seuil.

_____ 1988. 'Droite, gauche, centre. L'exception française: fin ou recommencement?', *Le Débat* 52: 4–10. (Reproduced in the 2nd edition of *La République du centre*, 1988, which includes a press review of the book and a postface by Pierre Rosanvallon).

_____ 1999 *La Faute aux élites*. Paris: Gallimard.

Julliard, J. and M. Winock, eds. 1996. *Dictionnaire des intellectuels français*. Paris: Seuil.

July, S. 1986. *Les Années Mitterrand: histoire baroque d'une normalisation inachevée*. Paris: Grasset.

Kahn, J.-F. 1995. *La Pensée unique*. Paris: Fayard.

Kaid, L., J. Gerstlé and K. Sanders. 1991. 'Commonalities, Differences, and Lessons Learned from Comparative Communication Research'. In L. Kaid, J. Gerstlé and K. Sanders (eds), *Mediated Politics in Two Cultures*. New York: Praeger.

Katz, E. and J.J. Feldman. 1968. 'The Debates in the Light of Research: A Survey of Surveys'. In S. Kraus (ed.), *The Great Debates. Background, Perspective, Effects*. Gloucester, Mass: Peter Smith.

Kauffer, R. 1999/2000. 'Le PCF et les enjeux politiques de la Résistance', *Les Cahiers d'histoire sociale* 13: 33–39.

Kavanagh, D. 1972. *Political Culture*. Basingstoke: Macmillan.

Kelly, M. 1997. 'French intellectuals and Zhdanovism'. *French Cultural Studies* 8, 22: 17–28.

_____ 2003. 'Comparing French and British Intellectuals: Towards a Cross-Channel Perspective', *French Cultural Studies* 14, 3: 336–48.

Kemp-Welch, A. and J. Jennings, eds. 1997. *Intellectuals in politics: from the Dreyfus affair to the Rushdie affair*. London: Routledge.

Kergoat, J. 1999a. 'Tribune libre', *L'Humanité*, 30 June.

_____ 1999b. 'La fin de la Fondation Saint-Simon vue par Jacques Kergoat', *L'Humanité*, 30 June.

Kesselman, M. 1991. 'La nouvelle cuisine en politique: la fin de l'exceptionnalité française'. In Y. Mény, (ed.), *Idéologies, partis politiques et groupes sociaux'*, 159–73. Paris: FNSP.

Kickert, W. 1997. 'Public Management in the United States and Europe'. In W. Kickert (ed.), *Public Management and Administrative Reform in Western Europe*. Cheltenham: Edward Elgar.

Kidd, W. and S. Reynolds, eds. 2000. *Contemporary French Cultural Studies*. London: Edward Arnold.

Kiegel, A. 1964. *Le Congrès de Tours*. Paris: Julliard.

Kitschelt, H. 1995. *The Radical Right in Western Europe: A Comparative Analysis*. Ann Arbor: University of Michigan Press.

Knapp, A. and V. Wright. 2001. *The Government and Politics of France*. London: Routledge.

Knigge, P. 1998. 'The Ecological Correlates of Right-wing Extremism in Western Europe', *European Journal of Political Research* 34, 2: 249–73.

Kouvélakis, E., ed. 2000. *Marx 2000*. Paris: Presses Universitaires de France.

Kramer, S.P. 1994. *Does France Still Count? The French Role in the New Europe*. Washington: Praeger (Washington Papers, no 164).

Kriegel, A and S. Courtois. 1997. *Eugène Fried. Le grand secret du PCF*. Paris: Seuil.

Kuhn, R. 1995. *The Media in France*. London: Routledge.

Kuisel, R. 2001. 'The Gallic Rooster Crows Again: the Paradox of French Anti-Americanism', *French Politics, Culture and Society* 19, 3: 1–16.

Laird, W. 1971. *French Nuclear Diplomacy*. Princeton: Princeton University Press.

Lardech, R. 2000. *Social-democracy and the Challenges of the European Union*. Boulder, Colorado: Lynne Rienner Press.

Lauer, S. 2001. 'Chez Michelin, les militants quittent la CFDT pour créer une SUD', *Le Monde*, 24 January.

Laurent, V. 1998. 'Enquête sur la Fondation Saint-Simon. Les architectes du social-libéralisme', *Le Monde diplomatique*. September.

Lavabre, M.-C. and F. Platone. 2003. *Que reste-t-il du PCF?*. Paris: Autrement-CEV-IFOP.

Lazar, M. 1992. *Maisons Rouges. Les partis communistes français et italien de la Libération à nos jours*. Paris: Aubier.

——— 1996. 'Le communisme français et italien fut-il un totalitarisme?', *Communisme* 47–48.

——— 2002. *Le communisme: une passion française*. Paris: Perrin.

Lazitch, B. 1976. *Le Rapport Khrouchtchev et son histoire*. Paris: Seuil.

Le Lay, P. 2001. 'Peut-on tout montrer à la télévision?', *Le Monde*, 11 May.

Le Monde (2003a): 'Larzac 2003, carrefour de la contestation sociale.' 8 August, p.5. (Written by Gaëlle Dupont)

Le Pen, J.-M. 1997 Discours à la dix-septième Fête des Bleu-Blanc-Rouge, http://www.frontnational.com/discours/2002/27.01.02.htm. Consulted on 12 July 2002.

——— 1999. Discours de Versailles lors de la manifestation contre le Traité d'Amsterdam, 17 January, http://www.frontnational.com/discours/2002/27.01.02.htm. Consulted on 12 July 2002.

——— 2001. Discours: une république référendaire, 4 February, http://www.frontnational.com/historique/indexc10.htm. Consulted on 11 March 2002.

——— 2002a. 'Grave crise des institutions', *Français d'abord!*, 367, June.

_____ 2002b. 'La France d'en haut intouchable', *Français d'abord!*, 368, July.

_____ 2002c 'La France retrouvée', *Profession de foi, élections présidentielles 2002, deuxième tour.*

_____ 2002d. Discours: immigration et souveraineté, 27 January, http://www.frontnational.com/discours/2002/27.01.02.htm. Consulted on 12 July 2002.

Le Goff, J. 1975. *Les Intellectuels au Moyen Age.* Paris: Seuil.

Le Roy Ladurie, E. 1990. *Entrer dans le XXI siècle. Essai sur l'avenir de l'identité française.* Paris: La Découverte/La Documentation Française.

Lefebvre, G. 1954. *Etudes sur la Révolution française.* Paris: Presses Universitaires de France.

Legavre, J.-B. 1991. 'Face to Face: the 1998 French Debate'. In L. Kaid, Gerstlé and K. Sanders (eds), *Mediated Politics in Two Cultures.* New York: Praeger.

Lelaube, A. 1997. *Le Travail toujours moins ou autrement.* Paris: Le Monde-Editions.

Lemaître, F. 2001a. 'Danone s'apprête à supprimer 3000 emplois en Europe dont 1700 en France', *Le Monde*, 11 January.

_____ 2001b. 'Les tensions salariales s'accentuent dans le secteur privé', *Le Monde*, 14–15 January.

Lenin, V.I. 1973. *The State and Revolution.* Peking: Foreign Languages Press.

Léotard, F. 1994. 'Nous allons assister à la naissance d'une sorte d'OTAN 2', *Les Echos*, 7–8 January.

Levy, D. 1999. *Europe's Digital Revolution.* London: Routledge.

Levy, J. 2000. 'France: Directing Adjustment?'. In F. Scharpf and V. Schmidt (eds), *Welfare and Work in the Open Economy,*Vol. 2. Oxford: Oxford University Press.

Leymarie, M. 2001. *Les Intellectuels et la politique en France.* Paris: Presses Universitaires de France.

Liaisons sociales. 2000. Supplément au numéro 13167, 30 May.

_____ 2001. 'Documents 94/2001. Les éléctions au comités d'entreprise en 1999', 18 December.

_____ 2002a. 'La loi Aubry', 30 May.

_____ 2002b.' Bref social: net recul des non-syndiqués aux élections aux CE en 2002', 26 December.

Lindenberg, D. 2002. *Rappel à l'ordre: enquête sur les nouveaux réactionnaires.* Paris: Seuil.

Lipietz, A. 1995. *Green Hopes: The Future of Political Ecology.* Cambridge: Polity Press.

Lipovetsky, G. 1983. *L'Ere du vide.* Paris: Gallimard.

Lipset, S.M. 1996. *American Exceptionalism: A Double-Edged Sword.* New York: Norton.

_____ 2000. 'Still the Exceptional Nation?', *The Wilson Quarterly*, Winter.

Loch, D. 2001.'La droite radicale en Allemagne: un cas particulier?'. In P. Perrineau (ed.), *Les Croisés de la société fermée: l'Europe des extrêmes droites.* La Tour d'Aigues: Editions de l'Aube.

Logeart, A. 1995.' Grand Oral', *Le Monde*, 4 May.

Looseley, D. 1995. *The Politics of Fun. Cultural Policy and Debate in Contemporary France.* London: Berg.

Lordon, F. 2001. 'The Logic and Limits of Désinflation Competitive'. In A. Glyn (ed.), *Social Democracy in Neoliberal Times*. Oxford: Oxford University Press.

Loupan, V. and P. Lorrain. 1994. *L'Argent de Moscou: l'histoire la plus secrète du PCF*. Paris: Plon.

Lovecy, J. 1992. 'Comparative Politics and the Fifth Republic: *la fin de l'exception française?*', *European Journal of Political Research*. 21: 385–408.

———— 1999.'The End of French Exceptionalism?', *West European Politics* 22, 4: 205–24.

Machin, H. 2001. 'Retooling the State Machine?'. In A. Guyomarch, H. Machin, P. Hall and J. Hayward (eds), Developments in French Politics. Basingstoke: Palgrave.

Maclean, M. 1999. 'Corporate Governance in France and the UK: Long-Term Perspectives on Contemporary Institutional Arrangements', *Business History* 41, 1: 88–116.

Madsen, D.L. 1998. *American Exceptionalism*. Edinburgh: Edinburgh University Press.

Mandraud, S. 2001. 'Le dispositif du gouvernement pour mieux encadrer les plans sociaux, cible les très grandes entreprises', *Le Monde*, 25 April.

Maréchal, S. 1996. *Ni Droite, ni gauche, français: contre la pensée unique, l'autre politique*. Charenton: Alizés.

Markovits, A. 2002. 'Austrian exceptionalism: Haider, the European Union and the Austrian past and present'. In R.Wodak and A. Pelinka (eds), *The Haider phenomenon in Austria*. London: Transaction Publishers.

Martelli, R. 1995. *Le Rouge et le Bleu*. Paris: Editions de l'Atelier.

Marx, K. [1871] 1968. 'The Civil War in France'. In K. Marx and F. Engels *Selected Works in One Volume*. London: Lawrence and Wishart.

Maschlet, G. 2001. 'Une municipalité communiste face à l'immigration algérienne et marocaine: Genevilliers, 1950–1972', *Genèse*, 45: 150–63.

Mason, J. 1989. 'Mitterrand, the Socialists, and French Nuclear Policy'. In P. Le Prestre (ed.), *French Security Policy in a Disarming World: Domestic Challenges and International Constraints*. Boulder: Lynne Rienner Publishers.

Mathy, J.-P. 1993. *Extreme Occident: French Intellectuals and America*. Chicago: University of Chicago Press.

Mayer, N. 1997 'Du vote lepéniste au vote frontiste', *Revue française de science politique* 47, 3–4: 438–53.

———— 1999. *Ces Français qui votent FN*. Paris: Flammarion.

———— 2002.'Les hauts et les bas du vote Le Pen', *Revue française de science politique* 52, 5–6: 505–20.

Mayer, N and P. Perrineau. 1992. 'Why do they vote Le Pen?', *European Journal of Political Research* 22, 1: 123–41.

McAllister, J. 2003a. ' Mad at America', *Time*, 20 January.

———— 2003b. 'War or Peace?', *Time*, 24 February.

McLellan, D., ed. 1981. *Karl Marx: Interviews and Recollections*. London: Macmillan.

McMillan, J. 2003. *Modern France 1880–2000*. Edinburgh: Edinburgh University Press.

McQuail, D. 2000. *McQuail's Mass Communication Theory*, 4th ed. London: Sage.

Meininger, M.-C. 2000. 'The Development and Current Features of the French Civil Service System'. In H. Bekke and F. van der Meer (eds), *Civil Service Systems in Western Europe.* Cheltenham: Edward Elgar.

Mendras, H. 1988. *La Seconde révolution française (1965–1984).* Paris: Gallimard.

Menon, A. 1995. 'From Independence to Cooperation: France, NATO and European Security.' *International Affairs* 71, 1: 19–34.

———— 2002. *France, NATO and the Limits of Independence 1981–1997.* Basingstoke: Macmillan.

Meny, Y. and Y. Surel. 2000. *Par le Peuple, pour le peuple. Le Populisme et les démocraties.* Paris: Fayard.

Mériaux, O. 1999. *Négocier l'emploi et la competitivité: Etudes pour le projet 'Collective Bargaining on Employment and Competitiveness'.* Dublin: European Foundation for the Improvement of Living and Working Conditions.

———— 2000. 'Eléments d'un régime post-fordiste de la négociation collective en France', *Relations Industrielles/Industrial Relations* 55, 4: 606–39.

Mériaux, O. and P. Trompette. 1997. 'Les accords d'entreprise sur l'emploi: quels processus de change?', *La Revue de l'IRES* 57: 119–48.

Merkl, P.-H. and L. Weinberg. 1997. *The Revival of Right-wing Extremism in the 90s.* London: Frank Cass.

Merleau-Ponty, M. 1996. *Sens et non-sens.* Paris: Gallimard.

Michelet, J. 1961. *Le Peuple.* Paris: Garnier-Flammarion.

———— 1963. *Histoire de France.* Paris: Editions J'ai Lu.

Mignon, P. and G.Truchot, eds. 2002 *Les Pratiques sportives en France.* Paris: Publications de l'INSEP.

Miller, A. and M. MacKuen. 1979. 'Learning about the Candidates: The 1976 Presidential Debates', *Public Opinion Quarterly.* 43: 326–46.

Millet, C. 2002. *La Vie sexuelle de Catherine M.* Paris: Seuil.

Milner, S. 2001. 'Globalisation and Employment in France: Between flexibility and protection?', *Modern and Contemporary France* 9, 3: 327–38.

Minc, A. 1994. *La France de l'an 2000.* Commissariat général du Plan. Paris: Editions Odile Jacob.

Ministère de la Culture et de la Communication.1992. *Etat et Culture. Le Cinéma.* Paris: La Documentation Française.

———— 1999. 'Dossier: Diversité culturelle et exception culturelle'. *La Lettre d'Information,* 56.

———— 2003. http://www.culture.gouv.fr./culture/historique/index.htm. Consulted on 9 September 2003.

Ministère de l'Economie, des Finances et du Budget. 2001. 'Projet de loi de finances pour 2002', *Les Notes Bleues,* Hors-série.

Ministère de l'Emploi et de la Solidarité (MES). 2000. *La Négociation Collective en 1999. Tome 1: La Tendance.* Paris: Editions législatives.

Ministère de la Fonction Publique, de la Réforme de l'Etat et de la Décentralisation. 1998. *La Fonction Publique de l'Etat: Rapport annuel mars 1997–mars 1998.* Paris: La Documentation Française.

———— 1999. *La Fonction Publique de l'Etat: Rapport annuel mars 1998–mars 1999.* Paris: La Documentation Française.

———— 2001. *Les principaux chantiers de la réforme*, http://www.fonction-publique.gouv.fr/lareforme/principauxchantiers/unetat.htm. Consulted 28 August 2001.

Ministère des Sports. 2002. *Les Chiffres clés du sport*. Paris: Mission Statistique.

Minkenberg, M. 2001. 'La nouvelle droite radicale, ses électeurs et ses milieux partisans: vote protestataire, phénoméne xenophobe ou *modernization losers*?'. In P. Perrineau (ed.), *Les Croisés de la société fermée: l'Europe des extrêmes droites*. La Tour d'Aigues: Editions de l'Aube.

Mitchell, A. 2000. 'The Great British Exception'. In S. Coleman (ed.), *Televised Election Debates. International Perspectives*. Basingstoke: Macmillan.

Mitterrand, F. 1964. *Le Coup d'état permanent*. Paris: Plon.

Monde, Le. 2001a. ' Le gouvernments face aux plans sociaux.', 24 April.

———— 2001b. 'Enquête sur le folie Loft-story', 4 May.

———— 2002. 'Dossier spécial: l'exception française', 15 April.

Monde, Le: dossiers et documents. 1988. 'La télévision en 1987: le grand chambardement'. Paris: Le Monde.

Monnot, C. 2001a. 'A Calais, Robert Hue fait sienne la mobilisation des Lu', *Le Monde*, 27 January.

———— 2001b. 'La nature obligatoire du PARE contesté en Conseil d'Etat', *Le Monde*, 6 July.

Montesquieu, C.L. 1961. *De l'Esprit des lois*. Paris: Garnier.

Montricher, N. de. 1995. 'Recent Developments in French Public Sector Reform'. Public service seminar, London School of Economics and Political Science.

Moore, B. Jr. 1966. *Social Origins of Dictatorship and Democracy*. London: Penguin.

Morin, F. 2000. 'A Transformation in the French Model of Shareholding and Management', *Economy and Society* 29, 1: 36–53.

Mudde, C. 1996a. 'Right-wing Extremism Analysed', *European Journal of Political Research* 27: 203–24.

———— 1996b.'The War of Words: Defining the Extreme-Right Party Family', *West European Politics* 19, 2: 225–48

———— 2000. *The Ideology of the Extreme Right*. Manchester: Manchester University Press.

———— 2002. 'Extremist movements'. In P. Heywood, E. Jones and M. Rhodes (eds), *Developments in West European Politics*. Basingstoke: Palgrave.

Muet, P.-A. 1998. 'Table ronde: comment appliquer les 35 heures?' *Revue politique et parlementaire* 993: 73–91.

———— 2000. *Achieving Full Employment*. London: Policy Network.

Muet, P.-A. and A. Fonteneau. 1985. *La Gauche face à la crise* Paris: FNSP.

Murdock, G. 2000. 'Digital Futures: European Television in the Age of Convergence'. In J. Wieten, G. Murdock and P. Dahlgren (eds), *Television Across Europe*. London: Sage.

Musso, P. 1999. 'Saint-Simon libéré', *Libération*, 6 July.

Negrine, R. 1994. *Politics and the Mass Media in Britain*, 2nd edn. London: Routledge.

Nelson, B. 1995. 'Forms of Commitment: Intellectuals in Contemporary France', *Monash Romance Studies:* 1. Melbourne: Dept. of Romance Languages Monash University.

Nizan, P. 1932. *Les Chiens de garde*. Paris: Rieder.

Noelle-Neumann, E. 1978. 'The Dual Climate of Opinion: the Influence of Television in the 1976 West German Federal Election'. In M. Kaase and K. von Beyme (eds), *Elections and Parties*. Beverley Hills: Sage.

Norpoth, H. and K.L. Baker. 1980. 'Mass Media Use and Electoral Choice in West Germany', *Comparative Politics* 13: 1–14.

Nysenholc, A. 1995. 'Cinéma américain, cinéma européen'. In F. Sojcher (ed.), *Cinéma européen et identités culturelles*. Brussels: Editions de l'Université de Bruxelles.

Ockrent, C. 1988. *Duel. Comment la télévision façonne un président*. Paris: Hachette.

OECD. 2000. *OECD Economic Surveys: France*. Paris: OECD.

OFCE. 1999. *L'Economie française 1999*. Paris: La Découverte.

———— 2001. *L'Economie française 2001*. Paris: La Découverte.

Ory, P. and J.-P. Sirinelli. 2002. *Les Intellectuels en France: De l'affaire Dreyfus à nos jour*, 3rd edn. Paris: A. Colin.

Osborn, A. 2001. 'Scorn poured on Berlusconi views', *The Guardian*, 28 September.

Oxford English Dictionary Online. 2003, at [http://www.dictionary.oed.com]. Consulted 17 August 2003,

Ozouf, M. 1983. 'Peut-on commémorer la Révolution française?', *Le Débat*, 26: 161–72.

Page, E. 1995 'Administering Europe'. In J. Hayward and E. Page (eds), *Governing the New Europe*. Cambridge: Polity Press.

Palmer, J. 1996. European Peace Role for NATO, *The Guardian*, 6 December.

Papathanassopoulos, S. 2002. *European Television in the Digital Age*. Cambridge: Polity.

Parks, T. 2003. 'Local Hero', *The Guardian*, 6 March.

Parti Socialiste. 1996. Final text of the National convention: 'Mondialisation, Europe, France', *Vendredi*, 276, 5 April.

Patriat, C. 1998. *La Culture, un besoin d'État: l'intervention politique dans la culture*. Paris: Hachette.

Pedder, S. 1999. 'The grand illusion', *The Economist* (US edition), 5 June.

Péguy, C. 1910. *Notre jeunesse*. Paris: Cahiers de la Quinzaine.

Perrineau, P. 1995. 'La dynamique du vote Le Pen: le poids du gaucho-lepénisme'. In P. Perrineau and C. Ysmal (eds), *Le vote de crise. L'élection présidentielle de 1995*. Paris: Presses de Science Po.

———— 1996. 'Le FN en 1995: une question de droite posée à gauche'. In J. Viard (ed.), *Aux sources du populisme nationaliste*. La Tour d'Aigues: Editions de l'Aube.

———— 1997. *Le Symptôme Le Pen: radiographie des électeurs du Front National*. Paris: Fayard.

———— 1998. 'L'exception française', *Pouvoirs*, 87: 35–42.

———— 2001. 'L'extrême-droite en Europe: des crispations face à la société ouverte'. In P. Perrineau (ed.), *Les Croisés de la société fermée: l'Europe des extrêmes-droites*. La Tour d'Aigues: Editions de l'Aube.

Perrot, M. 1974. *Les ouvriers en grève: France 1871–1890*, vol. 2. Paris: Mouton.

Perry, S. 1995. 'Political Television and the Creation of Conflict'. In R. Günther and J. Windebank (eds), *Violence and Conflict in Modern French Culture*. Sheffield: Sheffield Academic Press.

———— 1997. 'Television'. In S. Perry (ed.), *Aspects of Contemporary France*. London: Routledge.

Pierre, J. 1995. 'Comparative Public Administration: The State of the Art'. In J. Pierre (ed.), *Bureaucracy in the Modern State: An Introduction to Comparative Public Administration*. Aldershot: Edward Elgar.

Pingaud, D. 2000. *La Gauche de la gauche*. Paris: Seuil.

Pinto, D. 1988. 'The Atlantic influence and the mellowing of French identity'. In J. Howorth and G. Ross (eds), *Contemporary France: A Review of Inter-disciplinary Studies*, vol. 2. London: Frances Pinter.

Pisani-Ferry, J. 2000. 'Full Employment: France'. In P.-A. Muet (ed.), *Achieving Full Employment*. London: Policy Network.

Poirrier, P. 2002. *Les Politiques culturelles en France*. Paris: La Documentation Française.

Porter, M.E. 1990. *The Competitive Advantage of Nations*. Basingstoke: Macmillan.

Prost, A. 1968. *L'Enseignement en France*. Paris: A. Colin.

Racine, N. 2003. 'Les intellectuelles'. In M. Leymarie and J.-F. Sirinelli (eds), *L'histoire des intellectuels aujourd'hui*. Paris: Presses Universitaires de France.

Ramonet, I. 1995. 'La Pensée unique', *Le Monde diplomatique*, January.

Raynal, G.T. [1770] 1981. *Histoire philosophique et politique des deux Indes*. Paris: Maspero/ La Découverte.

Reader, K. 1987. *Intellectuals and the Left in France since 1968*. London: Macmillan.

Regourd, S. 2001. *Droit de la communication audiovisuel*. Paris: Presses Universitaires de France.

———— 2002. *L'Exception culturelle*. Paris: Presses Universitaires de France.

Rémond, R. 1985: 'Les Progrès du consensus', *Vingtième siècle*, 5: 123–32.

———— 1993. *La Politique n'est plus ce qu'elle était*. Paris: Calmann-Lévy.

Renaut, A., ed. 1999. *Histoire de la philosophie politique*, 5 vols. Paris: Calmann-Lévy.

Réseau Voltaire [http://: www.reseauvoltaire.net.] Consulted 9 November 2003

Ridley, F. 1996. 'The New Public Management in Europe Comparative Perspectives', *Public Policy and Administration* 11, 1: 16–29.

Rigaud, J. 1975. *La Culture pour vivre*. Paris: Gallimard.

———— 1990. *Libre culture*. Paris: Gallimard.

———— 1996. *L' Exception culturelle. Culture et pouvoirs sous la V République*. Paris: Grasset.

Robillard, S. 1999. *Cornerstone of the Information Society: Legal and Policy Implications of Convergence*. Düsseldorf: The European Institute for the Media.

Rollat, A. 1985. *Les Hommes de l'extrême-droite: Le Pen, Marie, Ortiz et les autres*. Paris: Calmann-Levy.

Roman, J., L. Ferry and O. Mongin. 1990. 'Le retour de l'exception française', *Esprit* 164, September: 65–102.

Rosanvallon, P. 2004. *Le modèle politique français*. Paris, Seuil.

Ross, G. 1991. 'Where have all the Sartres gone? The French Intelligensia Born Again'. In J. Hollifield and G. Ross (eds), *Searching for the New France*. London: Routledge.

Ross, G. and A. Martin. 1999. 'European Unions Face the Millennium'. In A. Martin and G. Ross (eds), *The Brave New World of European Labor: European Trade Unions at the Millennium*. Oxford: Berghahn.

Rouard, D. 2001. 'Pacte sur l'immigration entre Silvio Berlusconi et la Ligue du Nord', *Le Monde*, 7 April.

Rouban, L. 1990. 'La modernisation de l'Etat et la fin de la spécificité française', *Revue française de science politique* 40, 4: 63–87.

———— 1998a. *The French Civil Service*. Paris: La Documentation Française.

———— 1998b. 'Le Regard de l'opinion publique'. In F. Gallouédec-Genuys (ed.), *A propos de l'administration française*. Paris: La Documentation Française.

Rudé, G. 1959. *The Crowd in the French Revolution*. Westport, CN: Greenwood Press.

Ruggie, J. 1982. 'International Regimes, Transactions and Change: Embedded Liberalism in the Post-War Economic Order', *International Organization* 36, 2: 379–415.

Ruysseveldt, J. van and J. Visser. 1996. 'Contestation and state intervention forever? Industrial relations in France'. In J. van Ruysseveldt and J. Visser (eds), *Industrial Relations in Europe: Traditions and Transitions*. London: Sage.

Ryner, M. 2000. 'Swedish Employment Policy After EU-Membership', *Osterreichische Zeitschrift Fur Politikwissenschaft* 29, 3: 341–55.

Said, E.W. 1993. *Culture and Imperialism*. London: Chatto & Windus.

Saint-Etienne, C. 1992a. *L'Exception française: pour un nouveau modèle démocratique de croissance*. Paris: A. Colin.

———— 1992b. 'Moderniser l'exception française', *Le Débat*, 71: 66–71.

Sainteny, G. 1998. 'Variations sur l'exception française', *Commentaire*, special issue: 'Situations de la France', 81: 117–20.

Salant, R.S. 1979. 'The Good but not Great Nondebates: Some Random Personal Notes'. In S. Kraus (ed.), *The Great Debates. Carter vs Ford, 1976*. Bloomington: Indiana University Press.

Sartre, J.-P. 1948a. *Situations II*. Paris: Gallimard.

———— 1948b. 'Orphée noir'. Preface to L.S. Senghor, *Anthologie de la nouvelle poésie nègre et malgache*. Paris: Presses Universitaires de France.

———— 1949. *Situations III*. Paris: Gallimard.

———— 1952. *Saint Genet, comédien et martyr*. Paris: Gallimard.

———— 1966. Preface to Albert Memmi, *Portrait du colonisé*. Paris: Jean-Jacques Pauvert.

———— 1972. *Plaidoyer pour les intellectuels*. Paris: Gallimard.

———— [1961] 1987. 'Preface' to Frantz Fanon, *Les Damnés de la Terre*. Paris: La Découverte.

Sassoon, D. 1985. 'Political and Market Forces in Italian Broadcasting'. In R.Kuhn (ed.), *Broadcasting and Politics in Western Europe*. London: Frank Cass.

Sauviat, C. and J.-M. Pernot. 2000. 'Le poids croissant des investisseurs institutionnels'. In *L'Etat de la France, 2000–2001*. Paris: La Découverte & Syros.

Scharpf, F. 1991. *Crisis and Choice in European Social Democracy*. Ithaca: Cornell University Press.

Schmitt, J. 1986. *Fin de la France? Histoire d'une perte d'identité*. Paris: Nouvelles Editions Debresse.

Schmidt, V. 1996. *From State to Market? The Transformation of French Business and Government*. Cambridge: Cambridge University Press.

———— 1997. 'Running on Empty: The End of *Dirigisme* in French Economic Leadership', *Modern and Contemporary France* 5, 2: 229–41.

———— 1999. 'Privatisation in France: The Transformation of French Capitalism', *Environment and Planning* 17, 4: 445–61.

Schnapper, D. and C. Bachelier. 2000. *Qu'est-ce que la citoyenneté?* Paris: Gallimard.

Schoenbach, K. 1987. 'The Role of Mass Media in West German Election Campaigns', *Legislative Studies Quarterly* 12, 3: 373–94.

Schröder, G. 2000. Postscript. In B. Hombach (ed.), *The Politics of the New Centre*. Cambridge: Polity.

Schrott, P.R. 1990. 'Electoral Consequences of "Winning" Televised Campaign Debates', *Public Opinion Quarterly* 54: 567–85.

Scriven, M. and M. Lecomte. 1999. *Television Broadcasting in Contemporary France and Britain*. Oxford: Berghahn.

Scriven, M. and E. Roberts, eds. 2003. *Group Identities on French and British Television*. Oxford: Berghahn.

Séguin, P. 1992. 'Séguin-la-nation contre Léotard-l'Europe', *Nouvel observateur*, 7–13 May.

———— 1993. *Ce que j'ai dit*. Paris: Grasset.

Semetko, H.A. and K. Schoenbach. 1995. 'The Media and the Campaign in the New Germany'. In D.P. Conradt, G. Kleinfield, G. Romoser and C. Søsoe (eds), *Germany's New Politics: Parties and Issues in the 1990s*. Providence, RI and Oxford: Berghahn.

———— 2000. 'Parties, Leaders and Issues in the News'. In S. Padgett and T. Saalfeld (eds), *Bundestagswahl '98: End of an era?*. London: Frank Cass.

Senghor, L.S. 1948. Introduction, *Anthologie de la nouvelle poésie nègre et malgache*. Paris: Presses Universitaires de France.

Sergeant, J.-C. 2000. 'From Press Barons to Digital TV: Changing Media in France'. In W. Kidd and S. Reynolds (eds). *Contemporary French Cultural Studies*. London: Arnold.

Serreau, C. 2001. 'Le Carnet de bord de *Chaos*', site internet du film, http://www.chaos-lefilm.com/html/texte3/texte.htm. Consulted on 3 October 2001.

Shonfield, A. 1969. *Modern Capitalism: The Changing Balance of Public and Private Power*. London: Oxford University Press.

Shorter, E. and C. Tilly, C. 1974. *Strikes in France, 1930–1968*. Cambridge: Cambridge University Press.

Sieburg, F. 1991. *Dieu est-il français?* Paris: Grasset

Silguy, Y.-T. de. 2003. 'Moderniser l'Etat: Le cas de L'ENA' Rapport de la commission sur la réforme de l'ENA et la formation des cadres supérieurs des fonctions publiques, présidée par Y.T. de Silguy. Paris: Ministère de la Fonction Publique, de la Réforme de l'Etat et de l'Aménagement du Territoire, April.

Sirinelli, J.-F. 1990. *Intellectuels et passions françaises: manifestes et pétitions au XXe siè-cle*. Paris: Fayard.

Sojcher, F. 1995. *Cinéma européen et identités culturelles*. Brussels: Editions de l'U-niversité de Bruxelles.

Soubie, R. 1991. *Dieu est-il toujours français?* Paris: Editions de Fallois.

Stevens, A. 1987. 'Britain and France: Some Practical Comparisons' Memorandum for the House of Commons Treasury and Civil Service Select Committee, pub-lished in *Civil Service Recruitment Training and Manpower: Minutes of Evidence 1986–87 HCP 358-i*. London (HMSO) July: 99–106.

——— 1988. 'The French Civil Service Under the Mitterrand Government'. In J. Howorth and G. Ross (eds), *Contemporary France*, vol. 2. London: Frances Pinter.

——— 2003. *Government and Politics of France*. 3rd edn. Basingstoke: Palgrave Macmillan.

Stoffaes, C. 1989. 'Industrial Policy and the State: From Industry to Enterprise'. In P. Godt (ed.), *Policy-Making in France*. London: Pinter.

Straubhaar, J., O. Olsen, and M.C. Nunes. 1993. 'The Brazilian Case: Influencing the Voter'. In R.E. Skidmore (ed.), *Television, Politics and the Transition to Democracy in Latin America*. Baltimore and London: The John Hopkins University Press.

Suleiman, E. 1974. *Politics, Power and Bureaucracy in France*. Princeton N.J: Princeton University Press.

Supiot, A. 1994. *Critique du droit du travail*. Paris: Presses Universitaires de France.

Swyngedown, M. 2000. 'Belgium: Explaining the Relationship between the Vlaams Blok and the City of Antwerp'. In P. Hainsworth (ed.), *The Politics of the Extreme Right: From the Margins to the Mainstream*. London: Pinter.

Taggart, P. 1996. *New Populism and The New Politics New Protest Parties in Sweden in a Comparative Perspective*. London: St. Martins Press.

Taguieff, A. 1985. 'Les droites radicales en France. Nationalisme révolutionnaire et national-libéralisme', *Les Temps modernes*. 465: 1780–842.

——— 1997. 'Le populisme et la science politique: du mirage conceptuel aux vrais problèmes', *Vingtième siècle*, 56: 4–33.

Thompson, E.P. 1965. 'The Peculiarities of the English'. In *The Poverty of Theory and other Essays*. London: Merlin Press.

Tiersky, R. 1985. *Ordinary Stalinism: Democratic Centralism and the Question of Com-munist Political Development*. London: Allen & Unwin.

Tilly, C., L.Tilly, and R. Tilly. 1975. *The Rebellious Century 1830–1930*. London: Dent & Sons.

Tocqueville, A. de. 1928. *L'Ancien régime et la Révolution*. Paris: Calmann-Lévy.

——— 1966. *Democracy in America*. London: Macmillan/St. Martin's Press.

Tomlinson, J. 1999. *Globalization and Culture*. Cambridge: Polity Press.

Trouille, J.-M. 1996. 'The Franco-German Axis Since Unification'. In T. Chafer and B. Jenkins (eds), *France: From the Cold War to the New World Order*. Basingstoke: Macmillan.

Trouille, J.-M. and H.Uterwedde. 2001. 'Franco-German Relations, Europe and Globalisation', *Modern and Contemporary France* 9, 3: 339–54.

Tuchszirer, C. 2000. 'Quinze années d'érosion de l'assurance chômage'. In *L'Etat de la France 2000–2001*. Paris: La Découverte & Syros.

Utley, R. 2000. *The French Defence Debate: Consensus and Continuity in the Mitterrand Era.* Basingstoke: Macmillan.

Vacquin, H. 1999. 'Mutations dans le syndicalisme français', *Esprit*, 251: 219–29.

Vandenbroucke, F. 1999. 'European Social Democracy: Convergence, Divisions, and Shared Questions'. In A. Gamble and T. Wright (eds) *The New Social democracy.* Oxford: Blackwell.

Varouxakis, G. 1996. 'The Public Moralist versus Ethnocentrism: John Stuart Mill's French Enterprise', *European Review of History* 3, 1: 27–37.

Védrine, H and D. Moïsi. 2000. *Les Cartes de la France à l'heure de la mondialisation.* Paris: Fayard.

Verdès-Leroux, J. 1983. *Au service du Parti. Le Parti communiste, les intellectuels et la culture (1944–1956).* Paris: Fayard/Minuit.

Vernet, D. 1993. 'Nouveau pas de Paris vers L'OTAN', *Le Monde,* 12 March.

Vigarello, G. 2000. *Passion sport: histoire d'une culture.* Paris: Textuel.

Vincent, C. 2001. 'La politique contractuelle fonde-t-elle les relations sociales?', *L'Etat de la France, 2001–2002.* Paris: La Découverte & Syros.

Visser, J. 2000. 'France'. In B. Ebbinghaus and J. Visser (eds), *The Societies of Europe: Trade Unions in Western Europe since 1945.* Basingstoke: Macmillan.

Vulser, N. 2002. 'Industrie et médias: une dangereuse proximité', *Le Monde,* 14–15 April.

Wahl, A. 1989. *Les Archives du football. Sport et société en France (1880–1980).* Paris: Gallimard-Julliard.

Wahl, A. and P. Lanfranchi. 1995. *Les Footballeurs professionnels des années trente à nos jours.* Paris: La Vie Quotidienne-Hachette.

Ward, I. and M. Walsh. 2000. 'Leaders' Debates and Presidential Politics in Australia'. In S. Coleman (ed.), *Televised Election Debates. International Perspectives.* Basingstoke: Macmillan.

Webb, P. 2002. 'Party systems, electoral cleavages and government stability'. In P. Heywood, E. Jones and M. Rhodes (eds), *Developments in West European Politics.* Basingstoke: Palgrave.

Weber, E. 1977. *Peasants into Frenchmen: the Modernization of Rural France.* London: Chatto and Windus.

Webster, P. 2003a. 'Chirac the Hero at the Nation Unites.' *The Guardian.* 29 March.

———— 2003b. 'France Faces Isolation as Strain Shows in Anti-war Axis', *The Guardian,* 11 April.

Wehler, H.U. 1973. *Das deutsche Kaiserreich. 1871–1918.* Göttingen:Deutsche Geschichte, Bd. 9 / von J.Leuschner.

Weinberg, A. 1994. 'Vers la fin de l'exception française?', *Sciences Humaines,* special issue: La Société française en mouvement, 6: 6–10.

Westergaard, J. 1999. 'Where Does the Third Way Lead?', *New Political Economy* 4, 3: 429–36.

Wheen, F. 2000. *Karl Marx.* London: Fourth Estate.

Wieviorka, M. 1993. *La Démocratie à l'épreuve.* Paris: La Découverte.

Winock, M. 1986. *La Fièvre hexagonale.* Paris: Calmann-Lévy.

———— 1997. 'Populismes français', *Vingtième siècle,* 56: 77–91

———— 1999a. *Le Siècle des intellectuels.* Paris: Seuil.

_____ 1999b. *La France politique. XIX–XXe siècle.* Paris: Seuil.

_____ 2001. *Les Voix de la liberté. Les écrivains engagés au XIXe siècle.* Paris: Seuil.

_____ 2003. 'Le fin du mythe soviétique', *L'Histoire,* 276: 76–9.

Winock, M., ed. 1994. *Histoire de l'extrême-droite en France.* Paris: Seuil.

Wodak, R. and A. Pelinka, eds. 2002. *The Haider Phenomenon in Austria.* London: Transaction publishers.

Wright, V. 1994a. 'Reshaping the State: The Implications for Public Administration', *West European Politics* 17, 2: 102–37.

_____ 1994b. 'The Administrative Machine: Old Problems and New Dilemmas. In P. Hall, J. Hayward and H. Machin (eds), *Developments in French Politics.* London: Macmillan.

Wyplosz, C. 2000. 'Vices hexagonaux', *Libération,* 27 November.

'Y a-t-il une exception sociolinguistique française?' Conference at the University of Brest, Faculté des Lettres, 5–6 June 1997.http://www.linguist.org/issues/8/8-783.html. Consulted on 26 February 2001.

Zeldin, T. 1983. *The French.* London: Collins.

Zemmour, E. 2002 ' Le Pen IV, le retour', *Le Figaro,* hors série 57 984: 'La présidentielle qui a fait trembler la V République', June.

Zysman, J. 1983. *Government, Markets, Growth: Financial Systems and the Politics of Industrial Change.* Ithaca: Cornell University Press.

Notes on Contributors

Janet Bryant is senior lecturer in French Politics in the European and International Studies Division at the University of Portsmouth. Her area of research is French foreign and defence policy and aspects of European security. Her most recent publication is 'France and NATO from 1966 to Kosovo: Coming Full Circle?', *European Security* 9, 3 (Autumn 2000).

David S. Bell was one of the founder members of the Association for the Study of Modern and Contemporary France and worked with the committee from its inception until 1992. He is head of the School of Social Sciences and Law at the University of Leeds and is the author of numerous works on French political parties, including notably *French Politics Today* (Manchester University Press, 2002).

Tony Chafer is director of the Centre for European Studies Research at the University of Portsmouth. He has edited several books on francophone Africa and has written widely on contemporary Franco-African relations, including most recently 'Franco-African Relations: No Longer So Exceptional?', in *African Affairs* (2002). His monograph, *The End of Empire in French West Africa. France's Successful Decolonization?* was published by Berg in 2002.

Ben Clift is lecturer in International Political Economy in the Department of Politics and International Studies at the University of Warwick. His research interests include international and comparative political economy, social democracy and globalisation, and French party system change. In addition to his book *French Socialism in a Global Era* (Continuum 2003), he has written widely on comparative political economy and the French Socialists, including 'Social Democracy and Globalisation: the Cases of France and the UK', *Government and Opposition*, 2002. His new book *Where Are National Capitalisms Now?* (co-edited with Jonathon Perraton) is forthcoming (Palgrave 2004).

Sue Collard has been lecturer in French in the School of European Studies since 1986 and is now in the Sussex European Institute in the School of Social and Cultural Studies. Her research interests all derive from the analysis of contemporary French politics, with a particular interest in François Mitterrand and the *Grands Travaux*. She has mainly published on various aspects of cultural politics and policy, and on the relationship between France and Europe.

Emmanuel Godin is senior lecturer in French and European Studies at the University of Portsmouth. He has published articles on the French right and on French Catholic intellectuals and has just completed with Martin Evans a book on French history: *France 1815–2003* (Arnold, 2004).

Nick Hewlett is professor of French Studies at Oxford Brookes University. He is author of a number of books, including *Modern French Politics. Analysing Conflict and Consensus since 1945* (Polity, 1998); *Democracy and Modern France* (Continuum, 2003); *Currents in Contemporary French Intellectual Life* (with Christopher Flood, Palgrave, 2000). He is currently writing a book on the political thought of Alain Badiou and Jacques Rancière.

Michael Kelly is professor of French at the University of Southampton. He has published widely on French cultural and intellectual history, including books on catholic, Marxist and Hegelian thought, and on French cultural studies. His most recent book in this area is *French Culture and Society. The Essential Glossary* (Arnold, 2001). He is completing a book on the cultural reconstruction of France after the Second World War.

Raymond Kuhn is senior lecturer in the Department of Politics at Queen Mary, University of London. He has published widely on French media policy and political communication and is the author of *The Media in France* (Routledge, 1995), editor of *Broadcasting and Politics in Western Europe* (Frank Cass, 1985) and co-editor of *Political Journalism* (Routledge, 2002).

Margaret A. Majumdar is visiting professor of Francophone Studies at the University of Portsmouth and Honorary Secretary of the Association for the Study of Contemporary and Modern France. Her publications include *Althusser and the End of Leninism?* (Pluto, 1995); *Francophone Studies. The Essential Glossary* (Arnold, 2002); *Transition and Development. Patterns, Challenges and Implications of Change in Algeria* (co-edited with Mohammed Saad, Intellect, 2004).

Patrick Mignon is a researcher at the Institut National du Sport et de l'Education Physique (INSEP) in Paris. He has written widely on French sport, including *La Passion du football* (Editions Odile Jacob, 1998) and a recent chapter 'Another Side to French Exceptionalism: Football without Hooligans?'in E. Dunning. P. Murphy, Waddington I., Astrinakis A., eds, *Fighting Fans: Football Hooliganism as a world phenomenon* (University College Dublin Press, 2000).

Nick Parsons is senior lecturer in French at the School of European Studies, Cardiff University. He is the author of *Employee Participation in Europe: a Case Study of the British and French Gas Industries* (Ashgate, 1997), as well as of numerous articles and book chapters on British and French industrial relations.

Sheila Perry is lecturer in French Studies at the University of Nottingham where she specialises in contemporary French politics and the media. She is editor of *Aspects of Contemporary France* (Routledge, 1997) and co-editor of *Voices of France: Social, Political and Cultural Identity* (Pinter, 1997), *Population and Social Policy in France* (Pinter, 1997), and *Media Developments and Cultural Change* (UNN, 1999). She is co-founder of the Northern Media Research Group.

Brigitte Rollet is lecturer at the University of London-British Institute of Paris. She has published widely on French contemporary cinema. She is the author of *Coline Serreau* (MUP, 1998), and co-author with Carrie Tarr of *Cinema and the Second Sex. Twenty Years of Women's Filmmaking in France 1980s–1990s* (Continuum, 2001).

Anne Stevens is professor of European Studies in the School of Languages and European Studies, Aston University, Birmingham. Early experience as a civil servant gave her an ongoing interest in administration and government. She is the author of *The Government and Politics of France* (3rd edition, Palgrave Macmillan, 2003) and (with Handley Stevens) of *Brussels Bureaucrats: the Administrative Services of the European Union* (Palgrave, 2001).

INDEX